THE PROFITS OF RELIGION

Titles on Religion in
Prometheus's Great Minds Series

Thomas Henry Huxley
Agnosticism and Christianity and Other Essays

Ernest Renan
The Life of Jesus

Upton Sinclair
The Profits of Religion

Elizabeth Cady Stanton
The Woman's Bible

Voltaire
A Treatise on Toleration and Other Essays

See the back of this volume for a complete list of titles in Prometheus's
Great Books in Philosophy and Great Minds series.

THE PROFITS OF RELIGION

UPTON SINCLAIR

GREAT MINDS SERIES

 **Prometheus Books**

59 John Glenn Drive
Amherst, New York 14228-2197

Published 2000 by Prometheus Books
59 John Glenn Drive, Amherst, New York 14228-2197.
VOICE: 716-691-0133, ext. 207. FAX: 716-564-2711.
WWW.PROMETHEUSBOOKS.COM

Library of Congress Cataloging-in-Publication Data

Sinclair, Upton, 1878-1968.
    The profits of religion / Upton Sinclair.
        p. cm. — (Great minds paperback series)
    Originally published: Pasadena, Calif. : U. Sinclair, 1918.
    ISBN 1-57392-844-5 (alk. paper).
    1. Christianity—Controversial literature. I. Title. II. Great minds
series.

BL2775 .S55 2000
200—dc21   00-057579
                                                                CIP

Printed in the United States of America on acid-free paper

UPTON SINCLAIR was born on September 20, 1878, in Baltimore, Maryland. He received a bachelor's degree from the City College of New York in 1897 and was a graduate student at Columbia University. Sinclair took up writing for newspapers and published several unsuccessful novels before writing *The Jungle* for serialization in the socialist newspaper *Appeal to Reason*. Intended to lead to improved working conditions for the exploited immigrant workers in the meat-packing industry, *The Jungle* led to passage of the Pure Food and Drug Act, to protect consumers. Publication of the novel in 1906 placed Sinclair in the ranks of the early twentieth-century muckraking writers who used their pens to expose corruption and social injustice. He used the royalties from *The Jungle* to help found a cooperative-living venture, Helicon Hall, in Englewood, New Jersey.

His interest in social and industrial reform underlies most of his over eighty books, including the topical and polemical novels *The Money Changers* (1908), *King Coal* (1917), *Oil!* (1927), and *Boston* (1928); a cycle of eleven historical novels about a contemporary American, Lanny Budd; and many political and social studies such as *The Profits of Religion* (1918) and *The Goose-Step* (1923). Sinclair won the 1942 Pulitzer Prize for *Dragon's Teeth*, the third novel in the Lanny Budd series.

Joining the Socialist Party in 1902, Sinclair helped found the Intercollegiate Socialist Society in 1905. For many years he was active in California politics, running unsuccessfully as a Socialist candidate for the U.S. Congress in 1920 and 1922, and for governor of California in 1926 and 1930. In 1934 he received the Democratic nomination for governor of California, running on the Socialist reform platform EPIC (End Poverty In California). He founded the American Civil Liberties Union in California.

Sinclair died in Bound Brook, New Jersey, on November 25, 1968.

CONTENTS

Introductory

 Bootstrap-lifting 11
 Religion 16

Book One: The Church of the Conquerors

 The Priestly Lie 21
 The Great Fear 24
 Salve Regina! 27
 Fresh Meat 28
 Priestly Empires 31
 Prayer-wheels 33
 The Butcher-Gods 35
 The Holy Inquisition 38
 Hell-fire 41

Book Two: The Church of Good Society

 The Rain Makers 47
 The Babylonian Fire-God 50
 The Medicine-men 52
 The Canonization of Incompetence 55
 Gibson's Preservative 58
 The Elders 62
 Church History 66
 Land and Livings 68
 Graft in Tail 71
 Bishops and Beer 73
 Anglicanism and Alcohol 76
 Dead Cats 80
 "Suffer Little Children" 84
 The Court-circular 89
 Horn-blowing 92
 Trinity Corporation 94
 Spiritual Interpretation 97

Book Three: The Church of the Servant Girls

Charity..105
God's Armor...109
Thanksgivings...113
The Holy Roman Empire....................................115
Temporal Power..118
Knights of Slavery...120
Priests and Police...122
The Church Militant.......................................125
The Church Triumphant....................................128
God in the Schools..131
The Menace...133
King Coal...137
The Unholy Alliance.......................................141
Secret Service...144
Tax Exemption..146
Holy History..148
Das Centrum..152

Book Four: The Church of the Slavers

The Face of Caesar..161
Deutschland ueber Alles...................................163
Der Tag...164
King Cotton...167
Witches and Women..170
Moth and Rust..173
To Lyman Abbott..176
The Octopus...180
The Industrial Shelley.....................................183
The Outlook for Graft.....................................187
Clerical Camouflage.......................................191
The Jungle..195

Book Five: The Church of the Merchants

The Head Merchant..201
"Herr Beeble"...203
Holy Oil..207
Rhetorical Black-hanging..................................212
The Great American Fraud.................................214
Riches in Glory..217

Captivating Ideals.....................................219
Spook Hunting...222
Running the Rapids....................................225
Birth Control...227
Sheep...230

Book Six: The Church of the Quacks

Tabula Rasa 237
The Book of Mormon....................................239
Holy Rolling 242
Bible Prophecy..245
Koreshanity 248
Mazdaznan...250
Black Magic...253
Mental Malpractice....................................257
Science and Wealth....................................261
New Nonsense..264
"Dollars Want Me!"....................................267
Spiritual Financiering................................270
The Graft of Grace....................................273

Book Seven: The Church of the Social Revolution

Christ and Caesar.....................................281
Locusts and Wild Honey................................284
Mother Earth..287
The Soap Box 290
The Church Machine....................................292
The Church Redeemed...................................296
The Desire of Nations.................................300
The Knowable..302
"Nature's Insurgent Son"..............................305
The New Morality......................................308
Envoi...311

INTRODUCTORY

Bootstrap-lifting

Bootstrap-lifting? says the reader.

It is a vision I have seen: upon a vast plain, men and women are gathered in dense throngs, crouched in uncomfortable and distressing positions, their fingers hooked in the straps of their boots. They are engaged in lifting themselves; tugging and straining until they grow red in the face, exhausted. The perspiration streams from their foreheads, they show every symptom of distress; the eyes of all are fixed, not upon each other, nor upon their boot-straps, but upon the sky above. There is a look of rapture upon their faces, and now and then, amid grunts and groans, they cry out with excitement and triumph.

I approach one and say to him, "Friend, what is this you are doing?"

He answers, without pausing to glance at me, "I am performing spiritual exercises. See how I rise?"

"But," I say, "you are not rising at all!"

Whereat he becomes instantly angry. "You are one of the scoffers!"

"But, friend," I protest, "don't you feel the earth under your feet?"

"You are a materialist!"

"But, friend, I can see—"

"You are without spiritual vision!"

And so I move on among the sweating and groaning hordes. Being of a sympathetic turn of mind, I cannot help being distressed by the prevalence of this singular practice among so large a portion of the human race. How is it possible that none of them should suspect the futility of their procedure? Or can it really be that I am uncomprehending? That in some way they are actually getting off the ground, or about to get off the ground?

Then I observe a new phenomenon: a man gliding here and there among the bootstrap-lifters, approaching from the rear and slipping his hands into their pockets. The position of the spiritual exercisers greatly facilitates his work; their eyes being cast up to heaven, they do not see him, their thoughts being occupied, they do not heed him; he goes through their pockets at leisure, and transfers the contents to a bag he carries, and then moves on to the next victim. I watch him for a while, and finally approach and ask, "What are you doing, sir?"

He answers, "I am picking pockets."

"Oh," I say, puzzled by his matter-of-course tone. "But— I beg pardon—are you a thief?"

"Oh, no," he answers, smilingly, "I am the agent of the Wholesale Pickpockets' Association. This is Prosperity."

"I see," I reply. "And these people let you—"

"It is the law," he says. "It is also the gospel."

I turn, following his glance, and observe another person approaching—a stately figure, clad in scarlet and purple robes, moving with slow dignity. He gazes about at the sweating and grunting hordes; now and then he stops and lifts his hands in a gesture of benediction, and proclaims in rolling tones, "Blessed are the Bootstrap-lifters, for theirs is the kingdom of Heaven." He moves on, and after a bit stops and announces again, "Man doth not live by bread alone, but by every word that cometh out of the mouth of the prophets and priests of Bootstrap-lifting."

Watching a while longer, I see this majestic one approach the agent of the Wholesale Pickpockets' Association. The agent greets him as a friend, and proceeds to transfer to the pockets of his capacious robes a generous share of the loot which he has collected. The majestic one does not cringe, nor does he make any effort to hide what is going on. On the contrary he cries aloud, "It is more blessed to give than to receive!" And again he cries, "The laborer is worthy of his hire!" And a third time he cries, yet more sternly, "Render unto Caesar the things which are Caesar's!" And the Bootstrap-lifters pause long enough to answer: "Lord have mercy upon us, and incline our hearts to keep this law!" Then they renew their straining and tugging.

I step up, and in timid tones begin, "Reverend sir, will you tell me by what right you take this wealth?"

Instantly a frown comes upon his face, and he cries in a voice of thunder, "Blasphemer!" And all the Bootstrap-lifters desist from their lifting, and menace me with furious looks. There is a general call for a policeman of the Wholesale Pickpockets' Association; and so I fall silent, and slink away in the throng, and thereafter keep my thoughts to myself.

Over the vast plain I wander, observing a thousand strange and incredible and terrifying manifestations of the Bootstrap-lifting impulse. There is, I discover, a

regular propaganda on foot; a long time ago—no man
can recall how far back—the Wholesale Pickpockets
made the discovery of the ease with which a man's
pockets could be rifled while he was preoccupied with
spiritual exercises, and they began offering prizes for
the best essays in support of the practice. Now their
propaganda is everywhere triumphant, and year by year
we see an increase in the rewards and emoluments of
the prophets and priests of the cult. The ground is covered with stately temples of various designs, all of which
I am told are consecrated to Bootstrap-lifting. I come
to where a group of people are occupied in laying the
corner-stone of a new white marble structure; I inquire
and am informed it is the First Church of Bootstrap-
lifters, Scientist. As I stand watching, a card is handed
to me, informing me that a lady will do my Bootstrap-
lifting at five dollars per lift.

I go on to another building, which I am told is a
library containing volumes in defense of the Bootstrap-
lifters, published under the auspices of the Wholesale
Pickpockets. I enter, and find endless vistas of shelves,
also several thousand current magazines and papers. I
consult these—for my legs have given out in the effort to
visit and inspect all phases of the Bootstrap-lifting practice. I discover that hardly a week passes that some one
does not start a new cult, or revive an old one; if I had a
hundred life-times I could not know all the creeds and
ceremonies, the services and rituals, the litanies and
liturgies, the hymns, anthems and offertories of Bootstrap-lifting. There are the Holy Roman Bootstrap-lifters, whose priests are fed by Transubstantiation; the
established Anglican Bootstrap-lifters, whose priests live

by "livings"; the Baptist Bootstrap-lifters, whose preachers practice total immersion in Standard Oil. There are Yogi Bootstrap-lifters with flowing robes of yellow silk; Theosophist Bootstrap-lifters with green and purple auras; Mormon Bootstrap-lifters, Mazdaznan Bootstrap-lifters, Spiritualist and Spirit-Fruit, Millerite and Dowieite, Holy Roller and Holy Jumper, Come-to-glory negro, Billy Sunday base-ball and Salvation Army bass-drum Bootstrap-lifters. There are the thousand varieties of "New Thought" Bootstrap-lifters; the mystic and transcendentalist, Swedenborgian and Jacob Boehme Bootstrap-lifters; the Elbert Hubbard high-art Bootstrap-lifters with half a million magazinelets at two bits apiece; the "uplift" and "optimist," the Ralph Waldo Trine and Orison Swett Marden Bootstrap-lifters with a hundred thousand volumes at one dollar per volume. There are the Platonist and Hegelian and Kantian professors of collegiate metaphysical Bootstrap-lifting at several thousand dollars per year each. There are the Nietzschean Bootstrap-lifters, who lift themselves to the Superman, and the art-for-art's-sake, neo-Pagan Bootstrap-lifters, who lift themselves down to the Ape.

Excepting possibly the last-mentioned group, the priests of all these cults, the singers, shouters, prayers and exhorters of Bootstrap-lifting have as their distinguishing characteristic that they do very little lifting at their own bootstraps, and less at any other man's. Now and then you may see one bend and give a delicate tug, of a purely symbolical character: as when the Supreme Pontiff of the Roman Bootstrap-lifters comes once a year to wash the feet of the poor; or when the Sunday-school Superintendent of the Baptist Bootstrap-lifters shakes the hand of one of his Colorado mine-slaves. But for the most part the priests and preachers of Bootstrap-lifting walk haughtily erect, many of them being so swollen with prosperity that they could not reach their bootstraps if they wanted to. Their role in life is to exhort other men to more vigorous efforts at self-elevation, that the agents of the Wholesale Pickpockets' Association may ply their immemorial role with less chance of interference.

Religion

The reader, offended by this raillery, asks if I mean to impugn the sincerity of all who preach the supremacy of the soul. No; I admit the honesty of the heroes and madmen of history. All I ask of the preacher is that he shall make an effort to practice his doctrine. Let him be tormented like Don Quixote; let him go mad like Nietzsche; let him stand upon a pillar and be devoured by worms like Simeon Stylites—on these terms I grant to any dreamer the right to hold himself above economic science.

Man is an evasive beast, given to cultivating strange notions about himself. He is humiliated by his simian ancestry, and tries to deny his animal nature, to persuade himself that he is not limited by its weaknesses nor concerned in its fate. And this impulse may be harmless, when it is genuine. But what are we to say when we see the formulas of heroic self-deception made use of by unheroic self-indulgence? What are we to say when we see asceticism preached to the poor by fat and comfortable retainers of the rich? What are we to say when we see idealism become hypocrisy, and the moral and spiritual heritage of mankind twisted to the knavish purposes of class-cruelty and greed? What I say is—Boot-strap-lifting!

It is the fate of many abstract words to be used in two senses, one good and the other bad. Morality means the will to righteousness, or it means Anthony Comstock; democracy means the rule of the people, or it means Tammany Hall. And so it is with the word "Religion". In its true sense Religion is the most fundamental of the soul's impulses, the impassioned love of life, the feeling of its preciousness, the desire to foster and further it. In that sense every thinking man must be religious; in that sense Religion is a perpetually self-renewing force, the very nature of our being. In that sense I have no thought of assailing it, I would make clear that I hold it beyond assailment.

But we are denied the pleasure of using the word in that honest sense, because of another which has been given to it. To the ordinary man "Religion" means, not the soul's longing for growth, the "hunger and thirst after righteousness", but certain forms in which this hunger has manifested itself in history, and prevails to-day throughout the world; that is to say, institutions having fixed dogmas and "revelations", creeds and rituals, with an administering caste claiming supernatural sanction. By such institutions the moral strivings of the race, the affections of childhood and the aspirations of youth are made the prerogatives and stock in trade of ecclesiastical hierarchies. It is the thesis of this book that "Religion" in this sense is a source of income to parasites, and the natural ally of every form of oppression and exploitation.

If by my jesting at "Bootstrap-lifting" I have wounded some dear prejudice of the reader, let me endeavor to speak in a more persuasive voice. I am a man who has suffered, and has seen the suffering of others; I have devoted my life to analyzing the causes of the suffering, to find out if it be necessary and fore-ordained, or if by any chance there be a way of escape for future generations. I have found that the latter is the case; the suffering is needless, it can with ease and certainty be banished from the earth. I know this with the knowledge of science—in the same way that the navigator of a ship knows his latitude and longitude, and the point of the compass to which he must steer in order to reach the port.

Come, reader, let us put aside prejudice, and the terrors of the cults of the unknown. The power which made us has given us a mind, and the impulse to its use; let us see what can be done with it to rid the earth of its ancient evils. And do not be troubled if at the outset this book seems to be entirely "destructive". I assure you that I am no crude materialist, I am not so shallow as to imagine that our race will be satisfied with a barren rationalism. I know that the old symbols came out of the heart of man because they corresponded to certain needs of the heart of man. I know that new symbols will be found, corresponding more exactly to the needs of our time. If here I set to work to tear down an old and ramshackle building, it is not from blind destructfulness, but as an architect who means to put a new and sounder structure in its place. Before we part company, I shall submit the blue print of that new home of the spirit.

BOOK ONE

The Church of the Conquerors

I saw the Conquerors riding by
    With trampling feet of horse and men:
Empire on empire like the tide
    Flooded the world and ebbed again;

A thousand banners caught the sun,
    And cities smoked along the plain,
And laden down with silk and gold
    And heaped up pillage groaned the wain.

                   Kemp.

The Priestly Lie

When the first savage saw his hut destroyed by a bolt of lightning, he fell down upon his face in terror. He had no conception of natural forces, of laws of electricity; he saw this event as the act of an individual intelligence. To-day we read about fairies and demons, dryads and fauns and satyrs, Wotan and Thor and Vulcan, Freie and Flora and Ceres, and we think of all these as pretty fancies, play-products of the mind; losing sight of the fact that they were originally meant with entire seriousness—that not merely did ancient man believe in them, but was forced to believe in them, because the mind must have an explanation of things that happen, and an individual intelligence was the only explanation available. The story of the hero who slays the devouring dragon was not merely a symbol of day and night, of summer and winter; it was a literal explanation of the phenomena, it was the science of early times.

Men imagined supernatural powers such as they could comprehend. If the lightning god destroyed a hut, obviously it must be because the owner of the hut had given offense; so the owner must placate the god, using those means which would be effective in the quarrels of men—presents of roast meats and honey and fresh fruits, of wine and gold and jewels and women, accompanied by friendly words and gestures of submission. And when in spite of all things the natural evil did not cease, when the people continued to die of pestilence, then came the opportunity for hysterical or ambitious persons to discover new ways of penetrating the mind of the god. There would be dreamers of dreams and seers of visions and hearers of voices; readers of the entrails of beasts and interpreters of the flight of birds; there would be burning bushes and stone tablets on mountain-tops, and inspired words dictated to aged disciples on lonely islands. There would arise special castes of men and women, learned in these sacred matters; and these priestly castes would naturally emphasize the importance of their calling, would hold themselves aloof from the common herd, endowed with special powers and entitled to special privileges. They would interpret the oracles in ways favorable to themselves and their order; they would proclaim themselves friends and confidants of the god, walking with him in the night-time, receiving his messengers and angels, acting as his deputies in forgiving offenses, in dealing punishments and in receiving gifts. They would become makers of laws and moral codes. They would wear special costumes to distinguish them, they would go through elaborate ceremonies to impress their followers, employing all sensuous effects, architecture and sculpture and painting, music and poetry and dancing, candles and incense and bells and gongs

> And storied windows richly dight,
> Casting a dim religious light.
> There let the pealing organ blow,
> To the full-voiced choir below,
> In service high and anthem clear,
> As may with sweetness through mine ear
> Dissolve me into ecstacies,
> And bring all heaven before mine eyes.

So builds itself up, in a thousand complex and com-

plicated forms, the Priestly Lie. There are a score of
great religions in the world, each with scores or hundreds of sects, each with its priestly orders, its complicated creed and ritual, its heavens and hells. Each has
its thousands or millions or hundreds of millions of "true
believers"; each damns all the others, with more or less
heartiness—and each is a mighty fortress of Graft.

There will be few readers of this book who have not
been brought up under the spell of some one of these
systems of Supernaturalism; who have not been taught
to speak with respect of some particular priestly order,
to thrill with awe at some particular sacred rite, to seek
respite from earthly woes in some particular ceremonial
spell. These things are woven into our very fibre in
childhood ; they are sanctified by memories of joys and
griefs, they are confused with spiritual struggles, they
become part of all that is most vital in our lives. The
reader who wishes to emancipate himself from their
thrall will do well to begin with a study of the beliefs
and practices of other sects than his own—a field where
he is free to observe and examine without fear of sacri-
lege. Let him look into Madame Blavatsky's "Secret
Doctrine", or her "Isis Unveiled"—encyclopedias of the
fantastic inventions which terror and longing have wrung
out of the tortured soul of man. Here are mysteries and
solemnities, charms and spells, illuminations and trans-
migrations, angels and demons, guides, controls and
masters—all of which it is permissible to refuse to support with gifts. Let the reader then go to James Free-
man Clarke's "Ten Great Religions", and realize how
many billions of humans have lived and died in the solemn certainty that their welfare on earth and in heaven

depended upon their accepting certain ideas and practicing certain rites, all mutually exclusive and incompatible, each damning the others and the followers of the
others.   So gradually the realization will come to him
that the test of a doctrine about life and its welfare must
be something else than the fact that one was born to it.

The Great Fear

It was not the fault of primitive man that he was
ignorant, nor that his ignorance made him a prey to dread.
The traces of his mental suffering will inspire in us only
pity and sympathy; for Nature is a grim school-mistress,
and not all her lessons have yet been learned.   We have
a right to scorn and anger only when we see this dread
being diverted from its true function, a stimulus to a
search for knowledge, and made into a means of clamp-
ing down ignorance upon the mind of the race.   That
this has been the deliberate policy of institutionalized
Religion no candid student can deny.

The first thing brought forth by the study of any
religion, ancient or modern, is that it is based upon Fear,
born of it, fed by it—and that it cultivates the source
from which its nourishment is derived.   "The fear of
divine anger", says Prof. Jastrow, "runs as an undercur-
rent through the entire religious literature of Babylonia
and Assyria."   In the words of Tabi-utul-Enlil, King of
ancient Nippur:

Who is there that can grasp the will of the gods in heaven?
The plan of a god is full of mystery—who can understand it?
He who is still alive at evening is dead the next morning.
In an instant he is cast into grief, in a moment he is crushed.

And that cry might be duplicated from almost any
page of the Hebrew scriptures: the only difference being

that the Hebrews combined all their fears into one Great Fear. "The fear of the Lord is the beginning of wisdom," we are told by Solomon of the thousand wives; and the Psalmist repeats it. "Dominion and fear are with Him," cries Job. "How then can any man be just before God? Or how can he be clean that is born of a woman? Behold, even the moon hath no brightness, and the stars are not pure in His sight: How much less man, that is a worm? And the son of man, which is a worm?" He goes on, in his lyrical rapture, "Sheol is naked before Him, and Destruction hath no covering. . . . The pillars of heaven tremble and are astonished at His rebuke. . . . The thunder of His power who can understand?" That all this is some of the world's great poetry does not in the least alter the fact that it is an abasement of the soul, an hysterical perversion of the facts of life, and a preparation of the mind for the seeds of Priestcraft.

The Book of Job has been called a "Wisdom-drama": and what is the denouement of this drama, what is ancient Hebrew wisdom's last word about life? "Wherefore I abhor myself," says Job, "and repent in dust and ashes." The poor fellow has done nothing; we have been told at the beginning that he "was perfect and upright, and one that feared God, and eschewed evil." But the Sabeans and the Chaldeans rob him, and "the fire of God" falls from heaven and burns up his sheep and his servants, and "a great wind from the wilderness" kills his sons and daughters; and then his body becomes covered with boils—a phenomenon caused in part by worry, and the consequent nervous indigestion, but mainly by excess of starch and deficiency of mineral salts in the diet. Job, however, has never heard of the fasting cure for disease, and so he takes him a potsherd to scrape himself withal, and he sits among the ashes—a highly unsanitary procedure enforced by his religious ritual. So naturally he feels like a worm, and abhors himself, and cries out: "I know that Thou canst do all things, and that no purpose of Thine can be restrained." By which utter, unreasoning humility he succeeds in appeasing the Great Fear, and his friends make a sacrifice of seven bullocks and seven rams—a feast for a whole templeful of priests—and then "the Lord gave Job twice as much as he had before. . . . And after this Job lived an hundred and forty years, and saw his sons and his sons' sons, even four generations."

You do not have to look very deeply into this "Wisdom-drama" to find out whose wisdom it is. Confess your own ignorance and your own impotence, abandon yourself utterly, and then we, the sacred Caste, the Keepers of the Holy Secrets, will secure you pardon and respite—in exchange for fresh meat. Here are verses from a psalm of the ancient Babylonians, which "heathen" chant is identical in spirit and purpose with the utterances of Job:

The Sin that I have wrought, I know not;
The unclean that I have eaten, I know not;
The offense into which I have walked, I know not. . . .
The lord, in the wrath of his heart, hath regarded me;
The god, in the anger of his heart, hath surrounded me;
A goddess, known or unknown, hath wrought me sorrow. . . .
I sought for help, but no one took my hand;
I wept, but no one harkened to me. . . .
The feet of my goddess I kiss, I touch them;
To the god, known or unknown, I utter my prayer;
O god, known or unknown, turn thy countenance, accept my
    sacrifice;
O goddess, known or unknown, look mercifully on me, accept
    my sacrifice!

Salve Regina!

And now let tne reader leap three thousand years of
human history, of toil and triumph of the intellect of
man; and instead of a Hebrew manuscript or a Babylonian brick there confronts him a little publication,
printed on a modern rotary press in the capital of the
United States of America, bearing the date of October,
1914, and the title "Salve Regina". In it we find "a
beautiful prayer", composed by the late cardinal Ram-
polla; we are told that "Pius X attached to it an indulgence of 100 days, each time it is piously recited, appli-
cable to the souls in purgatory."

O Blessed Virgin, Mother of God, cast a glance from
Heaven, where thou sittest as Queen, upon this poor sinner,
your servant. Though conscious of his unworthiness. . . . he
blesses and exalts thee from his whole heart as the purest, the
most beautiful and the most holy of creatures. He blesses thy
holy name. He blesses thy sublime prerogatives as real Mother
of God, ever Virgin, conceived without stain of sin, as co-Re-
demptress of the human race. He blesses the Eternal Father
who chose you, etc. He blesses the Incarnate Word, etc. He
blesses the Divine Spirit, etc. He blesses, exalts and thanks
the most august Trinity, etc. O Virgin, holy and merciful. . . .
be pleased to accept this little homage of your servant, and
obtain for him also from your divine Son pardon for his sins,
Amen.

And then, looking more closely, we discover the purpose of this "beautiful prayer", and of the neat little
paper which prints it. "Salve Regina" is raising funds
for the "National Shrine of the Immaculate Conception", a home for more priests, and Catholic ladies who
desire to collect for it may receive little books which
they are requested to return within three months. Pius
X writes a letter of warm endorsement, and sets an ex-

ample by giving four hundred dollars "out of his poverty" —or, to be more precise, out of the poverty of the pitiful peasantry of Italy. There is included in the paper a form of bequest for "devoted clients of Our Blessed Mother", and at the top of the editorial page the most alluring of all baits for the loving hearts of the flock—that the names of deceased relatives and friends may be written in the collection books, and will be transferred to the records of the Shrine, and these persons "will share in all its spiritual benefits". In the days of Job it was with threats of boils and poverty that the Priestly Lie maintained itself; but in the case of this blackest of all Terrors, transplanted to our free Republic from the heart of the Dark Ages, the wretched victims see before their eyes the glare of flames, and hear the shrieks of their loved ones writhing in torment through uncounted ages and eternities.

Fresh Meat

In the days when I was experimenting with vegetarianism, I sought earnestly for evidence of a non-meat-eating race; but candor compelled me to admit that man was like the monkey and the pig and the bear—he was vegetarian when he could not help it. The advocates of the reform insist that meat as a diet causes muddy brains and dulled nerves; but you would certainly never suspect this from a study of history. What you find in history is that all men crave meat, all struggle for it, and the strongest and cleverest get it. Everywhere you find the subject classes living in the midst of animals which they tend, but whose flesh they rarely taste. Even in modern America, sweet land of liberty, our millions of tenant farmers raise chickens and geese and turkeys, and hardly venture to consume as much as an egg, but save everything for the summer-boarder or the buyer from the city. It would not be too much to say of the cultural records of early man that they all have to do, directly or indirectly, with the reserving of fresh meat to the masters. In J. T. Trowbridge's cheerful tale of the adventures of Captain Seaborn, we are told by the cannibal priest how idol-worship has ameliorated the morals of the tribe—

> For though some warriors of renown
>   Continue anthropophagous,
> 'Tis rare that human flesh goes down
>   The low-caste man's aesophagus!

I suspect that we should have to go back to the days of the cave-man to find the first lover of the flesh-pots who put a taboo upon meat, and promised supernatural favors to all who would exercise self-control, and instead of consuming their meat themselves, would bring it and lay it upon the sacred griddle, or altar, where the god might come in the night-time and partake of it. Certainly, at any rate, there are few religions of record in which such devices do not appear. The early laws of the Hebrews are more concerned with delicatessen for the priests than with any other subject whatever. Here, for example, is the way to make a Nazarite:

> He shall offer his offering up to the Lord, one he lamb of the first year without blemish for a burnt offering, and one ewe lamb of the first year without blemish for a sin offering, and one ram without blemish for peace offerings, and a basket of unleavened bread, cakes of fine flour mingled with oil, and wafers of unleavened bread anointed with oil, and their meat offerings.

And the law goes on to instruct the priests to take certain choice parts and "wave them for a wave offering

before the Lord: this is holy for the priest." What was
done with the other portions we are not told; but earlier
in this same "Book of Numbers" we find the general
law that

> Every offering of all the holy things of the children of
> Israel, which they bring unto the priest, shall be his. And ev-
> ery man's hallowed things shall be his: whatsoever any man
> giveth to the priest, it shall be his.

In the same way we are told by Viscount Amberley
that the priests of Ceylon first present the gifts to the
god, and then eat them. Among the Parsees, when a man
dies, the relatives must bring four new robes to the
priests; if they do this, the priests wear the robes; if they
fail to do it, the dead man appears naked before the judg-
ment-throne. The devotees are instructed that "he who
performs this rite succeeds in both worlds, and obtains
a firm footing in both worlds." Among the Buddhists,
the followers give alms to the monks, and are told specifically what advantages will thereby accrue to them. In
the Aitareyo Brahmanam of the Rig-Veda we read

> He who, knowing this, sacrifices according to this rite, is
> born from the womb of Agni and the offerings, participates in
> the nature of the Rik, Yajus, and Saman, the Veda (sacred
> knowledge), the Brahma (sacred element) and immortality, and
> is absorbed into the deity.

Among the Parsees the priest eats the bread and drinks
the haoma, or juice of a plant, considered to be both a
plant and a god. Among the Episcopalians, a contemporary Christian sect, the sacred juice is that of the
grape, and the priest is not allowed to throw away what
is left of it, but is ordered "reverently to consume it." In
as much as the priest is the sole judge of how much good

sherry wine he shall consecrate previous to the ceremony, it is to be expected that the priests of this cult should be lukewarm towards the prohibition movement, and should piously refuse to administer their sacrament with unfermented and uninteresting grape-juice.

Priestly Empires

In every human society of which we have record there has been one class which has done the hard and exhausting work, the "hewers of wood and drawers of water"; and there has been another, much smaller class which has done the directing. To belong to this latter class is to work also, but with the head instead of the hands; it is also to enjoy the good things of life, to live in the best houses, to eat the best food, to have choice of the most desirable women; it is to have leisure to cultivate the mind and appreciate the arts, to acquire graces and distinctions, to give laws and moral codes, to shape fashions and tastes, to be revered and regarded—in short, to have Power. How to get this Power and to hold it has been the first object of the thoughts of men from the beginning of time.

The most obvious method is by the sword; but this method is uncertain, for any man may take up a sword, and some may succeed with it. It will be found that empires based upon military force alone, however cruel they may be, are not permanent, and therefore not so dangerous to progress; it is only when resistance is paralyzed by the agency of Superstition, that the race can be subjected to systems of exploitation for hundreds and even thousands of years. The ancient empires were all priestly empires; the kings ruled because they obeyed the will of the priests, taught to them from childhood as the word of the gods.

Thus, for instance, Prescott tells us:

> Terror, not love, was the spring of education with the Aztecs. . . . Such was the crafty policy of the priests, who, by reserving to themselves the business of instruction, were enabled to mould the young and plastic mind according to their own wills, and to train it early to implicit reverence for religion and its ministers.

The historian goes on to indicate the economic harvest of this teaching:

> To each of the principal temples, lands were annexed for the maintenance of the priests. The estates were augmented by the policy or devotion of successive princes, until, under the last Montezuma, they had swollen to an enormous extent, and covered every district of the empire.

And this concerning the frightful system of human sacrifices, whereby the priestly caste maintained the prestige of its divinities:

> At the dedication of the temple of Huitzilopochtli, in 1486, the prisoners, who for some years had been reserved for the purpose, were ranged in files, forming a procession nearly two miles long. The ceremony consumed several days, and seventy thousand captives are said to have perished at the shrine of this terrible deity.

The same system appears in Professor Jastrow's account of the priesthood of Babylonia and Assyria:

> The ultimate source of all law being the deity himself, the original legal tribunal was the place where the image or symbol of the god stood. A legal decision was an oracle or omen, indicative of the will of the god. The power thus lodged in the priests of Babylonia and Assyria was enormous. They virtually held in their hands the life and death of the people.

And of the business side of this vast religious system:

The temples were the natural depositories of the legal arch-
ives, which in the course of centuries grew to veritably enormous proportions. Records were made of all decisions; the
facts were set forth, and duly attested by witnesses. Business
and marriage contracts, loans and deeds of sale were in like
manner drawn up in the presence of official scribes, who were
also priests. In this way all commercial transactions received
the written sanction of the religious organization. The temples themselves—at least in the large centres—entered into
business relations with the populace. In order to maintain the
large household represented by such an organization as that of
the temple of Enlil of Nippur, that of Ningirsu at Lagash, that
of Marduk at Babylon, or that of Shamash at Sippar, large holdings of land were required which, cultivated by agents for the
priests, or farmed out with stipulations for a goodly share of
the produce, secured an income for the maintenance of the
temple officials. The enterprise of the temples was expanded
to the furnishing of loans at interest—in later periods, at 20%—
to barter in slaves, to dealings in lands, besides engaging labor
for work of all kinds directly needed for the temples. A large
quantity of the business documents found in the temple arch-
ives are concerned with the business affairs of the temple, and we
are justified in including the temples in the large centres as
among the most important business institutions of the country.
In financial or monetary transactions the position of the temples was not unlike that of national banks. . . .

And so on. We may venture the guess that the
learned professor said more in that last sentence that he
himself intended for his lectures were delivered in that
temple of plutocracy, the University of Pennsylvania,
and paid out of an endowment which specifies that "all
polemical subjects shall be positively excluded!"

Prayer-wheels

These priestly empires exist in the world today. If
we wish to find them we have only to ask ourselves:

What countries are making no contribution to the progress of the race? What countries have nothing to give us, whether in art, science, or industry?

For example, Gervaise tells us of the Talapoins, or priests of Siam, that "they are exempted from all public charges, they salute nobody, while everybody prostrates himself before them. They are maintained at the public expense." In the same way we read of the negroes of the Caribbean islands that "their priests and priestesses exercise an almost unlimited power." Miss Kingsley, in her "West African Studies", tells us that if we desire to understand the institutions of this district, we must study the native's religion.

For his religion has so firm a grasp upon his mind that it influences everything he does. It is not a thing apart, as the religion of the Europeans is at times. The African cannot say, "Oh, that is all right from a religious point of view, but one must be practical." To be practical, to get on in the world, to live the day and night through, he must be right in the religious point of view, namely, must be on working terms with the great world of spirits around him. The knowledge of this spirit world constitutes the religion of the African, and his customs and ceremonies arise from his idea of the best way to influence it.

Or consider Henry Savage Landor's account of Thibet:

In Lhassa and many other sacred places fanatical pilgrims make circumambulations, sometimes for miles and miles, and for days together, covering the entire distance lying flat upon their bodies. . . . From the ceiling of the temple hang hundreds of long strips, katas, offered by pilgrims to the temple, and becoming so many flying prayers when hung up—for mechanical praying in every way is prominent in Thibet. . . . Thus instead of having to learn by heart long and varied prayers, all you have to do is to stuff the entire prayer-book into a prayer-wheel,

and revolve it while repeating as fast as you can four words
meaning, "O God, the gem emerging from the lotus-flower.". . . .
The attention of the pilgrims is directed to a large box, or often
a big bowl, where they may deposit whatever offerings they can
spare, and it must be said that their religious ideas are so
strongly developed that they will dispose of a considerable portion of their money in this fashion. . . . The Lamas are very
clever in many ways, and have a great hold over the entire
country. They are ninety per cent of them unscrupulous
scamps, depraved in every way and given to every sort of vice.
So are the women Lamas. They live and sponge on the credulity and ignorance of the crowds; it is to maintain this ignorance, upon which their luxurious life depends, that foreign influence of every kind is strictly kept out of the country.

The Butcher-Gods

In this last sentence we have summed up the fundamental fact about institutionalized religion. Wherever
belief and ritual have become the means of livelihood of
a class, all innovation will of necessity be taken as an
attack upon that class; it will be literally a crime—
robbing the priests of their age-long privileges. And of
course they will oppose the robber—using every weapon
of terrorism, both of this world and the next. They will
require the submission, not merely of their own people,
but of their neighbors, and their jealousy of rival priestly
castes will be a cause of wars. The story of the early
days of mankind is a sickening record of torture and
slaughter in the name of ten thousand butcher-gods.

Thus, for example, we read in the Hebrew religious
records how the priests were engaged in establishing the
prestige of a fetish called "the ark"; and how the people
of one tribe violated this fetish and wakened the wrath
of Jehovah, the god.

> And he smote the men of Beth-shemesh, because they had looked into the ark of the Lord, even he smote of the people fifty thousand and three score and ten men; and the people lamented, because the Lord had smitten many of the people with a great slaughter. And the men of Beth-shemesh said, Who is able to stand before this holy Lord God?

This terrible old Hebrew divinity said of himself that he was "a jealous god". Throughout the time of his sway he issued through his ministers precise instructions for the most revolting cruelties, the extermination of whole nations of men, women and children, whose sole offense was that they did not pay tribute to Jehovah's priests. Thus, for example, the chief of his prophets, Moses, called the people together, and with all solemnity, and with many warnings, handed down ten commandments graven upon stone tablets; he went on to set forth how the people were to set upon and rob their neighbors, and gave them these blood-thirsty instructions:

> When the Lord thy God shall bring thee into the land whither thou goest to possess it, and hath cast out many nations before thee, the Hittites, and the Girgashites, and the Amorites, and the Canaanites, and the Perizzites, and the Hivites, and the Jebusites, seven nations greater and mightier than thou; And when the Lord thy God shall deliver them before thee; thou shalt smite them, and utterly destroy them; thou shalt make no covenant with them, nor shew mercy unto them: . . . But thus shall ye deal with them; ye shall destroy their altars, and break down their images, and cut down their groves, and burn their graven images with fire. For thou art a holy people unto the Lord thy God: the Lord thy God hath chosen thee to be a special people unto himself, above all people that are upon the face of the earth.

The records of this Jehovah are full of similar horrors. He sent his chosen people out to destroy the Midianites, and they slew all the males, but this was not sufficient, and Moses was wroth, and commanded them to kill all the married women, and to take the single women "for themselves". We are told that sixteen thousand single women were spared, of whom "the Lord's tribute was thirty and two!" In the Book of Joshua we read that he had an interview with a supernatural personage called "the captain of the Lord's host", and how this captain had given to him a magic spell which would destroy the city of Jericho. The city should be accursed, "even it and all that are therein, to the Lord"; every living thing except one traitor-harlot was to be slaughtered, and all the wealth of the city reserved to the priestly caste. This was carried out to the letter, except that "Achan, the son of Carmi, the son of Zabdi, the son of Zerah, of the tribe of Judah, took of the accursed thing"—that is, he hid some gold and silver in his tent; whereupon the army met with a defeat, and everybody knew that something was wrong, and Joshua rent his clothes and fell to the earth upon his face before the ark of the Lord, and got another message from Jehovah, to the effect that the guilty man should be burned with fire, "he and all that he hath."

And Joshua, and all Israel with him, took Achan the son of Zerah, and the silver, and the garment, and the wedge of gold, and his sons, and his daughters, and his oxen, and his asses, and his sheep, and his tent, and all that he had: and they brought them unto the Valley of Achor. And Joshua said, Why hast thou troubled us? the Lord shall trouble thee this day. And all Israel stoned him with stones, and burned them with fire, after they had stoned him with stones.

We have no means of knowing what was the character of the unfortunate inhabitants of the city of Jericho, nor of the Hittites and the Girgashites and the Amorites and all the rest of the victims of Jehovah. To be sure, we are told by the Hebrew priests that they sacrificed their children to their gods; but then, consider what we should believe about the Hebrew religion, if we took the word of rival priestly castes! Consider, for example, that in this twentieth century we saw an orthodox Jew tried in a Russian court of law for having made a sacrifice of Christian babies; nevertheless we know that the Jews represent a considerable part of the intelligence and idealism of Russia. We know in the same way that the Moors had most of the culture and all of the scientific knowledge of Spain, that the Huguenots had most of the conscience and industry of France; and we know that they were massacred or driven out to death by the priestly castes of the Middle Ages.

The Holy Inquisition

Let us have one glimpse of the conditions in those mediaeval times, so that we may know what we ourselves have escaped. In the fifteenth century there was established in Europe the cult of a three-headed god, whose priests had won lordship over a continent. They were enormously wealthy, and unthinkably corrupt; they sold to the rich the license to commit every possible crime, and they held the poor in ignorance and degradation. Among the comparatively intelligent and freedom-loving people of Bohemia there arose a great reformer, John Huss, himself a priest, protesting against the corruptions of his order. They trapped him into their power by means of a "safe-conduct"—which they repudiated because no promise to a heretic could have validity. They found him guilty of having taught the hateful doctrine that a priest who committed crimes could not give absolution for the crimes of others; and they held an **auto de fe**—which means a "sentence of faith." As we read in Lea's "History of the Inquisition":

The cathedral of Constance was crowded with Sigismund (the Emperor) and his nobles, the great officers of the empire with their insignia, the prelates in their splendid robes. While mass was sung, Huss, as an excommunicate, was kept waiting at the door; when brought in he was placed on an elevated bench by a table on which stood a coffer containing priestly vestments. After some preliminaries, including a sermon by the Bishop of Lodi, in which he assured Sigismund that the events of that day would confer on him immortal glory, the articles of which Huss was convicted were recited. In vain he protested that he believed in transubstantiation and in the validity of the sacrament in polluted hands. He was ordered to hold his tongue, and on his persisting the beadles were told to silence him, but in spite of this he continued to utter protests. The sentence was then read in the name of the council, condemning him both for his written errors and those which had been proven by witnesses. He was declared a pertinacious and incorrigible heretic who did not desire to return to the Church; his books were ordered to be burned, and himself to be degraded from the priesthood and abandoned to the secular court. Seven bishops arrayed him in priestly garb and warned him to recant while yet there was time. He turned to the crowd, and with broken voice declared that he could not confess the errors which he never entertained, lest he should lie to God, when the bishops interrupted him, crying that they had waited long enough, for he was obstinate in his heresy. He was degraded in the usual manner, stripped of his sacerdotal vestments, his fingers scraped; but when the tonsure was to be disposed of, an absurd quarrel arose among the bishops as to whether the head should be shaved with a razor or the tonsure be destroyed with scissors. Scissors won the day, and a cross was cut in his hair. Then on his head was placed a conical paper cap, a cubit in height, adorned with painted devils and the inscription, "This is the heresiarch."

The place of execution was a meadow near the river, to which he was conducted by two thousand armed men, with Palsgrave Louis at their head, and a vast crowd, including many nobles, prelates, and cardinals. The route followed was circuitous, in order that he might be carried past the episcopal palace, in front of which his books were burning, whereat he smiled. Pity from man there was none to look for, but he sought comfort on high, repeating to himself, "Christ Jesus, Son of the living God, have mercy upon us!" and when he came in sight of the stake he fell on his knees and prayed. He was asked if he wished to confess, and said that he would gladly do so if there were space. A wide circle was formed, and Ulrich Schorand, who, according to custom, had been providently empowered to take advantage of final weakening, came forward, saying, "Dear sir and master, if you will recant your unbelief and heresy, for which you must suffer, I will willingly hear your confession; but if you will not, you know right well that, according to canon law, no one can administer the sacrament to a heretic." To this Huss answered, "It is not necessary: I am not a mortal sinner." His paper crown fell off and he smiled as his guards replaced it. He desired to take leave of his keepers, and when they were brought to him he thanked them for their kindness, saying that they had been to him rather brothers than jailers. Then he commenced to address the crowd in German, telling them that he suffered for errors which he did not hold, and he was cut short. When bound to the stake, two cartloads of fagots and straw were piled up around him, and the palsgrave and vogt for the last time adjured him to abjure. Even yet he could save himself, but only repeated that he had been convicted by false witnesses on errors never entertained by him. They clapped their hands and then withdrew, and the executioners applied the fire. Twice Huss was heard to exclaim, "Christ Jesus, Son of the living God, have mercy upon me!" then a wind springing up and blowing the flames and smoke into his face checked further utterances, but his head was seen to shake and his lips to move while one might twice or thrice recite a paternoster. The tragedy was over; the sorely-tried soul had escaped from its tormentors, and the bitterest enemies of the reformer could not refuse to him the praise that no philosopher of old had faced death with more composure than he had shown in his dreadful extremity. No faltering of the voice had betrayed an internal struggle. Palsgrave Louis, seeing Huss's mantle on the arm of one of the executioners, ordered it thrown into the flames lest it should be reverenced as a relic, and promised the man to compensate him. With the same view the body was carefully reduced to ashes and thrown into the Rhine, and even the earth around the stake was dug up and carted off; yet the Bohemians long hovered around the spot and carried home fragments of the neighboring clay, which they reverenced as relics of their martyr. The next day thanks were returned to God in a solemn procession in which figured Sigismund and his queen, the princes and nobles, nineteen cardinals, two patriarchs, seventy-seven bishops, and all the clergy of the council. A few days later Sigismund, who had delayed his departure for Spain to see the matter concluded, left Constance, feeling that his work was done.

Hell-Fire

If such a scene could be witnessed in the world today, it would only be in some remote and wholly savage place, such as the mountains of Hayti, or the Solomon Islands. It could no longer happen in any civilized country; the reason being, not any abatement of the pretensions of the priesthood, but solely the power of science, embodied in the physical arm of a secular State. The advance of that arm the church has fought systematically, in every country, and at every point. To quote Buckle: "A careful study of the history of religious toleration will prove that in every Christian country where it has been adopted, it has been forced upon the clergy by the authority of the secular classes." The wolf of superstition has been driven into its lair, but it has backed away snarling, and it still crouches, watching for a chance to spring. The Church which

burned John Huss, which burned Giordano Bruno for
teaching that the earth moves round the sun—that same
church, in the name of the same three-headed god, sent
out Francesco Ferrer to the firing-squad; if it does not
do the same thing to the author of this book, it will be
solely because of the police.   Not being allowed to burn
me here, the clergy will vent their holy indignation by
sentencing me to eternal burning in a future world which
they have created, and which they run to suit themselves.

It is a fact, the significance of which cannot be ex-
aggerated, that the measure of the civilization which any
nation has attained is the extent to which it has cur-
tailed the power of institutionalized religion.   Those peoples which are wholly under the sway of the priesthood,
such as Thibetans and Koreans, Siamese and Caribbeans,
are peoples among whom the intellectual life does not
exist.   Farther in advance are Hindoos and Turks, who
are religious, but not exclusively.   Still farther on the
way are Spaniards and Irish; here, for example, is a flash-
light of the Irish peasantry, given by one of their number, Patrick MacGill:

> The merchant was a great friend of the parish priest, who
> always told the people if they did not pay their debts they
> would burn for ever and ever in hell.   "The fires of eternity
> will make you sorry for the debts that you did not pay," said the
> priest.   "What is eternity?" he would ask in a solemn voice
> from the altar steps.   "If a man tried to count the sands on
> the sea-shore and took a million years to count every single
> grain, how long would it take him to count them all?   A long
> time, you'll say.   But that time is nothing to eternity.   Just
> think of it!   Burning in hell while a man, taking a million years
> to count a grain of sand, counts all the sand on the sea-shore.
> And this because you did not pay Farley McKeown his lawful

debts, his lawful debts within the letter of the law." That concluding phrase, "within the letter of the law," struck terror
into all who listened, and no one, maybe not even the priest
himself, knew what it meant.

There is light in Ireland to-day, and hope for an
Irish culture; the thing to be noted is that it comes from
two movements, one for agricultural co-operation and
the other for political independence—both of them definitely and specifically non-religious. This same thing
has been true of the movements which have helped on
happier nations, such as the republics of France and
America, which have put an end to the power of the
priestly caste to take property by force, and to dominate
the mind of the child without its parents' consent.

This is as far as any nation has so far gone; it has
apparently not yet occurred to any legislature that the
State may owe a duty to the child to protect its mind
from being poisoned, even though it has the misfortune
to be born of poisoned parents. It is still permitted that
parents should terrify their little ones with images of a
personal devil and a hell of eternal brimstone and sul-
phur; it is permitted to found schools for the teaching
of devil-doctrines; it is permitted to organize gigantic
campaigns and systematically to infect whole cities full
of men, women and children with hell-fire phobias. In
the American city where I write one may see gather-
ings of people sunk upon their knees, even rolling on the
ground in convulsions, moaning, sobbing, screaming to
be delivered from such torments. I open my morning
paper and read of the arrest of five men and seven
women in Los Angeles, members of a sect known as the
"Church of the Living God", upon a charge of having
disturbed the peace of their neighbors. The police of-

ficers testified that the accused claimed to be possessed
of the divine spirit, and that as signs of this possession
they "crawled on the floor, grunted like pigs and barked
like dogs." There were "other acts, even more startling", about which the newspapers did not go into details. And again, a week or two later, I read how a woman has been heard screaming, and found tied to a bed-
post, being whipped by a man. She belonged to a religious sect which had found her guilty of witchcraft. Another woman was about to shoot her, but this woman's
nerve failed, and the "high priest" was called in, who
decreed a whipping. The victim explained to the police
that she would have deserved to be whipped had she
really been a witch, but a mistake had been made—it
was another woman who was the witch. And again in
the Los Angeles "Times" I read a perfectly serious news
item, telling how a certain man awakened one morning,
and found on his pillow where his head had lain a perfect reproduction of the head of Christ with its crown of
thorns. He called in his neighbors to witness the mir-
acle, and declared that while he was not superstitious,
he knew that such a thing could not have happened by
chance, and he knew what it was intended to signify—
he would buy more Liberty Bonds and be more ardent
in his support of the war!

And this is the world in which our scientists and
men of culture think that the battle of the intellect is
won, and that it is no longer necessary to spend our
energies in fighting "Religion!"

BOOK TWO

The Church of Good Society

Within the House of Mammon his priesthood stands
    alert
By mysteries attended, by dusk and splendors girt,
Knowing, for faiths departed, his own shall still endure,
And they be found his chosen, untroubled, solemn, sure.

Within the House of Mammon the golden altar lifts
Where dragon-lamps are shrouded as costly incense
    drifts—
A dust of old ideals, now fragrant from the coals,
To tell of hopes long-ended, to tell the death of souls.

Sterling.

The Rain Makers

I begin with the Church of Good Society, because it happens to be the Church in which I was brought up. Reading this statement, some of my readers suspected me of snobbish pride. I search my heart; yes, it brings a hidden thrill that as far back as I can remember I knew this atmosphere of urbanity, that twice every Sunday those melodious and hypnotizing incantations were chanted in my childish ears! I take up the book of ritual, done in aristocratic black leather with gold lettering, and the old worn volume brings me strange stirrings of recollected awe. But I endeavor to repress these vestigial emotions and to see the volume— not as a message from God to Good Society, but as a landmark of man's age-long struggle against myth and dogma used as a source of income and a shield to privilege.

In the beginning, of course, the priest and the magician ruled the field. But today, as I examine this "Book of Common Prayer", I discover that there is at least one spot out of which he has been cleared entirely; there appears no prayer to planets to stand still, or to comets to go away. The "Church of Good Society" has discovered astronomy! But if any astronomer attributes this to his instruments with their marvelous accuracy, let him at least stop to consider my "economic interpretation" of the phenomenon—the fact that the heavenly bodies affect the destinies of mankind so little that there has not been sufficient emolument to justify the priest in holding on to his job as astrologer.

But when you come to the field of meteorology, what a difference! Has any utmost precision of barometer

been able to drive the priest out of his prerogatives as
rainmaker? Not even in the most civilized of countries; not in that most decorous and dignified of institutions, the Protestant Episcopal Church of America!
I study with care the passage wherein the clergyman
appears as controller of the fate of crops. I note a
chastened caution of phraseology; the church will not
repeat the experience of the sorcerer's apprentice, who set
the demons to bringing water, and then could not make
them stop! The spell invokes "moderate rain and show-
ers"; and as an additional precaution there is a counter-
spell against "excessive rains and floods": the weather-
faucet being thus under exact control.

I turn the pages of this "Book of Common Prayer",
and note the remnants of magic which it contains. There
are not many of the emergencies of life with which the
priest is not authorized to deal; not many natural phenomena for which he may not claim the credit. And in
case anything should have been overlooked, there is a
blanket order upon Providence: "Graciously hear us,
that those evils which the craft or subtilty of the devil
or man worketh against us, be brought to nought!" I
am reminded of the idea which haunted my childhood,
reading fairy-stories about the hero who was allowed
three wishes that would come true. I could never understand why the hero did not settle the matter once for
all—by wishing that everything he wished might come
true!

Most of these incantations are harmless, and some are
amiable; but now and then you come upon one which is
sinister in its implications. The volume before me happens to be of the Church of England, which is even more

forthright in its confronting of the Great Magic. Many
years ago I remember talking with an English army officer, asking how he could feel sure of his soldiers in case
of labor strikes; did it never occur to him that the men
had relatives among the workers, and might some time
refuse to shoot them? His answer was that he was
aware of it, the military had worked out its technique with
care. He would never think of ordering his men to fire
upon a mob in cold blood; he would first start the spell
of discipline to work, he would march them round the
block, and get them in the swing, get their blood moving to military music; then, when he gave the order, in
they would go. I have never forgotten the gesture, the
animation with which he illustrated their going—I could
hear the grunting of bayonets in the flesh of men. The
social system prevailing in England has made necessary
the perfecting of such military technique; also, you discover, English piety has made necessary the providing of
a religious sanction for it. After the job has been done
and the bayonets have been wiped clean, the company is
marched to church, and the officer kneels in his family
pew, and the privates kneel with the parlor-maids, and
the clergyman raises his hands to heaven and intones:
"We bless thy Holy Name, that it hath pleased Thee to
appease the seditious tumults which have been lately
raised up among us!"

And sometimes the clergyman does more than bless
the killers—he even takes part in their bloody work. In
the Home Office Records of the British Government I
read (vol 40, page 17) how certain miners were on strike
against low wages and the "truck" system, and the Vicar
of Abergavenny put himself at the head of the yeomanry

and the Greys. He wrote the Home Office a lively account of his military operations. All that remained was to apprehend certain of the strikers, "and then I shall be able to return to my Clerical duties." Later he wrote of the "sinister influences" which kept the miners from returning to their work, and how he had put half a dozen of the most obstinate in prison.

The Babylonian Fire-god

So we come to the most important of the functions of the tribal god, as an ally in war, an inspirer to martial valour. When in ancient Babylonia you wished to overcome your enemies, you went to the shrine of the Fire-god, and with awful rites the priest pronounced incantations, which have been preserved on bricks and handed down for the use of modern churches. "Pronounce in a whisper, and have a bronze image therewith," commands the ancient text, and runs on for many strophes in this fashion:

> Let them die, but let me live!
> Let them be put under a ban, but let me prosper!
> Let them perish, but let me increase!
> Let them become weak, but let me wax strong!
> O, fire-god, mighty, exalted among the gods,
> Thou art the god, thou art my lord, etc.

This was in heathen Babylon, some three thousand years ago. Since then, the world has moved on—

> Three thousand years of war and peace and glory,
>   Of hope and work and deeds and golden schemes,
> Of mighty voices raised in song and story,
>   Of huge inventions and of splendid dreams—

And in one of the world's leading nations the people stand up and bare their heads, and sing to their god to save their king and punish those who oppose him—

O Lord our God, arise,
Scatter his enemies,
And make them fall;
Confound their politics,
Frustrate their knavish tricks,
On him our hopes we fix,
God save us all.

Recently, I understand, it has become the custom to
omit this stanza from the English national anthem; but
it is clear that this is because of its crudity of expression,
not because of objection to the idea of praying to a god
to assist one nation and injure others; for the same sen-
timent is expressed again and again in the most carefully edited of prayer-books:

Abate their pride, assuage their malice, and confound their
devices.
Defend us, Thy humble servants, in all assaults of our enemies.
Strengthen him (the King) that he may vanquish and overcome
all his enemies.
There is none other that fighteth for us, but only Thou, O God.

Prayers such as these are pronounced in every so-
called civilized nation today.   Behind every battle-line
in Europe you may see the priests of the Babylonian Fire-
god with their bronze images and their ancient incantations; you may see magic spells being wrought, magic
standards sanctified, magic bread eaten and magic wine
drunk, fetishes blessed and hoodoos lifted, eternity ran-
sacked to find means of inciting soldiers to the mood
where they will "go in".   Throughout all civilization, the
phobias and manias of war have thrown the people back
into the toils of the priest, and that church which tortured Galileo in the dungeons of the Inquisition, and shot
Ferrer beneath the walls of the fortress of Montjuich, is
rejoicing in a "rebirth of religion".

The Medicine-men

Andrew D. White tells us that

It was noted that in the 14th century, after the great plague, the Black Death, had passed, an immensely increased proportion of the landed and personal property of every European country was in the hands of the Church. Well did a great ecclesiastic remark that "pestilences are the harvests of the ministers of God."

And so naturally the clergy hold on to their prerogative as banishers of epidemics. Who knows what day the Lord may see fit to rebuke the upstart teachers of impious and atheistical inoculation, and scourge the people back into His fold as in the good old days of Moses and Aaron? Viscount Amberley, in his immensely learned and half-suppressed work, "The Analysis of Religious Belief", quotes some missionaries to the Fiji islanders, concerning the ideas of these benighted heathen on the subject of a pestilence. It was the work of a "disease-maker", who was burning images of the people with incantations; so they blew horns to frighten this disease-maker from his spells. The missionaries undertook to explain the true cause of the affliction—and thereby revealed that they stood upon the same intellectual level as the heathen they were supposed to instruct! It appeared that the natives had been at war with their neighbors, and the missionaries had commanded them to desist; they had refused to obey, and God had sent the epidemic as punishment for savage presumption!

And on precisely this same Fijian level stands the "Book of Common Prayer" of our most decorous and cultured of churches. I remember as a little child lying on a bed of sickness, occasioned by the prevalence in our home of the Southern custom of hot bread three times a day; and there came an amiable clerical gentleman and recited the service proper to such pastoral calls: "Take therefore in good part the visitation of the Lord!" And again, when my mother was ill, I remember how the clergyman read out in church a prayer for her, specifying all sickness, "in mind, body or estate". I was thinking only of my mother, and the meaning of these words passed over my childish head; I did not realize that the elderly plutocrat in black broadcloth who knelt in the pew in front of me was invoking the aid of the Almighty so that his tenements might bring in their rentals promptly; so that his little "flyer" in cotton might prove successful; so that the children in his mills might work with greater speed.

Somebody asked Voltaire if you could kill a cow by incantations, and he answered, "Yes, if you use a little strychnine with it." And that would seem to be the attitude of the present-day Anglican church-member; he calls in the best physician he knows, he makes sure that his plumbing is sound, and after that he thinks it can do no harm to let the Lord have a chance. It makes the women happy, and after all, there are a lot of things we don't yet know about the world. So he repairs to the family pew, and recites over the venerable prayers, and contributes his mite to the maintenance of an institution which, fourteen Sundays every year, proclaims the terrifying menaces of the Athanasian Creed:

Whoever will be saved, before all things it is necessary that he hold the Catholick faith. Which faith, except one do keep whole and undefiled; without doubt he shall perish everlastingly.

For the benefit of the uninitiated reader, it may be

explained that the "Catholick faith" here referred to is not the Roman Catholic, but that of the Church of England and the Protestant Episcopal Church of America. This creed of the ancient Alexandrian lays down the truth with grim and menacing precision—forty-four paragraphs of metaphysical minutiae, closing with the final doom: "This is the Catholick faith: which except a man believe faithfully, he cannot be saved."

You see, the founders of this august institution were not content with cultured complacency; what they believed they believed really, with their whole hearts, and they were ready to act upon it, even if it meant burning their own at the stake. Also, they knew the ceaseless impulse of the mind to grow; the terrible temptation which confronts each new generation to believe that which is reasonable. They met the situation by setting out the true faith in words which no one could mistake. They have provided, not merely the Creed of Athanasius, but also the "Thirty-nine Articles"—which are thirty-nine separate and binding guarantees that one who holds orders in the Episcopal Church shall be either a man of inferior mentality, or else a sophist and hypocrite. How desperate some of them have become in the face of this cruel dilemma is illustrated by the tale which is told of Dr. Jowett, of Balliol College, Oxford: that when he was required to recite the "Apostle's Creed" in public, he would save himself by inserting the words "used to" between the words "I believe", saying the inserted words under his breath, thus, "I used to believe in the Father, the Son, and the Holy Ghost." Perhaps the eminent divine never did this; but the fact that his students told it, and thought it funny, is sufficient indication of their attitude toward their "Religion." The son of William George Ward tells in his biography how this leader of the "Tractarian Movement" met the problem with cynicism which seems almost sublime: "Make yourself clear that you are justified in deception; and then lie like a trooper!"

The Canonization of Incompetence

The supreme crime of the church to-day is that everywhere and in all its operations and influences it is on the side of sloth of mind; that it banishes brains, it sanctifies stupidity, it canonizes incompetence. Consider the power of the Church of England and its favorite daughter here in America; consider their prestige with the press and in politics, their hold upon literature and the arts, their control of education and the minds of children, of charity and the lives of the poor: consider all this, and then say what it means to society that such a power must be, in every new issue that arises, on the side of reaction and falsehood. "So it was in the beginning, is now, and ever shall be," runs the church's formula; and this per se and a priori, of necessity and in the nature of the case.

Turn over the pages of history and read the damning record of the church's opposition to every advance in every field of science, even the most remote from theological concern. Here is the Reverend Edward Massey, preaching in 1772 on "The Dangerous and Sinful Practice of Inoculation"; declaring that Job's distemper was probably confluent small-pox; that he had been inoculated doubtless by the devil; that diseases are sent by Providence for the punishment of sin; and that the proposed attempt to prevent them is "a diabolical operation". Here

are the Scotch clergy of the middle of the nineteenth
century denouncing the use of chloroform in obstetrics,
because it is seeking "to avoid one part of the primeval
curse on woman". Here is Bishop Wilberforce of Oxford anathematizing Darwin: "The principle of natural
selection is absolutely incompatible with the word of
God"; it "contradicts the revealed relation of creation to
its creator"; it "is inconsistent with the fulness of His
glory"; it is "a dishonoring view of nature". And the
Bishop settled the matter by asking Huxley whether he
was descended from an ape through his grandmother or
grandfather.

Think what it means, friends of progress, that these
ecclesiastical figures should be set up for the reverence of
the populace, and that every time mankind is to make an
advance in power over Nature, the pioneers of thought
have to come with crow-bars and derricks and heave
these figures out of the way! And you think that conditions are changed to-day? But consider syphilis and
gonorrhea, about which we know so much, and can do
almost nothing; consider birth-control, which we are sent
to jail for so much as mentioning! Consider the divorce
reforms for which the world is crying—and for which it
must wait, because of St. Paul! Realize that up to date
it has proven impossible to persuade the English Church
to permit a man to marry his deceased wife's sister!
That when the war broke upon England the whole nation
was occupied with a squabble over the disestablishment
of the church of Wales! Only since 1888 has it been
legally possible for an unbeliever to hold a seat in Parliament; while up to the present day men are tried for
blasphemy and convicted under the decisions of Lord

Hale, to the effect that "it is a crime either to deny the truth of the fundamental doctrines of the Christian religion or to hold them up to contempt or ridicule." Said Mr. Justice Horridge, at the West Riding Assizes, 1911: "A man is not free in any public place to use common ridicule on subjects which are sacred."

The purpose, as outlined by the public prosecutor in London, is "to preserve the standard of outward decency." And you will find that the one essential to prosecution is always that the victim shall be obscure and helpless; never by any chance is he a duke in a drawing-room. I will record an utterance of one of the obscure victims of the British "standard of outward decency", a teacher of mathematics named Holyoake, who presumed to discuss in a public hall the starvation of the working classes of the country. A preacher objected that he had discussed "our duty to our neighbor" and neglected "our duty to God"; whereupon the lecturer replied: "Our national Church and general religious institutions cost us, upon accredited computation, about twenty million pounds annually. Worship being thus expensive, I appeal to your heads and your pockets whether we are not too poor to have a God. While our distress lasts, I think it would be wise to put deity upon half pay." And for that utterance the unfortunate teacher of mathematics served six months in the common Gaol at Gloucester!

While men were being tried for publishing the "Free-thinker", the Premier of England was William Ewart Gladstone. And if you wish to know what an established church can do by way of setting up dullness in high places, get a volume of this "Grand Old Man's" writings on theological and religious questions. Read his "Juventus Mundi", in the course of which he establishes a mystic connection between the trident of Neptune and the Christian Trinity! Read his efforts to prove that the writer of Genesis was an inspired geologist! This writer of Genesis points out in Nature "a grand, fourfold division, set forth in an orderly succession of times: First, the water population; secondly, the air population; thirdly, the land population of animals; fourthly, the land population consummated in man." And it seems that this division and sequence "is understood to have been so affirmed in our time by natural science that it may be taken as a demonstrated conclusion and established fact." Hence we must conclude of the writer of Genesis that "his knowledge was divine"! Consider that this was actually published in one of the leading British monthlies, and that it was necessary for Professor Huxley to answer it, pointing out that so far is it from being true that "a fourfold division and orderly sequence" of water, air and land animals "has been affirmed in our time by natural science", that on the contrary, the assertion is "directly contradictory to facts known to everyone who is acquainted with the elements of natural science". The distribution of fossils proves that land animals originated before sea-animals, and there has been such a mixing of land, sea and air animals as utterly to destroy the reputation of both Genesis and Gladstone as possessing a divine knowledge of Geology.

Gibson's Preservative

I have a friend, a well-known "scholar", who permits me the use of his extensive library. I stand in the middle and look about me, and see in the dim shadows walls lined from floor to ceiling with decorous and grave-looking books, bound for the most part in black, many of them fading to green with age. There are literally thousands of such, and their theme is the pseudo-science of "divinity". I close my eyes, to make the test fair, and walk to the shelves and put out my hand and take a book. It proves to be a modern work, "A History of the English Prayer-book in Relation to the Doctrine of the Eucharist". I turn the pages and discover that it is a study of the variations of one minute detail of church doctrine. This learned divine—he has written many such works, as the advertisements inform us—fills up the greater part of his pages with foot-notes from hundreds of authorities, arguments and counter-arguments over supernatural subtleties. I will give one sample of these footnotes—asking the reader to be patient:

I add the following valuable observation, of Dean Goode: ("On Eucharist", II p 757. See also Archbishop Ware in Gibson's "Preservative", vol X, Chap II) "One great point for which our divines have contended, in opposition to Romish errors, has been the reality of that presence of Christ's Body and Blood to the soul of the believer which is affected through the operation of the Holy Spirit notwithstanding the absence of that Body and Blood in Heaven. Like the Sun, the Body of Christ is both present and absent; present, really and truly present, in one sense—that is, by the soul being brought into immediate communion with—but absent in another sense—that is, as regards the contiguity of its substance to our bodies. The authors under review, like the Romanists, maintain that this is not a Real Presence, and assuming their own interpretation of the phrase to be the only true one, press into their service the testimony of divines who, though using the phrase, apply it in a sense the reverse of theirs. The ambiguity of the phrase, and its misapplication by the Church of Rome, have induced many of our divines to repudiate it, etc."

Realize that of the work from which this "valuable

observation" is quoted, there are at least two volumes, the second volume containing not less than 757 pages! Realize that in Gibson's "Preservative" there are not less than ten volumes of such writing! Realize that in this twentieth century a considerable portion of the mental energies of the world's greatest empire is devoted to that kind of learning!

I turn to the date upon the volume, and find that it is 1910. I was in England within a year of that time, and so I can tell what was the condition of the English people while printers were making and papers were reviewing and book-stores were distributing this work of ecclesiastical research. I walked along the Embankment and saw the pitiful wretches, men, women and sometimes children, clad in filthy rags, starved white and frozen blue, soaked in winter rains and shivering in winter winds, homeless, hopeless, unheeded by the doctors of divinity, unpreserved by Gibson's "Preservative". I walked on Hampstead Heath on Easter day, when the population of the slums turns out for its one holiday; I walked, literally trembling with horror, for I had never seen such sights nor dreamed of them. These creatures were hardly to be recognized as human beings; they were some new grotesque race of apes. They could not walk, they could only shamble; they could not laugh, they could only leer. I saw a hand-organ playing, and turned away—the things they did in their efforts to dance were not to be watched. And then I went out into the beautiful English country; cultured and charming ladies took me in swift, smooth motor-cars, and I saw the pitiful hovels and the drink-sodden, starch-poisoned inhabitants—slum-populations everywhere, even on the land! When the news-

paper reporters came to me, I said that I had just come
from Germany, and that if ever England found herself at
war with that country, she would regret that she had let
the bodies and the minds of her people rot; for which expression I was severely taken to task by more than one
British divine.

The bodies—and the minds; the rot of the latter being
the cause of the former. All over England in that year
of 1910, in thousands of schools, rich and poor, and in the
greatest centres of learning, men like Dean Goode were
teaching boys dead languages and dead sciences and dead
arts; sending them out to life with no more conception
of the modern world than a monk of the Middle Ages;
sending them out with minds made hard and inflexible,
ignorant of science, indifferent to progress, contemptuous
of ideas. And then suddenly, almost overnight, this terrified people finds itself at war with a nation ruled and
disciplined by modern experts, scientists and technicians.
The awful muddle that was in England during the first
two years of the war has not yet been told in print; but
thousands know it, and some day it will be written, and
it will finish forever the prestige of the British ruling
caste. They rushed off an expedition to Gallipoli, and
somebody forgot the water-supply, and at one time they
had ninety-five thousand cases of dysentery!

They always "muddle through", they tell you; that is
the motto of their ruling caste. But this time they did not
"muddle through"—they had to come to America for
help. As I write, our Congress is voting billions and tens
of billions of dollars, and a million of the best of our
young manhood are being taken from their homes—because in 1910 the mind of England was occupied with

Dean Goode "On Eucharist", and the ten volumes of Gibson's "Preservative".

The Elders

What the Church means in human affairs is the rule of the aged. It means old men in the seats of authority, not merely in the church, but in the law-courts and in Parliament, even in the army and navy. For a test I look up the list of bishops of the Church of England in Whitaker's Almanac; it appears that there are 40 of these functionaries, including the archbishops, but not the suffragans; and that the total salary paid to them amounts to more than nine hundred thousand dollars a year. This, it should be understood, does not include the pay of their assistants, nor the cost of maintaining their religious establishments; it does not include any private incomes which they or their wives may possess, as members of the privileged classes of the Empire. I look up their ages in Who's Who, and I find that there is only one below fifty-three; the oldest of them is ninety-one, while the average age of the goodly company is seventy. There have been men in history who have retained their flexibility of mind, their ability to adjust themselves to new circumstances at the age of seventy, but it will always be found that these men were trained in science and practical affairs, never in dead languages and theology. One of the oldest of the English prelates, the Archbishop of Canterbury, recently stated to a newspaper reporter that he worked seventeen hours a day, and had no time to form an opinion on the labor question.

And now—here is the crux of the argument—do these aged gentlemen rule of their own power? They do not! They do literally nothing of their own power; they could not make their own episcopal robes, they could not even cook their own episcopal dinners. They have to be maintained in all their comings and goings. Who supports them, and to what end?

The roots of the English Church are in the English land system, which is one of the infamies of the modern world. It dates from the days of William the Norman, who took possession of Britain with his sword, and in order to keep possession for himself and his heirs, distributed the land among his nobles and prelates. In those days, you understand, a high ecclesiastic was a man of war, who did not stoop to veil his predatory nature under pretense of philanthropy; the abbots and archbishops of William wore armor and had their troops of knights like the barons and the dukes. William gave them vast tracts, and at the same time he gave them orders which they obeyed. Says the English chronicler, "Stark he was. Bishops he stripped of their bishopricks, abbots of their abbacies". Green tells us that "the dependence of the church on the royal power was strictly enforced. Homage was exacted from bishop as from baron." And what was this homage? The bishop knelt before William, bareheaded and without arms, and swore: "Hear my lord, I become liege man of yours for life and limb and earthly regard, and I will keep faith and loyalty to you for life and death, God help me."

The lands which the church got from William the Norman, she has held, and always on the same condition —that she shall be "liege man for life and limb and earthly regard". In this you have the whole story of the church of England, in the twentieth century as in the eleventh. The balance of power has shifted from time

to time; old families have lost the land and new families
have gotten it; but the loyalty and homage of the church
have been held by the land, as the needle of the compass
is held by a mass of metal. Some two hundred and fifty
years ago a popular song gave the general impression—

> For this is law that I'll maintain
> Until my dying day, sir:
> That whatsoever king shall reign
> I'll still be vicar of Bray, sir!

So, wherever you take the Anglican clergy, they are
Tories and Royalists, conservatives and reactionaries,
friends of every injustice that profits the owning class.
And always among themselves you find them intriguing
and squabbling over the dividing of the spoils; always
you find them enjoying leisure and ease, while the people suffer and the rebels complain. One can pass down
the corridor of English history and prove this statement
by the words of Englishmen from every single generation. Take the fourteenth century; the "Good Parliament" declares that

> Unworthy and unlearned caitiffs are appointed to benefices
> of a thousand marks, while the poor and learned hardly ob-
> tain one of twenty. God gave the sheep to be pastured, not to
> be shaven and shorn.

And a little later comes the poet of the people, Piers
Plowman—

> But now is Religion a rider, a roamer through the streets,
> A leader at the love-day, a buyer of the land,
> Pricking on a palfrey from manor to manor,
> A heap of hounds at his back, as tho he were a lord;
> And if his servant kneel not when he brings his cup,
> He loureth on him asking who taught him courtesy.
> Badly have lords done to give their heirs' lands

Away to the Orders that have no pity;
Money rains upon their altars.
There where such parsons be living at ease
They have no pity on the poor; that is their "charity".
Ye hold you as lords; your lands are too broad,
But there shall come a king and he shall shrive you all
And beat you as the bible saith for breaking of your Rule.

Another step through history, and in the early part
of the sixteenth century here is Simon Fish, addressing
King Henry the Eighth, in the "Supplicacyon for the
Beggars", complaining of the "strong, puissant and coun-
terfeit holy and ydell" which "are now increased under
your sight, not only into a great nombre, but ynto a
kingdome."

They have begged so importunatly that they have gotten
ynto their hondes more than a therd part of all youre Realme.
The goodliest lordshippes, maners, londes, and territories, are
theyres. Besides this, they have the tenth part of all the
corne, medowe, pasture, grasse, wolle, coltes, calves, lambes,
pigges, gese and chikens. Ye, and they looke so narowly uppon
theyre proufittes, that the poore wyves must be countable to
thym of every tenth eg, or elles she gettith not her rytes at
ester, shal be taken as an heretike. . . . Is it any merveille
that youre people so compleine of povertie? The Turke nowe,
in your tyme, shulde never be abill to get so moche grounde of
christendome . . . And whate do al these gredy sort of
sturdy, idell, holy theves? These be they that have made an
hundredth thousand idell hores in your realme. These be they
that catche the pokkes ot one woman, and bere them to an
other.

The petitioner goes on to tell how they steal wives
and all their goods with them, and if any man protest
they make him a heretic, "so that it maketh him wisshe
that he had not done it". Also they take fortunes for
masses and then don't say them. "If the Abbot of west-

minster shulde sing every day as many masses for his
founders as he is bounde to do by his foundacion, 1000
monkes were too few." The petitioner suggests that the
king shall "tie these holy idell theves to the cartes, to be
whipped naked about every market towne till they will
fall to laboure!"

Church History

King Henry did not follow this suggestion precisely,
but he took away the property of the religious orders for
the expenses of his many wives and mistresses, and forced
the clergy in England to forswear obedience to the Pope
and make his royal self their spiritual head. This was
the beginning of the Anglican Church, as distinguished
from the Catholic; a beginning of which the Anglican
clergy are not so proud as they would like to be. When
I was a boy, they taught me what they called "church
history", and when they came to Henry the Eighth they
used him as an illustration of the fact that the Lord is
sometimes wont to choose evil men to carry out His
righteous purposes. They did not explain why the Lord
should do this confusing thing, nor just how you were
to know, when you saw something being done by a murderous adulterer, whether it was the will of the Lord
or of Satan; nor did they go into details as to the motives which the Lord had been at pains to provide, so as
to induce his royal agent to found the Anglican Church.
For such details you have to consult another set of authorities—the victims of the plundering.

When I was in college my professor of Latin was a
gentleman with bushy brown whiskers and a thundering
voice of which I was often the object—for even in those
early days I had the habit of persisting in embarrassing

questions. This professor was a devout Catholic, and
not even in dealing with ancient Romans could he re-
strain his propaganda impulses. Later on in life he became editor of the "Catholic Encyclopedia", and now
when I turn its pages, I imagine that I see the bushy
brown whiskers, and hear the thundering voice: "Mr.
Sinclair, it is so because I tell you it is so!"

I investigate, and find that my ex-professor knows all
about King Henry the Eighth, and his motives in founding the Church of England; he is ready with an "economic interpretation", as complete as the most rabid
muckraker could desire! It appears that the king wanted
a new wife, and demanded that the Pope should grant
the necessary permission; in his efforts to browbeat the
Pope into such betrayal of duty, King Henry threatened
the withdrawal of the "annates" and the "Peter's pence".
Later on he forced the clergy to declare that the Pope
was "only a foreign bishop", and in order to "stamp out
overt expression of disaffection, he embarked upon a ver-
itable reign of terror".

In Anglican histories, you are assured that all this
was a work of religious reform, and that after it the
Church was the pure vehicle of God's grace. There were
no more "holy idell theves", holding the land of England
and plundering the poor. But get to know the clergy,
and see things from the inside, and you will meet some
one like the Archbishop of Cashell, who wrote to one of
his intimates:

I conclude that a good bishop has nothing more to do than
to eat, drink and grow fat, rich and die; which laudable example I propose for the remainder of my days to follow.

If you say that might be a casual jest, hear what

Thackeray reports of that period, the eighteenth century, which he knew with peculiar intimacy:

> I read that Lady Yarmouth (my most religious and gracious King's favorite) sold a bishopric to a clergyman for 5000 pounds. (She betted him the 5000 pounds that he would not be made a bishop, and he lost, and paid her.) Was he the only prelate of his time led up by such hands for consecration? As I peep into George II's St. James, I see crowds of cassocks pushing up the back-stairs of the ladies of the court; stealthy clergy slipping purses into their laps; that godless old king yawning under his canopy in his Chapel Royal, as the chaplain before him is discoursing. Discoursing about what?—About righteousness and judgment? Whilst the chaplain is preaching, the king is chattering in German and almost as loud as the preacher; so loud that the clergyman actually burst out crying in his pulpit, because the defender of the faith and the dispenser of bishoprics would not listen to him!

Land and Livings

And how is it in the twentieth century? Have conditions been much improved? There are great Englishmen who do not think so. I quote Robert Buchanan, a poet who spoke for the people, and who therefore has still to be recognized by English critics. He writes of the "New Rome", by which he means present-day England:

> The gods are dead, but in their name
> Humanity is sold to shame,
> While (then as now!) the tinsel'd priest
> Sitteth with robbers at the feast,
> Blesses the laden, blood-stained board,
> Weaves garlands round the butcher's sword,
> And poureth freely (now as then)
> The sacramental blood of Men!

You see, the land system of England remains—the changes having been for the worse. William the Con-

queror wanted to keep the Saxon peasantry contented, so
he left them their "commons"; but in the eighteenth century these were nearly all filched away. We saw the
same thing done within the last generation in Mexico,
and from the same motive—because developing capitalism needs cheap labor, whereas people who have access
to the land will not slave in mills and mines. In England, from the time of Queen Anne to that of William
and Mary, the parliaments of the landlords passed some
four thousand separate acts, whereby more than seven
million acres of the common land were stolen from the
people. It has been calculated that these acres might
have supported a million families; and ever since then
England has had to feed a million paupers all the time.

As an old song puts the matter:

> Why prosecute the man or woman
> Who steals a goose from off the common,
> And let the greater felon loose
> Who steals the common from the goose?

In our day the land aristocracy is rooted like the native oak in British soil: some of them direct descendants
of the Normans, others children of the court favorites
and panders who grew rich in the days of the Tudors and
the unspeakable Stuarts. Seven men own practically all
the land of the city and county of London, and collect
tribute from seven millions of people. The estates are
entailed—that is, handed down from father to oldest son
automatically; you cannot buy any land, but if you want
to build, the landlord gives you a lease, and when the
lease is up, he takes possession of your buildings. The
tribute which London pays is more than a hundred million dollars a year. So absolute is the right of the land-

owner that he can sue for trespass the driver on an aeroplane which flies over him; he imposes on fishermen a tax upon catches made many hundred of yards from the shore.

And in this graft, of course, the church has its share. Each church owns land—not merely that upon which it stands, but farms and city lots from which it derives income. Each cathedral owns large tracts; so do the schools and universities in which the clergy are educated. The income from the holdings of a church constitutes what is called a "living"; these livings, which vary in size, are the prerogatives of the younger sons of the ruling families, and are intrigued and scrambled for in exactly the fashion which Thackeray describes in the eighteenth century.

About six thousand of these "livings" are in the gift of great land owners; one noble lord alone disposes of fifty-six such plums; and needless to say, he does not present them to clergymen who favor radical land-taxes. He gives them to men like himself—autocratic to the poor, easy-going to members of his own class, and cynical concerning the grafts of grace.

In one English village which I visited the living was worth seven hundred pounds, with the use of a fine mansion; as the incumbent had a large family, he lived there. In another place the living was worth a thousand pounds, and the incumbent hired a curate, himself appearing twice a year, on Christmas day and on the King's birthday, to preach a sermon; the rest of the time he spent in Paris. It is worth noting that in 1808 a law was proposed compelling absentee pluralists—that is, clergymen holding more than one "living"—to furnish curates to do their work; it might be interesting to note that this law met with strenuous clerical opposition, the house of Bishops voting against it without a division. Thus we may understand the sharp saying of Karl Marx, that the English clergy would rather part with thirty-eight of their thirty-nine articles than with one thirty-ninth of their income.

There is always a plentiful supply of curates in England. They are the sons of the less influential ruling families, and of the clergy; they have been trained at Oxford or Cambridge, and possess the one essential qualification, that they are gentlemen. Their average price is two hundred and fifty pounds a year; their function was made clear to me when I attended my first English tea-party. There was a wicker table, perhaps a foot and a half square, having three shelves, one below the other —on the top layer the plates and napkins, on the next the muffins, and on the lowest the cake. Said the hostess, "Will you pass the curate, please?" I looked puzzled, and she pointed. "We call that the curate, because it does the work of a curate."

Graft in Tail

As one of America's head muck-rakers, I found that I was popular with the British ruling classes; they found my books useful in their campaigns against democracy, and they were surprised and disconcerted when they found I did not agree with their interpretation of my writings. I had told of corruption in American politics; surely I must know that in England they had no such evils! I explained that they did not have to; their graft, to use their own legal phrase, was "in tail"; the grafters had, as a matter of divine right, the things which in

America they had to buy. In America, for instance, we had a Senate, a "Millionaire's Club", for admission to which the members paid in cash; but in England the same men came to the same position as their birth-right. Political corruption is not an end in itself, it is merely a means to exploitation; and of exploitation England has even more than America. When I explained this, my popularity with the British ruling classes vanished quickly.

As a matter of fact, England is more like America than she realizes; her British reticence has kept her ignorant about herself. I could not carry on my business in England, because of the libel laws, which have as their first principle "the greater the truth, the greater the libel". Englishmen read with satisfaction what I write about America; but if I should turn my attention to their own country, they would send me to jail as they sent Frank Harris. The fact is that the new men in England, the lords of coal and iron and shipping and beer, have bought their way into the landed aristocracy for cash, just as our American senators have done; they have bought the political parties with campaign gifts, precisely as in America; they have taken over the press, whether by outright purchase like Northcliffe, or by advertising subsidy—both of which methods we Americans know. Within the last decade or two another group has been coming into control; and not merely is this the same class of men as in America, it frequently consists of the same invididuals. These are the big money-lenders, the international financiers who are the fine and final flower of the capitalist system. These gentlemen make the world their home—or, as Shakespeare puts it,

their oyster. They know how to fit themselves to all
environments; they are Catholics in Rome and Vienna,
country gentlemen in London, **bons vivants** in Paris,
democrats in Chicago, Socialists in Petrograd, and Hebrews wherever they are.

And of course, in buying the English government,
these new classes have bought the English Church.
Skeptics and men of the world as they are, they know
that they must have a Religion. They have read the
story of the French revolution, and the shadow of the
guillotine is always over their thoughts; they see the
giant of labor, restless in his torment, groping as in a
nightmare for the throat of his enemy. Who can blind
the eyes of this giant, who can chain him to his couch of
slumber? There is but one agent, without rival—the
Keeper of the Holy Secrets, the Deputy of the Almighty
Awfulness, the Giver and Withholder of Eternal Life.
Tremble, slave! Fall down and bow your forehead in
the dust! I can see in my memory the sight that
thrilled my childhood—my grim old Bishop, clad in his
gorgeous ceremonial robes, stretching out his hands over
the head of the new priest, and pronouncing that most
deadly of all the Christian curses:

"Whose sins thou dost forgive, they are forgiven; and
whose sins thou dost retain, they are retained!"

Bishops and Beer

For example, the International Shylocks wanted the
diamond mines of South Africa—wanted them more
firmly governed and less firmly taxed than could be
arranged with the Old Man of the Boers. So the armies
of England were sent to subjugate the country. You
might think they would have had the good taste to

leave the lowly Jesus out of this affair—but if so, you have missed the essential point about established religion. The bishops, priests, and deacons are set up for the populace to revere, and when the robber-classes need a blessing upon some enterprise, then is the opportunity for the bishops, priests and deacons to earn their "living." During the Boer war the blood-lust of the English clergy was so extreme that writers in the dignified monthly reviews felt moved to protest against it. When the pastors of Switzerland issued a collective protest against cruelties to women and children in the South African concentration-camps, it was the Right Reverend Bishop of Winchester who was brought forward to make reply. Nowadays all England is reading Bernhardi, and shuddering at Prussian glorification of war; but no one mentions Bishop Welldon of Calcutta, who advocated the Boer war as a means of keeping the nation "virile"; nor Archbishop Alexander, who said that it was God's way of making "noble natures".

The British God had other ways of improving nations—for example, the opium traffic. The British traders had been raising the poppy in India and selling its juice to the Chinese. They had made perhaps a hundred million "noble natures" by this method; and also they were making a hundred million dollars a year. The Chinese, moved by their new "virility," undertook to destroy some opium, and to stop the traffic; whereupon it was necessary to use British battle-ships to punish and subdue them. Was there any difficulty in persuading the established church of Jesus to bless this holy war? There was not! Lord Shaftesbury, himself the most devout of Anglicans, commented with horror upon the attitude of the clergy, and wrote in his diary:

> I rejoice that this cruel and debasing opium war is terminated. We have triumphed in one of the most lawless, unnecessary, and unfair struggles in the records of history; and Christians have shed more heathen blood in two years, than the heathens have shed of Christian blood in two centuries.

That was in 1843; for seventy years thereafter pious England continued to force the opium traffic upon protesting China, and only in the last two or three years has the infamy been brought to an end. Throughout the long controversy the attitude of the church was such that Li Hung Chang was moved to assert in a letter to the Anti-Opium Society:

> Opium is a subject in the discussion of which England and China can never meet on a common ground. China views the whole question from a moral standpoint, England from a fiscal.

And just as the Chinese people were poisoned with opium, so the English people are being poisoned with alcohol. Both in town and country, labor is sodden with it. Scientists and reformers are clamoring for restriction—and what prevents? Head and front of the opposition for a century, standing like a rock, has been the Established Church. The Rev. Dawson Burns, historian of the early temperance movement, declares that "among its supporters I cannot recall one Church of England minister of influence." When Asquith brought in his bill for the restriction of the traffic in beer, he was confronted with petitions signed by members of the clergy, protesting against the act. And what was the basis of their protest? That beer is a food and not a poison? Yes, of course; but also that there was property invested in brewing it. Three hundred and thirty-two clergy of the diocese of Peterborough declared:

> We do strongly protest against the main provisions of the present bill as creating amongst our people a sense of grave injustice as amounting to a confiscation of private property, spelling ruin for thousands of quite innocent people, and provoking deep and widespread resentment, which must do harm to our cause and hinder our aims.

I have come upon references to another and even more plainspoken petition, signed by 1,280 clergymen; but war-time facilities for research have not enabled me to find the text. In Prof. Henry C. Vedder's "Jesus Christ and the Social Question," we read:

> It was authoritatively stated a short time ago that Mr. Asquith's temperance bill was defeated in Parliament through the opposition of clergymen who had invested their savings in brewery stock, the profits of which might have been lessened by the bill.

Also the power of the clergy, combined with the brewer, was sufficient to put through Parliament a provision that no prohibition legislation should ever be passed without providing for compensation to the owners of the industry. Today, all over America, appeals are being made to the people to eat less grain; the grain is being shipped to England, some of it to be made into beer; and a high Anglican prelate, his Grace the Archbishop of York, comes to America to urge us to increased sacrifices, and in his first newspaper interview takes occasion to declare that his church is not in favor of prohibition as a measure of war-time economy!

Anglicanism and Alcohol

This partnership of Bishops and Beer is painfully familiar to British radicals; they see it at work in

every election—the publican confusing the voters with
spirits, while the parson confuses them with spirituality. There are two powerful societies in England employing this deadly combination—the "Anti-Socialist
Union" and the "Liberty and Property Defense
League." If you scan the lists of the organizers, directors and subsidizers of these satanic institutions,
you find Tory politicians and landlords, prominent
members of the higher clergy, and large-scale dealers
in drunkenness. I attended in London a meeting called
by the "Liberty and Property Defense League," to list-
en to a denunciation of Socialism by W. H. Mallock, a
master sophist of Roman Catholicism; upon the platform were a bishop and half a dozen members of the
Anglican clergy, together with the secretary of the
Federated Brewers' Association, the Secretary of the
Wine, Spirit, and Beer Trade Association, and three or
four other alcoholic magnates.

In every public library in England and many in
America you will find an assortment of pamphlets published by these organizations, and scholarly volumes
endorsed by them, in which the stock misrepresenta-
tions of Socialism are perpetuated. Some of these writings are brutal—setting forth the ethics of exploitation in the manner of the Rev. Thomas Malthus, the
English clergyman who supplied for capitalist depre-
dation a basis in pretended natural science. Said this
shepherd of Jesus:

A man who is born into a world already possessed, if he
cannot get subsistence from his parents, and if society does not
want his labor, has no claim of right to the smallest portion of
food, and in fact has no business to be where he is. At Nature's

mighty feast there is no cover for him. She tells him to be gone, and will quickly execute her own orders.

Such was the tone of the ruling classes in the nineteenth century; but it was found that for some reason this failed to stop the growth of Socialism, and so in our time the clerical defenders of Privilege have grown subtle and insinuating. They inform us now that they have a deep sympathy with our fundamental purposes; they burn with pity for the poor, and they would really and truly wish happiness to everyone, not merely in Heaven, but right here and now. However, there are so many complications—and so they proceed to set out all the anti-Socialist bug-a-boos. Here for example, is the Rev. James Stalker, D. D., expounding "The Ethics of Jesus," and admonishing us extremists:

> Efforts to transfer money and property from one set of hands to another may be inspired by the same passions as have blinded the present holders to their own highest good, and may be accompanied with injustice as extreme as has ever been manifested by the rich and powerful.

And again, the Rev. W. Sanday, D. D., an especially popular clerical author, gives us this sublime utterance of religion on wage-slavery:

> The world is full of mysteries, but some clear lines run through them, of which this is one. Where God has been so patient, it is not for us to be impatient.

And again, Professor Robert Flint, of Edinburgh University, a clergyman, author of a big book attacking Socialism, and bringing us back to the faith of our fathers:

> The great bulk of human misery is due, not to social arrangements, but to personal vices.

I study Professor Flint's volume in the effort to find just what, if anything, he would have the church do about the evils of our time. I find him praising the sermons of Dr. Westcott, Bishop of Durham, as being the proper sort for clergymen to preach. Bishop Westcott, whether he is talking to a high society congregation, or to one of workingmen, shows "an exquisite sense of knowing always where to stop." So I consulted the Bishop's volume, "The Social Aspects of Christianity" and I see at once why he is popular with the anti-Socialist propagandists—neither I or any other man can possibly discover what he really means, or what he really wants done.

I was fascinated by this Wescott problem; I thought maybe if I kept on the good Bishop's trail, I might in the end find something a plain man could understand; so I got the beautiful two-volume "Life of Brooke Westcott, by his Son"—and there I found an exposition of the social purposes of bishops! In the year 1892 there was a strike in Durham, which is in the coal country; the employers tried to make a cut in wages, and some ten thousand men walked out, and there was a long and bitter struggle, which wrung the episcopal heart. There was much consultation and correspondence on episcopal stationery, and at last the masters and men were got together, with the Bishop as arbitrator, and the dispute was triumphantly settled—how do you suppose? On the basis of a ten per cent reduction in wages!

I know nothing quainter in the history of English graft than the **naiveté** with which the Bishop's biographer and son tells the story of this episcopal venture into reality. The prelate came out from the conference "all smiles, and well satisfied with the result of his day's work." As for his followers, they were in ecstacies; they "seized and waltzed one another around on the carriage drive as madly as ever we danced at a flower show ball. Hats and caps are thrown into the air, and we cheer ourselves hoarse." The Bishop proceeds to his palace, and sends one more communication on episcopal stationery—an order to all his clergy to "offer their humble and hearty thanks to God for our happy deliverance from the strife by which the diocese has been long afflicted." Strange to say, there were a few varlets in Durham who did not appreciate the services of the bold Bishop, and one of them wrote and circulated some abusive verses, in which he made reference to the Bishop's comfortable way of life. The biographer then explains that the Bishop was so tender-hearted that he suffered for the horses who drew his episcopal coach, and so ascetic that he would have lived on tea and toast if he had been permitted to. A curious condition in English society, where the Bishop would have lived on tea and toast, but was not permitted to; while the working people, who didn't want to live on tea and toast, were compelled to!

Dead Cats

For more than a hundred years the Anglican clergy have been fighting with every resource at their command the liberal and enlightened men of England who wished to educate the masses of the people. In 1807 the first measure for a national school-system was denounced by the Archbishop of Canterbury as "derogatory to the authority of the Church." As a counter-

measure, his supporters established the "National Society for Promoting the Education of the Poor in the
Doctrines of the Established Church"; and the founder
of the organization, a clergyman, advocated a barn as
a good structure for a school, and insisted that the children of the workers "should not be taught beyond their
station." In 1840 a Committee of the Privy Council on
Education was appointed, but bowed to the will of the
Archbishops, setting forth the decree of "their lord-
ships" that "the first purpose of all instruction must be
the regulation of the thoughts and habits of the children by the doctrine and precepts of revealed religion."
In 1850 a bill for secular education was denounced as
presenting to the country "a choice between Heaven or
Hell, God or the Devil." In 1870, Forster, author of the
still unpassed bill, wrote that while the parsons were
disputing, the children of the poor were "growing into
savages."

As with Education, so with Social Reform. During
the struggle to abolish slavery in the British colonies,
some enthusiasts endeavored to establish the doctrine
that Christian baptism conferred emancipation upon
negroes who accepted it; whereupon the Bishop of London laid down the formula of exploitation: "Christianity and the embracing of the gospel do not make the
least alteration of civil property."

Gladstone, who was a democrat when he was not
religious, spoke of the cultured classes of England:

In almost every one, if not every one, of the greatest political
controversies of the last fifty years, whether they affected the
franchise, whether they affected commerce, whether they affected
religion, whether they affected the bad and abominable institu-

tion of slavery, or what subject they touched, these leisured classes, these educated classes, these titled classes have been in the wrong.

The "Great Commoner" did not add "these religious classes," for he belonged to the religious classes himself; but a study of the record will supply the gap. The Church opposed all the reform measures which Gladstone himself put through. It opposed the Reform Bill of 1832. It opposed all the social reforms of Lord Shaftesbury. This noble-hearted Englishman complained that at first only a single minister of religion supported him, and to the end only a few. He expressed himself as distressed and puzzled "to find support from infidels and non-professors; opposition or coldness from religionists or declaimers."

And to our own day it has been the same. In 1894 the House of Bishops voted solidly against the Employers' Liability Law. The House of Bishops opposed Home Rule, and beat it; the House of Bishops opposed Womans' Suffrage, and voted against it to the end. Concerning this establishment Lord Shaftesbury, himself the most devout of Englishmen, used the vivid phrase: "this vast aquarium full of cold-blooded life." He told the Bishops that he would give up preaching to them about ecclesiastical reform, because he knew that they would never begin. Another member of the British aristocracy, the Hon. Geo. Russell, has written of their record and adventures:

They were defenders of absolutism, slavery, and the bloody penal code; they were the resolute opponents of every political or social reform; and they had their reward from the nation outside Parliament. The Bishop of Bristol had his palace sacked and burnt; the Bishop of London could not keep an engagement to preach lest the congregation should stone him. The Bishop of Litchfield barely escaped with his life after preaching at St. Bride's, Fleet Street. Archbishop Howley, entering Canterbury for his primary visitation, was insulted, spat upon, and only brought by a circuitous route to the Deanery, amid the execrations of the mob. On the 5th of November the Bishops of Exeter and Winchester were burnt in effigy close to their own palace gates. Archbishop Howley's chaplain complained that a dead cat had been thrown at him, when the Archbishop—a man of apostolic meekness—replied: "You should be thankful that it was not a live one."

The people had reason for this conduct—as you will always find they have, if you take the trouble to inquire. Let me quote another member of the English ruling classes, Mr. Conrad Noel, who gives "an instance of the procedure of Church and State about this period":

In 1832 six agricultural labourers in South Dorsetshire, led by one of their class, George Loveless, in receipt of 9s. a week each, demanded the 10s. rate of wages usual in the neighbourhood. The result was a reduction to 8s. An appeal was made to the chairman of the local bench, who decided that they must work for whatever their masters chose to pay them. The parson, who had at first promised his help, now turned against them, and the masters promptly reduced the wage to 7s., with a threat of further reduction. Loveless then formed an agricultural union, for which all seven were arrested, treated as convicts, and committed to the assizes. The prison chaplain tried to bully them into submission. The judge determined to convict them, and directed that they should be tried for mutiny under an act of George III, specially passed to deal with the naval mutiny at the Nore. The grand jury were landowners, and the petty jury were farmers; both judge and jury were churchmen of the prevailing type. The judge summed up as follows: "Not for anything that you have done, or that I can prove that you intend to do, but for an example to others I consider it my duty to pass the sentence of seven years' penal transportation across His Majesty's high seas upon each and every one of you."

Suffer Little Children

The founder of Christianity was a man who specialized in children. He was not afraid of having His discourses disturbed by them, He did not consider them superfluous. "Of such is the Kingdom of Heaven", He said; and His Church is the inheritor of this tradition—"feed my lambs". There were children in Great Britain in the early part of the nineteenth century, and we may see what was done with them by turning to Gibbin's "Industrial History of England":

> Sometimes regular traffickers would take the place of the manufacturer, and transfer a number of children to a factory district, and there keep them, generally in some dark cellar, till they could hand them over to a mill owner in want of hands, who would come and examine their height, strength, and bodily capacities, exactly as did the slave owners in the American markets. After that the children were simply at the mercy of their owners, nominally as apprentices, but in reality as mere slaves, who got no wages, and whom it was not worth while even to feed and clothe properly, because they were so cheap and their places could be so easily supplied. It was often arranged by the parish authorities, in order to get rid of imbeciles, that one idiot should be taken by the mill owner with every twenty sane children. The fate of these unhappy idiots was even worse than that of the others. The secret of their final end has never been disclosed, but we can form some idea of their awful sufferings from the hardships of the other victims to capitalist greed and cruelty. The hours of their labor were only limited by exhaustion, after many modes of torture had been unavailingly applied to force continued work. Children were often worked sixteen hours a day, by day and by night.

In the year 1819 an act of Parliament was proposed limiting the labor of children nine years of age to four-

teen hours a day. This would seem to have been a
reasonable provision, likely to have won the approval of
Christ; yet the bill was violently opposed by Christian
employers, backed by Christian clergymen. It was in
terfering with freedom of contract, and therefore with
the will of Providence; it was anathema to an established Church, whose function was in 1819, as it is in
1918, and was in 1918 B. C., to teach the divine origin
and sanction of the prevailing economic order. "Anu
and Baal called me, Hammurabi, the exalted prince,
worshipper of the gods"....so begins the oldest legal
code which has come down to us, from 2250 B. C.; and
the coronation service of the English church is made
whole out of the same thesis. The duty of submission,
not merely to divinely chosen King, but to divinely
chosen Landlord and divinely chosen Manufacturer, is
implicit in the church's every ceremony, and explicit in
many of its creeds. In the Litany the people petition
for "increase of grace to hear meekly Thy Word"; and
here is this "Word," as little children are made to learn
it by heart. If there exists in the world a more perfect
summary of slave ethics, I do not know where to find it.

My duty towards my neighbour is.....To honour and obey
the King, and all that are put in authority under him; To submit myself to all my governours, teachers, spiritual pastors, and
masters: To order myself lowly and reverently to all my betters
....Not to covet nor desire other men's goods; But to learn and
labour truly to get mine own living, and to do my duty in that
state of life, unto which it shall please God to call me.

A hundred years ago one of the most popular of
British writers was Hannah More. She and her sister
Martha went to live in the coal-country, to teach this

"catechism" to the children of the starving miners. The "Mendip Annals" is the title of a book in which they tell of their ten years' labors in a village popularly known as "Little Hell." In this place two hundred people were crowded into nineteen houses. "There is not one creature in it that can give a cup of broth if it would save a life." In one winter eighteen perished of "a putrid fever", and the clergyman "could not raise a sixpence to save a life."

And what did the pious sisters make of all this? From cover to cover you find in the "Mendip Annals" no single word of social protest, not even of social suspicion. That wages of a shilling a day might have anything to do with moral degeneration was a proposition beyond the mental powers of England's most popular woman writer. She was perfectly content that a woman should be sentenced to death for stealing butter from a dealer who had asked what the woman thought too high a price. When there came a famine, and the children of these mine-slaves were dying like flies, Hannah More bade them be happy because God had sent them her pious self. "In suffering by the scarcity, you have but shared in the common lot, with the pleasure of knowing the advantage you have had over many villages in your having suffered no scarcity of religious instruction." And in another place she explained that the famine was caused by God to teach the poor to be grateful to the rich!

Let me remind you that probably that very scarcity has been permitted by an all-wise and gracious Providence to unite all ranks of people together, to show the poor how immediately they are dependent upon the rich, and to show both rich and poor that they are all dependent upon Himself. It has also enabled you to see more clearly the advantages you derive from the government and constitution of this country—to observe the benefits flowing from the distinction of rank and fortune, which has enabled the high to so liberally assist the low.

It appears that the villagers were entirely convinced by this pious reasoning; for they assembled one Saturday night and burned an effigy of Tom Paine! This proceeding led to a tragic consequence, for one of the "common people," known as Robert, "was overtaken by liquor," and was unable to appear at Sunday School next day. This fall from grace occasioned intense remorse in Robert. "It preyed dreadfully upon his mind for many months," records Martha More, "and despair seemed at length to take possession of him." Hannah had some conversation with him, and read him some suitable passages from "The Rise and Progress". "At length the Almighty was pleased to shine into his heart and give him comfort."

Nor should you imagine that this saintly stupidity was in any way unique in the Anglican establishment. We read in the letters of Shelley how his father tormented him with Archdeacon Paley's "Evidences" as a cure for atheism. This eminent churchman wrote a book, which he himself ranked first among his writings, called "Reasons for Contentment, addressed to the Labouring Classes of the British Public." In this book he not merely proved that religion "smooths all inequalities, because it unfolds a prospect which makes all earthly distinctions nothing"; he went so far as to prove that, quite apart from religion, the British exploiters were less fortunate than those to whom they paid a shilling a day.

Some of the conditions which poverty (if the condition of the labouring part of mankind must be so called) imposes, are not hardships, but pleasures. Frugality itself is a pleasure. It is an exercise of attention and contrivance, which, whenever it is successful, produces satisfaction.....This is lost among abundance.

And there was William Wilberforce, as sincere a philanthropist as Anglicanism ever produced, an ardent supporter of Bible societies and foreign missions, a champion of the anti-slavery movement, and also of the ruthless "Combination Laws," which denied to British wage-slaves all chance of bettering their lot. Wilberforce published a "Practical View of the System of Christianity", in which he told unblushingly what the Anglican establishment is for. In a chapter which he described as "the basis of all politics," he explained that the purpose of religion is to remind the poor

That their more lowly path has been allotted to them by the hand of God; that it is their part faithfully to discharge its duties, and contentedly to bear its inconveniences; that the objects about which worldly men conflict so eagerly are not worth the contest; that the peace of mind, which Religion offers indiscriminately to all ranks, affords more true satisfaction than all the expensive pleasures which are beyond the poor man's reach; that in this view the poor have the advantage; that if their superiors enjoy more abundant comforts, they are also exposed to many temptations from which the inferior classes are happily exemptted; that, "having food and raiment, they should be therewith content," since their situation in life, with all its evils, is better than they have deserved at the hand of God; and finally, that all human distinctions will soon be done away, and the true followers of Christ will all, as children of the same Father, be alike admitted to the possession of the same heavenly inheritance. Such are the blessed effects of Christianity on the temporal well-being of political communities.

The Court Circular

The Anglican system of submission has been transplanted intact to the soil of America. When King George the Third lost the sovereignty of the colonies, the bishops of his divinely inspired church lost the control of the clergy across the seas; but this revolution was purely one of Church politics—in doctrine and ritual the "Protestant Episcopal Church of America" remained in every way Anglican. The little children of our free republic are taught the same slave-catechism, "to order myself lowly and reverently to all my betters." The only difference is that instead of being told "to honour and obey the King," they are told "to honour and obey the civil authority."

It is the Church of Good Society in England, and it is the same in Boston, New York, Philadelphia, Baltimore, Washington, Charleston. Just as our ruling classes have provided themselves with imitation English schools and imitation English manners and imitation English clothes—so in their Heaven they have provided an imitation English monarch. I wonder how many Americans realize the treason to democracy they are committing when they allow their children to be taught a symbolism and liturgy based upon absolutist ideas. I take up the hymn-book—not the English, but the sturdy, independent, democratic American hymn-book. I have not opened it for twenty years, yet the greater part of its contents is as familiar to me as the syllables of my own name. I read:

Holy, holy, holy! All the saints adore Thee,
Casting down their golden crowns around the glassy sea;
Cherubim and seraphim bowing down before Thee,
Which wert, and art, and ever more shall be!

One might quote a hundred other hymns made thus out of royal imagery. I turn at random to the part headed "General," and find that there is hardly one hymn in which there is not "king," "throne," or some image of homage and flattery. The first hymn begins—

> Ancient of days, Who sittest, throned in glory;
> To Thee all knees are bent, all voices pray.

And the second—

> Christ, whose glory fills the skies—

And the third—

> Lord of all being, throned afar,
> Thy glory flames from sun and star.

There is a court in Heaven above, to which all good Britons look up, and about which they read with exactly the same thrills as they read the Court Circular. The two courts have the same ethical code and the same manners; their Sovereigns are jealous, greedy of attention, self-conscious and profoundly serious, punctilious and precise; their existence consisting of an endless round of ceremonies, and they being incapable of boredom. No member of the Royal Family can escape this regime even if he wishes; and no more can any member of the Holy Family—not even the meek and lowly Jesus, who chose a carpenter's wife for his mother, and showed all his earthly days a preference for low society.

This unconventional Son lived obscurely; he never carried weapons, he could not bear to have so much as a human ear cut off in his presence. But see how he figures in the Court Circular:

> The Son of God goes forth to war,
>   A kingly crown to gain:
> His blood-red banner streams afar:
>   Who follows in His train?

This carpenter's son was one of the most unpretentious men on earth; utterly simple and honest—he would not even let anyone praise him. When some one called him "good Master," he answered, quickly, "Why callest thou me good? There is none good save one, that is, God." But this simplicity has been taken with deprecation by his church, which persists in heaping compliments upon him in conventional, courtly style:

> The company of angels
> Are praising Thee on high;
> And mortal men, and all things
> Created, make reply:
> All Glory, laud and honour,
> To Thee, Redeemer, King. . . . .

The impression a modern man gets from all this is the unutterable boredom that Heaven must be. Can one imagine a more painful occupation than that of the saints —casting down their golden crowns around the glassy sea—unless it be that of the Triumvirate itself, compelled to sit through eternity watching these saints, and listening to their mawkish and superfluous compliments!

But one can understand that such things are necessary in a monarchy; they are necessary if you are going to have Good Society, and a Good Society church. For Good Society is precisely the same thing as Heaven; that is, a place to which only a few can get admission, and those few are bored. They spend their time going through costly formalities—not because they enjoy it, but because of its effect upon the populace, which reads about them and sees their pictures in the papers, and now and then is allowed to catch a glimpse of their physical Presences, as at the horse-show, or the opera, or the coaching-parade.

Horn-blowing

I know the Church of Good Society in America, having studied it from the inside. I was an extraordinarily devout little boy; one of my earliest recollections—I cannot have been more than four years of age—is of carrying a dust-brush about the house as the choir-boy carried the golden cross every Sunday morning. I remember asking if I might say the "Lord's prayer" in this fascinating play; and my mother's reply: "If you say it reverently." When I was thirteen, I attended service, of my own volition and out of my own enthusiasm, every single day during the forty days of Lent; at the age of fifteen I was teaching Sunday-school. It was the Church of the Holy Communion, at Sixth Avenue and Twentieth Street, New York; and those who know the city will understand that this is a peculiar location—precisely half way between the homes of some of the oldest and most august of the city's aristocracy, and some of the vilest and most filthy of the city's slums. The aristocracy were paying for the church, and occupied the best pews; they came, perfectly clad, **aus dem Ei gegossen,** as the Germans say, with the manner they so carefully cultivate, gracious, yet infinitely aloof. The service was made for them—as all the rest of the world is made for them; the populace was permitted to occupy a fringe of vacant seats.

The assistant clergyman was an Englishman, and a gentleman; orthodox, yet the warmest man's heart I have ever known. He could not bear to have the church remain entirely the church of the rich; he would go persistently into the homes of the poor, visiting the old slum women in their pitifully neat little kitchens, and luring their children with entertainments and Christmas candy.

They were corralled into the Sunday-school, where it was my duty to give them what they needed for the health of their souls.

I taught them out of a book of lessons; and one Sunday it would be Moses in the Bulrushes, and next Sunday it would be Jonah and the Whale, and next Sunday it would be Joshua blowing down the walls of Jericho. These stories were reasonably entertaining, but they seemed to me futile, not to the point. There were little morals tagged to them, but these lacked relationship to the lives of little slum-boys. Be good and you will be happy, love the Lord and all will be well with you; which was about as true and as practical as the procedure of the Fijians, blowing horns to drive away a pestilence.

I had a mind, you see, and I was using it. I was reading the papers, and watching politics and business. I followed the fates of my little slum-boys—and what I saw was that Tammany Hall was getting them. The liquor-dealers and the brothel-keepers, the panders and the pimps, the crap-shooters and the petty thieves—all these were paying the policeman and the politician for a chance to prey upon my boys; and when the boys got into trouble, as they were continually doing, it was the clergyman who consoled them in prison—but it was the Tammany leader who saw the judge and got them out. So these boys got their lesson, even earlier in life than I got mine—that the church was a kind of amiable fake, a pious horn-blowing; while the real thing was Tammany.

I talked about this with the vestrymen and the ladies of Good Society; they were deeply pained, but I noticed that they did nothing practical about it; and gradually, as I went on to investigate, I discovered the reason—

that their incomes came from real estate, traction, gas and other interests, which were contributing the main part of the campaign expenses of the corrupt Tammany machine, and of its equally corrupt rival. So it appeared that these immaculate ladies and gentlemen, aus dem Ei gegossen, were themselves engaged, unconsciously, perhaps, but none the less effectively, in spreading the pestilence against which they were blowing their religious horns!

So little by little I saw my beautiful church for what it was and is: a great capitalist interest, an integral and essential part of a gigantic predatory system. I saw that its ethical and cultural and artistic features, however sincerely they might be meant by individual clergymen, were nothing but a bait, a device to lure the poor into the trap of submission to their exploiters. And as I went on probing into the secret life of the great Metropolis of Mammon, and laying bare its infamies to the world, I saw the attitude of the church to such work; I met, not sympathy and understanding, but sneers and denunciation—until the venerable institution which had once seemed dignified and noble became to me as a sepulchre of corruption.

Trinity Corporation

There stands on the corner of Broadway and Wall Street a towering brown-stone edifice, one of the most beautiful and most famous churches in America. As a child I have walked through its church yard and read the quaint and touching inscriptions on its gravestones; when I was a little older, and knew Wall Street, it seemed to me a sublime thing that here in the very heart of the world's infamy there should be raised,

like a finger of warning, this symbol of Eternity and
Judgment. Its great bell rang at noon-time, and all the
traders and their wage-slaves had to listen, whether
they would or no! Such was Old Trinity to my young
soul; and what is it in reality?

The story was told some ten years ago by Charles
Edward Russell. Trinity Corporation is the name of
the concern, and it is one of the great landlords of New
York. In the early days it bought a number of farms,
and these it has held, as the city has grown up around
them, until in 1908 their value was estimated at anywhere from forty to a hundred million dollars. The true
amount has never been made public; to quote Russell's
words:

The real owners of the property are the communicants of the
church. For 94 years none of the owners has known the extent
of the property, nor the amount of the revenue therefrom, nor
what is done with the money. Every attempt to learn even the
simplest fact about these matters has been baffled. The management is a self perpetuating body, without responsibility and
without supervision.

And the writer goes on to describe the business
policy of this great corporation, which is simply the
English land system complete. It refuses to sell the
land, but rents it for long periods, and the tenant builds
the house, and then when the lease expires, the Corporation takes over the house for a nominal sum. Thus it
has purchased houses for as low as $200, and made
them into tenements, and rented them to the swarming
poor for a total of fifty dollars a month. The houses
were not built for tenements, they have no conveni-
ences, they are not fit for the habitation of animals.

The article, in Everybody's Magazine for July, 1908, gives pictures of them, which are horrible beyond belief. To quote the writer again:

Decay, neglect and squalor seem to brood wherever Trinity is an owner. Gladly would I give to such a charitable and benevolent institution all possible credit for a spirit of improvement manifested anywhere, but I can find no such manifestation. I have tramped the Eighth Ward day after day with a list of Trinity properties in my hand, and of all the tenement houses that stand there on Trinity land, I have not found one that is not a disgrace to civilization and to the City of New York.

It happens that I once knew the stately prelate who presided over this Corporation of Corruption. I imagine how he would have shivered and turned pale had some angel whispered to him what devilish utterances were some day to proceed from the lips of the little cherub with shining face and shining robes, who carried one half the bishop's train in the stately ceremonials of the Church! Truly, even into the goodly company of the elect, even to the most holy places of the temple, Satan makes his treacherous way! Even under the consecrated hands of the bishop! For while the bishop was blessing me and taking me into the company of the sanctified, I was thinking about what the papers had reported, that the bishop's wife had been robbed of fifty thousand dollars worth of jewels! It did not seem quite in accordance with the doctrine of Jesus that a bishop's wife should possess fifty thousand dollars worth of jewels, or that she should be setting the bloodhounds of the police on the train of a human being. I asked my clergyman friend about it, and remember his patient explanation—that the bishop had to know all classes and conditions of men; his wife had to go among the rich as well as the poor, and must be able to dress so that she would not be embarrassed. The Bishop at this time was making it his life-work to raise a million dollars for the beginning of a great Episcopal cathedral; and this of course compelled him to spend much time among the rich!

The explanation satisfied me; for of course I thought there had to be cathedrals—despite the fact that both St. Stephen and St. Paul had declared that "the Lord dwelleth not in temples made with hands." In the twenty-five years which have passed since that time the good Bishop has passed to his eternal reward, but the mighty structure which is a monument to his visitations among the rich towers over the city from its vantage-point on Morningside Heights. It is called the Cathedral of St. John the Divine; and knowing what I know about the men who contributed its funds, and about the general functions of the churches of the Metropolis of Mammon, it would not seem to me less holy if it were built, like the monuments of ancient ravagers, out of the skulls of human beings.

Spiritual Interpretation

There remains to say a few words as to the intellectual functions of the Fifth Avenue clergy. Let us realize at the outset that they do their preaching in the name of a proletarian rebel, who was crucified as a common criminal because, as they said, "He stirreth up the people." An embarrassing "Savior" for the church of Good Society, you might imagine; but they manage to fix him up and make him respectable.

I remember something analogous in my own boyhood. All day Saturday I ran about with the little street rowdies, I stole potatoes and roasted them in vacant lots, I threw mud from the roofs of apartment-houses; but on Saturday night I went into a tub and was lathered and scrubbed, and on Sunday I came forth in a newly brushed suit, a clean white collar and a shining tie and a slick derby hat and a pair of tight gloves which made me impotent for mischief. Thus I was taken and paraded up Fifth Avenue, doing my part of the duties of Good Society. And all church-members go through this same performance; the oldest and most venerable of them steal potatoes and throw mud all week —and then take a hot bath of repentance and put on the clean clothing of piety. In this same way their ministers of religion are occupied to scrub and clean and dress up their disreputable Founder—to turn him from a proletarian rebel into a stained-glass-window divinity.

The man who really lived, the carpenter's son, they take out and crucify all over again. As a young poet has phrased it, they nail him to a jeweled cross with cruel nails of gold. Come with me to the New Golgotha and witness this crucifixion; take the nails of gold in your hands, try the weight of the jeweled sledges! Here is a sledge, in the form of a dignified and scholarly volume, published by the exclusive house of Scribner, and written by the Bishop of my boyhood, the Bishop whose train I carried in the stately ceremonials: "The Citizen in His Relation to the Industrial Situation," by the Right Reverend Henry Codman Potter, D. D., L. L. D., D. C. L.—a course of lectures delivered before the sons of our predatory classes at Yale University, under the endowment of a millionaire mining king, founder of the Phelps-Dodge corporation, which the other day carried out the deportation from their homes of a thousand striking miners at Bisbee, Arizona. Says my Bishop:

> Christ did not denounce wealth any more than he denounced pauperism. He did not abhor money; he used it. He did not abhor the company of rich men; he sought it. He did not invariably scorn or even resent a certain profuseness of expenditure.

And do you think that the late Bishop of J. P. Morgan and Company stands alone as an utterer of scholarly blasphemy, a driver of golden nails? In the course of this book there will march before us a long line of the clerical retainers of Privilege, on their way to the New Golgotha to crucify the carpenter's son: the Rector of the Money Trust, the Preacher of the Coal Trust, the Priest of the Traction Trust, the Archbishop of Tammany, the Chaplain of the Millionaires' Club, the Pastor of the Pennsylvania Railroad, the Religious Editor of the New Haven, the Sunday-school Superintendent of Standard Oil. We shall try the weight of their jewelled sledges—books, sermons, newspaper-interviews, after-dinner speeches—wherewith they pound their golden nails of sophistry into the bleeding hands and feet of the proletarian Christ.

Here, for example, is the Rev. F. G. Plummer, late Professor of Christian Morals at Harvard University. Prof. Plummer has written several books on the social teachings of Jesus; he quotes the most rabid of the carpenter's denunciations of the rich, and says:

> Is it possible that so obvious and so limited a message as this, a teaching so slightly distinguished from the curbstone

rhetoric of a modern agitator, can be an adequate reproduction
of the scope and power of the teaching of Jesus?

The question answers itself: Of course not! For
Jesus was a gentleman; he is the head of a church attended by gentlemen, of universities where gentlemen
are educated. So the Professor of Christian Morals
proceeds to make a subtle analysis of Jesus' actions;
demonstrating therefrom that there are three proper
uses to be made of great wealth: first, for almsgiving
—"The poor ye have always with you!"; second, for
beauty and culture—buying wine for wedding-feasts,
and ointment-boxes and other **objets de vertue;** and
third, "stewardship," "trusteeship"—which in plain
English is "Big Business."

I have used the illustration of soap and hot water;
one can imagine he is actually watching the scrubbing
process, seeing the proletarian Founder emerging all
new and respectable under the brush of this capitalist
professor. The professor has a rule all his own for
reading the scriptures; he tells us that when there are
two conflicting sayings, the rule of interpretation is
that "the more spiritual is to be preferred." Thus, one
gospel makes Jesus say: "Blessed are ye poor." Another puts it: "Blessed are the poor in spirit." The first
one is crude and literal; obviously the second must be
what Jesus meant! In other words, the professor and
his church have made for their economic masters a
treacherous imitation virtue to be taught to wage-
slaves, a quality of submissiveness, impotence and futility, which they call by the name of "spirituality". This
virtue they exalt above all others, and in its name they

cut from the record of Jesus everything which has relation to the realities of life!

So here is Francis Greenwood Peabody, successor
to the Plummer chair at Harvard, writing on "Jesus
Christ and the Social Question," and explaining:

The fallacy of the Socialist program is not in its radicalism,
but in its externalism. It proposes to accomplish by economic
change what can be attained by nothing less than spiritual regeneration.

And here is "The Churchman," organ of the Episcopalians of New York, warning us:

It is necessary to remember that something more than material and temporal considerations are involved. There are things
of more importance to the purposes of God and to the welfare
of humanity than economic readjustments and social amelioration.

And again:

Without doubt there is a strong temptation today, bearing
upon clergy and laity alike, to address their religious energies
too exclusively to those tasks whereby human life may be made
more abundant and wholesome materially.....We need constantly to be reminded that spiritual things come first.

There come before my mental eye the elegant ladies
and gentlemen for whom these comfortable sayings are
prepared: the vestrymen and pillars of the Church, with
black frock coats and black kid gloves and shiny top-
hats; the ladies of Good Society with their Easter costumes in pastel shades, their gracious smiles and their
sweet intoxicating odors. I picture them as I have seen
them at St. George's, where that aged wild boar, Pier-
pont Morgan, the elder, used to pass the collection
plate; at Holy Trinity, where they drove downtown in
old-fashioned carriages with grooms and footmen sit-
ting like twin statues of insolence; at St. Thomas',

where you might see all the "Four Hundred" on exhibition at once; at St. Mary the Virgin's, where the choir paraded through the aisles, swinging costly incense into my childish nostrils, the stout clergyman walking alone with nose upturned, carrying on his back a jewelled robe for which some adoring female had paid sixty thousand dollars. "Spiritual things come first?" Ah, yes! "Seek first the kingdom of God, and the jewelled robes shall be added unto you!" And it is so dreadful about the French and German Socialists, who, as the "Churchman" reports, "make a creed out of materialism." But then, what is this I find in one issue of the organ of the "Church of Good Society"?

Business men contribute to the Y. M. C. A. because they realize that if their employes are well cared for and religiously influenced, they can be of greater service in business!

Who let that material cat out of the spiritual bag?

BOOK THREE

The Church of the Servant-girls

Was it for this—that prayers like these
  Should spend themselves about thy feet,
And with hard, overlabored knees
  Kneeling, these slaves of men should beat
Bosoms too lean to suckle sons
And fruitless as their orisons?

Was it for this—that men should make
  Thy name a fetter on men's necks,
Poor men made poorer for thy sake,
  And women withered out of sex?
Was it for this—that slaves should be—
Thy word was passed to set men free?

Swinburne.

Charity

As everyone knows, the "society lady" is not an in-dependent and self-sustaining phenomenon. For every one of these exquisite, sweet-smelling creatures that you meet on Fifth Avenue, there must be at home a large number of other women who live sterile and empty lives, and devote themselves to cleaning up after their luckier sisters. But these "domestics" also are human beings; they have emotions—or, in religious parlance, "souls;" it is necessary to provide a discipline to keep them from appropriating the property of their mistresses, also to keep them from becoming enceinte. So it comes about that there are two cathedrals in New York: one, St. John the Divine, for the society ladies, and the other, St. Patrick's, for the servant-girls. The latter is located on Fifth Avenue, where its towering white spires divide with the homes of the Vanderbilts the interest of the crowds of sight-seers. The land on which it stands was the price of religious support for the most infamous of New York's political gangs, that of Boss Tweed, which sold to the trustees of the cathe-dral a whole city block, from 50th to 51st Streets, and from Fourth to Fifth Avenues, for the sum of eighty-three dollars and thirty-two cents! And now, early every Sunday morning, before "Good Society" has open-ed its eyes, you may see the devotees of the Irish snake-charmer hurrying to their orisons, each with a little black prayer-book in her hand. What is it they do in-side? What are they taught about life? This is the question to which we have next to give attention.

Some years ago Mr. Thomas F. Ryan, traction and in-

surance magnate of New York, favored me with his justification of his own career and activities. He mentioned
his charities, and, speaking as one man of the world to
another, he said: "The reason I put them into the hands
of Catholics is not religious, but because I find they are
efficient in such matters. They don't ask questions, they
do what you want them to do, and do it economically."

I made no comment; I was absorbed in the implications of the remark—like Agassiz when some one gave
him a fossil bone, and his mind set to work to recon-
struct the creature.

When a man is drunk, the Catholics do not ask if it
was long hours and improper working-conditions which
drove him to desperation; they do not ask if police and
politicians are getting a rake-off from the saloon, or if
traction magnates are using it as an agency for the controlling of votes; they do not plunge into prohibition
movements or good government campaigns—they simply
take the man in, at a standard price, and the patient
slave-sisters and attendants get him sober, and then turn
him out for society to make him drunk again. That is
"charity," and it is the special industry of Roman Catholicism. They have been at it for a thousand years, cleaning up loathsome and unsightly messes—"plague, pestilence and famine, battle and murder and sudden death."
Yet—puzzling as it would seem to anyone not religious
—there were never so many messes, never so many different kinds of messes, as now at the end of the thousand
years of charitable activity!

But the Catholics go on and on; like the patient
spider, building and rebuilding his web across a door-

way; like soldiers under the command of a ruling class
with a "muddling through" tradition—

> Theirs not to reason why,
> Theirs but to do and die.

And so of course all magnates and managers of industry
who have messes to be cleaned up, human garbage-heaps
to be carted away quickly and without fuss, turn to the
Catholic Church for this service, no matter what their
personal religious beliefs or lack of beliefs may be. Somewhere in the neighborhood of every steel-mill, every
coal-mine or other place of industrial danger, you will
find a Catholic hospital, with its slave-sisters and attendants. Once when I was "muck-raking" near Pittsburgh,
I went to one of these places to ask information as to the
frequency of industrial accidents and the fate of the victims. The "Mother Superior" received me with a look
of polite dismay. "These concerns pay us!" she said.
"You must see that as a matter of business it would not
do for us to talk about them."

Obey and keep silence: that is the Catholic law. And
precisely as it is with the work of nursing and almsgiving, so it is with the work of vote-getting, the elaborate
system of policemen and saloon-keepers and ward-heelers
which the Catholic machine controls. This industry of
vote-getting is a comparatively new one; but the Church
has been handling the masses for so many centuries that
she quickly learned this new way of "democracy," and
has established her supremacy over all rivals. She has
the schools for training the children, the confessional for
controlling the women; she has the intellectual machinery, the purgatory and the code of slave-ethics. She has
the supreme advantage that the rank and file of her

mighty host really believe what she teaches; they do not
have to listen to table-rappings and flounder through
swamps of automatic writings in order to bolster their
hope of the survival of personality after death!

So it comes about that our captains of industry and
finance have been driven to a more or less reluctant alliance with the Papacy. The Church is here, and her followers are here, before the war several hundred thousand
of them pouring into the country every year. It is no
longer possible to do without Catholics in America; not
merely do ditches have to be dug, roads graded, coal
mined, and dishes washed, but franchises have to be
granted, tariff-schedules adjusted, juries and courts manipulated, police trained and strikes crushed. Under our
native political system, for these purposes millions of
votes are needed; and these votes belong to people of a
score of nationalities—Irish and German and Italian and
French-Canadian and Bohemian and Mexican and Portuguese and Polish and Hungarian. Who but the Catholic
Church can handle these polyglot hordes? Who can furnish teachers and editors and politicians familiar with all
these languages?

Considering how complex is the service, the price is
extremely moderate—the mere actual expenses of the
campaign, the cost of red fire and torch-lights, of liquor
and newspaper advertisements. The rest may come out
of the public till, in the form of exemption from taxation
of church buildings and lands, a share of the public funds
for charities and schools, the control of the police for
saloon-keepers and district leaders, the control of police-
courts and magistrates, of municipal administrations and
boards of education, of legislatures and governors; with

a few higher offices now and then, to flatter our sacred self-esteem, a senator or a justice on the Supreme Court Bench; and on state occasions, to keep up our necessary prestige, some cabinet-members and legislators and justices to attend High Mass, and be blessed in public by Catholic prelates and dignitaries.

You think this is empty rhetoric—you comfortable, easy-going, ultra-cultured Americans? You professors in your classic shades, absorbed in "the passionless pursuit of passionless intelligence"—while the world about you slides down into the pit! You ladies of Good Society, practicing your "sweet little charities," pursuing your "dear little ideals," raising your families of one or two lovely children—while Irish and French-Canadians and Italians and Portuguese and Hungarians are breeding their dozens and scores, and preparing to turn you out of your country!

God's Armor

You remember "Bishop Blougram's Apology," Browning's study of the psychology of a modern Catholic ecclesiastic. He is not unaware of modern thought, this bishop; he is a man of culture, who wants to have beauty about him, to be a "cabin passenger":

> There's power in me and will to dominate
> Which I must exercise, they hurt me else;
> In many ways I need mankind's respect,
> Obedience, and the love that's born of fear.

He wishes that he had faith—faith in anything; he understands that faith is all-important—

> Enthusiasm's the best thing, I repeat.

But you cannot get faith just by wishing for it—

> But paint a fire, it will not therefore burn!

He tries to imagine himself going on a crusade for truth, but he asks what there would be in it for him—

> State the facts,
> Read the text right, emancipate the world—
> The emancipated world enjoys itself
> With scarce a thank-you. Blougram told it first
> It could not owe a farthing,—not to him
> More than St. Paul!

So the bishop goes on with his role, but uneasily conscious of the contempt of intellectual people.

> I pine among my million imbeciles
> (You think) aware some dozen men of sense
> Eye me and know me, whether I believe
> In the last winking virgin as I vow,
> And am a fool, or disbelieve in her,
> And am a knave.

But, as he says, you have to keep a tight hold upon the chain of faith, that is what

> Gives all the advantage, makes the difference,
> With the rough, purblind mass we seek to rule.
> We are their lords, or they are free of us,
> Just as we tighten or relax that hold.

So he continues, but not with entire satisfaction, in his role of shepherd to those whom he calls "King Bomba's lazzaroni," and "ragamuffin saints."

I wander into a Catholic bookstore and look to see what Bishop Blougram is doing with his lazzaroni and his ragamuffin saints here in this new country of the far West. It is easy to acquire the information, for the saleswoman is polite and the prices fit my purse. America is going to war, and Catholic boys are being drafted to be trained for battle; so for ten cents I obtain a firmly bound little pamphlet called "God's Armor, a Prayer Book for Soldiers." It is marked "Copyright by the G. R. C. Central-Verein," and bears the "Nihil Obstat" of the "Censor Theolog." and the "Imprimatur" of "Johannes Josephus, Archiepiscopus Sti. Ludovici" —which last you may at first fail to recognize as a well-known city on the Mississippi River. Do you not feel the spell of ancient things, the magic of the past creeping over you, as you read those Latin trade-marks? Such is the Dead Hand, and its cunning, which can make even St. Louis sound mysterious!

In this booklet I get no information as to the commercial causes of war, nor about the part which the clerical vote may have played throughout Europe in supporting military systems. I do not even find anything about the sacred cause of democracy, the resolve of a self-governing people to put an end to feudal rule. Instead I discover a soldier-boy who obeys and keeps silent, and who, in his inmost heart, is in the grip of terrors both of body and soul. Poor, pitiful soldier-boy, marking yourself with crosses, performing genuflexions, mumbling magic formulas in the trenches—how many billions of you have been led out to slaughter by the greeds and ambitions of your religious masters, since first this accursed Antichrist got its grip upon the hearts of men!

I quote from this little book:

Start this day well by lifting up your heart to God. Offer yourself to Him, and beg grace to spend the day without sin. Make the sign of the cross. Most Holy Trinity, Father, Son, and Holy Ghost, behold me in Thy Divine Presence. I adore Thee and give Thee thanks. Grant that all I do this day be for Thy Glory, and for the salvation of my immortal soul.

During the day lift your heart frequently to God. Your prayers need not be long nor read from a book. Learn a few of these short ejaculations by heart and frequently repeat them. They will serve to recall God to your heart and will strengthen you and comfort you.

You remember a while back about the prayer-wheels of the Thibetans. The Catholic religion was founded before the Thibetan, and is less progressive; it does not welcome mechanical devices for saving labor. You have to use your own vocal apparatus to keep yourself from hell; but the process has been made as economical as possible by kindly dispensations of the Pope. Thus, each time that you say "My God and my all," you get fifty days indulgence; the same for "My Jesus, mercy," and the same for "Jesus, my God, I love Thee above all things." For "Jesus, Mary, Joseph," you get three hundred days—which would seem by all odds the best investment of your spare breath.

And then come prayers for all occasions: "Prayer before Battle"; "Prayer for a Happy Death"; "Prayer in Temptation"; "Prayer before and after Meals"; "Prayer when on Guard"; "Prayer before a long March"; "Prayer of Resignation to Death"; "Prayer for Those in their Agony"—I cannot bear to read them, hardly to list them. I remember standing in a cathedral "somewhere in France" during the celebration of some special Big Magic. There was brilliant white light, and a suffocating strange odor, and the thunder of a huge organ, and a clamor of voices, high, clear voices of young boys mounting to heaven, like the hands of men in a pit reaching up, trying to climb over the top of one another. It sent a shudder into the depths of my soul. There is nothing left in the modern world which can carry the mind so far back into the ancient night-

mare of anguish and terror which was once the mental
life of mankind, as these Roman Catholic incantations
with their frantic and ceaseless importunity. They have
even brought in the sex-spell; and the poor, frightened
soldier-boy, who has perhaps spent the night with a
prostitute, now prostrates himself before a holy Wom-
an-being who is lifted high above the shames of the
flesh, and who stirs the thrills of awe and affection
which his mother brought to him in early childhood.
Read over the phrases of this "Litany of the Blessed
Virgin":

Holy Mary, Pray for us. Holy Mother of God. Holy Virgin
of Virgins. Mother of Christ. Mother of divine grace. Mother
most pure. Mother most chaste. Mother inviolate. Mother undefiled. Mother most amiable. Mother most admirable. Mother
of good counsel. Mother of our Creator. Mother of our Savior.
Virgin most prudent. Virgin most venerable. Virgin most re-
nowned. Virgin most powerful. Virgin most merciful. Virgin
most faithful. Mirror of justice. Seat of wisdom. Cause of our
joy. Spiritual vessel. Vessel of honor. Singular vessel of devotion. Mystical rose. Tower of David. Tower of ivory. House
of gold. Ark of the covenant. Gate of heaven. Morning Star.
Health of the sick. Refuge of sinners. Comforter of the afflicted.
Help of Christians. Queen of Angels. Queen of Patriarchs.
Queen of Prophets. Queen of Apostles. Queen of Martyrs.
Queen of Confessors. Queen of Virgins. Queen of all Saints.
Queen conceived without original sin. Queen of the most holy
Rosary. Queen of Peace, Pray for us.

Thanksgivings

For another five cents—how cheaply a man of insight can obtain thrills in this fantastic world!—I purchase a copy of the "Messenger of the Sacred Heart",
a magazine published in New York, the issue for October, 1917. There are pages of advertisements of

schools and colleges with strange titles: "Immaculata Seminary", "Holy Cross Academy", "Holy Ghost Institute", "Ladycliff", "Academy of Holy Child Jesus". The leading article is by a Jesuit, on "The Spread of the Apostleship of Prayer among the Young"; and then "Sister Clarissa" writes a poem telling us "What are Sorrows"; and then we are given a story called "Prayer for Daddy"; and then another Jesuit father tells us about "The Hills that Jesus Loved". A third father tells us about the "Eucharistic Propaganda"; and we learn that in July, 1917, it distributed 11,699 beads, and caused the expenditure of 57,714 hours of adoration; and then the faithful are given a form of letter which they are to write to the Honorable Baker, Secretary of War, imploring him to intimate to the French government that France should withdraw from one of her advances in civilization, and join with mediaeval America in exempting priests from being drafted to fight for their country. And then there is a "Question Box"—just like the Hearst newspapers, only instead of asking whether she should allow him to kiss her before he has told her that he loves her, the reader asks what is the Pauline Privilege, and what is the heroic Act, and is Robert a saint's name, and if food remains in the teeth from the night before, would it break the fast to swallow it before Holy Communion. (No, I am not inventing this.)

I quoted the Episcopal Book of Common Prayer, and pointed out how deftly the Church has managed to slip in a prayer for worldly prosperity. But the Catholic Church does not show any squeamishness in dealing with its "million imbeciles", its "rough, purblind mass".

There is a department of the little magazine entitled
"Thanksgiving", and a statement at the top that "the
total number of Thanksgivings for the month is 2,143,-
911." I am suspicious of that, as of German reports of
prisoners taken; but I give the statement as it stands,
not going through the list and picking out the crudest,
but taking them as they come, classified by states:

GENERAL FAVORS: For many of these favors Mass and
publication were promised, for others the Badge of Promoter's
Cross was used, for others the prayers of the Associates had
been asked.

Alabama—Jewelry found, relief from pain, protection during
storm.

Alaska—Safe return, goods found.

Arizona—Two recoveries, suitable boarding place, illness
averted, safe delivery.

British Honduras—Successful operation.

California—Seventeen recoveries, six situations, two successful examinations, house rented, stocks sold, raise in salary, return to religious duties, sight regained, medal won, Baptism,
preservation from disease, contract obtained, success in business,
hearing restored, Easter duty made, happy death, automobile
sold, mind restored, house found, house rented, successful jour-
ney, business sold, quarrel averted, return of friends, two successful operations.

And for all these miraculous performances the
Catholic machine is harvesting the price day by day—
harvesting with that ancient fervor which the Latin
poet described as "auri sacra fames". As Christopher
Columbus wrote from Jamaica in 1503: "Gold is a
wonderful thing. By means of gold we can even get
souls into Paradise."

The Holy Roman Empire

The system thus self-revealed you admit is appalling

in its squalor; but you say that at least it is milder and less perilous than the Church which burned Giordano Bruno and John Huss. But the very essence of the Catholic Church is that it does not change; **semper eadem** is its motto: the same yesterday, today and forever—the same in Washington as in Rome or Madrid—the same in a modern democracy as in the Middle Ages. The Catholic Church is not primarily a religious organization; it is a political organization, and proclaims the fact, and defies those who would shut it up in the religious field. The Rev. S. B. Smith, a Catholic doctor of divinity, explains in his "Elements of Ecclesiastical Law":

> Protestants contend that the entire power of the Church consists in the right to teach and exhort, but not in the right to command, rule, or govern; whence they infer that she is not a perfect society or sovereign state. This theory is false; for the Church, as was seen, is vested **Jure divino** with power, (1) to make laws; (2) to define and apply them (**potestas judicialis**); (3) to punish those who violate her laws (**potestas coercitiva**).

And this is not one scholar's theory, but the formal and repeated proclamation of infallible popes. Here is the "Syllabus of Errors", issued by Pope Pius IX, Dec. 8th, 1864, declaring in precise language that

> The state has not the right to leave every man free to profess and embrace whatever religion he shall deem true.

> It has not the right to enact that the ecclesiastical power shall require the permission of the civil power in order to the exercise of its authority.

Then in the same Syllabus the rights and powers of the Church are affirmed thus:

> She has the right to require the state not to leave every man free to profess his own religion.

She has the right to exercise her power without the permission or consent of the state.

She has the right of perpetuating the union of church and state.

She has the right to require that the Catholic religion shall be the only religion of the state, to the exclusion of all others.

She has the right to prevent the state from granting the public exercise of their own worship to persons immigrating from it.

She has the power of requiring the state not to permit free expression of opinion.

You see, the Holy Office is unrepentant and unchastened. You, who think that liberty of conscience is the basis of civilization, ought at least to know what the Catholic Church has to say about the matter. Here is Mgr. Segur, in his "Plain Talk About Protestantism of Today", a book published in Boston and extensively circulated by American Catholics:

Freedom of thought is the soul of Protestantism; it is likewise the soul of modern rationalism and philosophy. It is one of those impossibilities which only the levity of a superficial reason can regard as admissable. But a sound mind, that does not feed on empty words, looks upon this freedom of thought only as simply absurd, and, what is more, as sinful.

You take the liberty of thinking, nevertheless; you feel safe because the Law will protect you. But do you imagine that this "Law" applies to your Catholic neighbors? Do you imagine that they are bound by the restraints that bind **you**? Here is Pope Leo XIII, in his Encyclical of 1890—and please remember that Leo XIII was the **beau ideal** of our capitalist statesmen and editors, as wise and kind and gentle-souled a pope as ever roasted a heretic. He says:

If the laws of the state are openly at variance with the laws of God—if they inflict injury upon the Church—or set at naught the authority of Jesus Christ which is vested in the Supreme Pontiff, then indeed it becomes a duty to resist them, a sin to render obedience.

And consider how many fields there are in which the laws of a democratic state do and forever must contravene the "laws of God" as interpreted by the Catholic Church. Consider for example, that the Pope, in his decree **Ne Temere,** has declared that all persons who have been married by civil authorities or by Protestant clergymen are living in "filthy concubinage"! Consider, in the same way, the problems of education, burial, prison discipline, blasphemy, poor relief, incorporation, mortmain, religious endowments, vows of celibacy. To the above list, as given by Gladstone, one might add many issues, such as birth control, which have arisen since his time.

What the Church means is to rule. Her literature is full of expressions of that intention, set forth in the boldest and haughtiest and most uncompromising manner. For example, Cardinal Manning, in the Pro-Cathedral at Kensington, speaking in the name of the Pope:

> I acknowledge no civil power; I am the subject of no prince; I claim more than this—I claim to be the supreme judge and director of the consciences of men—of the peasant that tills the field, and of the prince that sits upon the throne; of the household of privacy, and the legislator that makes laws for kingdoms; I am the sole, last supreme judge of what is right and wrong.

Temporal Power

What this means is, that here in our American democracy the Catholic Church is a rebel; a prisoner of war who bides his time, watching for the moment to rise in revolt, and meantime making no secret of his intentions. The pious Leo XIII, addressing all true believers in America, instructed them as to their attitude in captivity:

The Church amongst you, unopposed by the Constitution and government of your nation, fettered by no hostile legislation, protected against violence by the common laws and the impartiality of the tribunals, is free to live and act without hindrance. Yet, though all this is true, it would be very erroneous to draw the conclusion that in America is to be sought the type of the most desirable status of the church, or that it would be universally lawful or expedient for state and church to be, as in America, dissevered and divorced. The fact that Catholicity with you is in good condition, nay, is even enjoying a prosperous growth, is by all means to be attributed to the fecundity with which God has endowed His Church....But she would bring forth more abundant fruits if, in addition to liberty, she enjoyed the favor of the laws and patronage of the public authority.

Accordingly, here is Father Phelan of St. Louis, addressing his flock in the "Western Watchman", June 27, 1913:

Tell us we are Catholics first and Americans or Englishmen afterwards; of course we are. Tell us, in the conflict between the church and the civil government we take the side of the church; of course we do. Why, if the government of the United States were at war with the church, we would say tomorrow, To hell with the government of the United States; and if the church and all the governments of the world were at war, we would say, To hell with all the governments of the world....Why is it that in this country, where we have only seven per cent of the population, the Catholic church is so much feared? She is loved by all her children and feared by everybody. Why is it that the Pope has such tremendous power? Why, the Pope is the ruler of the world. All the emperors, all the kings, all the princes, all the presidents of the world, are as these altar boys of mine. The Pope is the ruler of the world.

You recall what I said at the outset about Power;

the ability to control the lives of other men, to give laws and moral codes, to shape fashions and tastes, to be revered and regarded. Here is a man swollen to bursting with this Power. Dressed in his holy robes, with his holy incense in his nostrils, and the faces of the faithful gazing up at him awe-stricken, hear him proclaim:

The Church gives no bonds for her good behavior. She is the judge of her own rights and duties, and of the rights and duties of the state.

And lest you think that an extreme example of ultramontanist arrogance, listen to the Boston "Pilot", April 6, 1912, speaking for Cardinal O'Connell, whose official organ it is:

It must be borne in mind that even though Cardinals Farley, O'Connell and Gibbons are at heart patriotic Americans and members of an American hierachy, yet they are as cardinals foreign princes of the blood, to whom the United States, as one of the great powers of the world, is under an obligation to concede the same honors that they receive abroad.

Thus, were Cardinal Farley to visit an American man-of-war, he would be entitled to the salutes and to naval honors reserved for a foreign royal personage, and at any official entertainment at Washington the Cardinal will outrank not merely every cabinet officer, the speaker of the house and the vice-president, but also the foreign ambassadors, coming immediately next to the chief magistrate himself.

Incidentally, it may be mentioned that when a royal personage not of sovereign rank visits New York it is his duty to make the first call on Cardinal Farley.

Knights of Slavery

Such is the worldly station of these apostles of the lowly Jesus. And what is their attitude towards their brothers in God, the rank and file of the membership, whose pennies grease the wheels of the ecclesiastical machine? His Holiness, the Pope, sent over a delegate to represent him in America, and at a convention of the Federation of Catholic Societies held in New Orleans in November, 1910, this gentleman, Diomede Falconio, delivered himself on the subject of Capital and Labor. We have heard the slave-code of the Anglican disciples of Jesus, the revolutionary carpenter; now let us hear the slave-code of his Roman disciples:

Human society has its origin from God and is constituted of two classes of people, the rich and the poor, which respectively represent Capital and Labor.

Hence it follows that according to the ordinance of God, human society is composed of superiors and subjects, masters and servants, learned and unlettered, rich and poor, nobles and plebians.

And lest this should not be clear enough, the Pope sent a second representative, Mgr. John Bonzano, who, speaking at a general meeting of the German Catholic Central-Verein, St. Louis, 1917, declared:

One of the worst evils that may grow out of the European war is the spreading of the doctrine of Socialism, and the Catholic Church must be ready to counteract such doctrines. We must be ready to prevent the spread of Socialism and to work against it. As I understand, you have a society of wealthy people in St. Louis ready for such a campaign. You have experienced leaders who are masters in their kind of work. They are always insistent to show that this wealth was and is in close touch with the Church, and therefore it will not fail.

This, you perceive, is the complete thesis of the present book, which therefore no doubt will be entitled to the 'Nihil Obstat" of the "Censor Theolog.", and the "Imprimatur" of "Johannes Josephus, Archiepiscopus Sti. Ludovici." No wonder that the "experienced leaders" of America, our captains of industry and exploiters of labor, are forced, whatever their own faith may be, to make use of this system of subjection. A few years ago we read in our papers how a Jewish millionaire of Baltimore was presenting a fortune to the Catholic Church, to be used in its war upon Socialism. The late Mark Hanna, the shrewdest and most far-seeing man that Big Business ever brought into power, said that in twenty years there would be two parties in America, a capitalist and a socialist; and that it would be the Catholic church that would save the country from Socialism. That prophecy was widely quoted, and sank into the souls of our steel and railway and money magnates; from which time you might see, if you watched political events, a new tone of deference to the Roman Hierarchy on the part of our ruling classes. Today you cannot get an expression of opinion hostile to Catholicism into any newspaper of importance. The Associated Press does not handle news unfavorable to the Church, and from top to bottom, the politician takes off his hat when the Sacred Host goes by. Said Archbishop Quigley, speaking before the children of the Mary Sodality:

I'd like to see the politician who would try to rule against the church in Chicago. His reign would be short indeed.

Priests and Police

And how is it in our national capital, the palladium of our liberties? As a means of demonstrating the power of the church and the subservience of our politicians, the Catholics have invented what they call the "Cardinal's Day Mass": An elaborate procession of high ecclesiastics, dressed in gorgeous robes and jewels, through the streets of Washington, accompanied by a

small army of policemen, paid by non-Catholic tax-
payers. The Cardinal seats himself upon a throne, and
our political rulers make obeisance before him. On
Sunday, January 14, 1917, there were present at this
political mass the following personages: Four cabinet
members and their wives; the speaker of the House; a
large group of senators and representatives; a general
of the army and his wife; an admiral of the navy and
his wife; the Chief Justice of the Supreme Court and
his wife, and another Justice of the Supreme Court and
his wife.

And understand that the church makes no secret of
its purpose in conducting such public exhibitions. Here
is the pious Pope Leo XIII again, in his Encyclical of
Nov. 1, 1885:

> All Catholics must make themselves felt as active elements
> in daily political life in the countries where they live. They must
> penetrate, wherever possible, in the administration of civil af-
> fairs; must constantly exert the utmost vigilance and energy to
> prevent the usages of liberty from going beyond the limits fixed
> by God's law. All Catholics should do all in their power to cause
> the constitutions of states and legislation to be modeled on the
> principles of the true Church.

And following these instructions, the Catholics are
organized for political work. There are the various
Catholic Societies, such as the Knights of Columbus,
secret, oath-bound organizations, the military arm of
the Papal Power. These societies boast some three million members, and control not less than that many
votes. The one thing that you can be certain about these
votes is that on every public question, of whatever nature, they will be cast on the side of ignorance and reaction. Thus, it was the influence of the Catholic So-

cieties which put upon our national statute books the
infamous law providing five years imprisonment and
five thousand dollars fine for the sending through the
mail of information about the prevention of conception. It is their influence which keeps upon the statute-
books of New York state the infamous law which permits divorce only for infidelity, and makes it "collusion"
if both parties desire the divorce. It is these societies
which, in every city and town in America, are pushing
and plotting to get Catholics upon library boards, so
that the public may not have a chance to read scientific
books; to get Catholics into the public schools and on
school-boards, so that children may not hear about
Galileo, Bruno, and Ferrer; to have Catholics in control
of police and on magistrates benches, so that priests
who are caught in brothels may not be exposed or punished.

You are shocked at this, you think it a vulgar jest,
perhaps; but during a period of "vice raids" in New
York I was told by a captain of police, himself a Catholic, that it was a common thing for them to get priests
in their net. "Of course," the official added, good-
naturedly, "we let them slip out." I understood that he
had to do that; for the Pope, in his "Motu Proprio" decree, has forbidden Catholics to bring a priest into court
for any civil crime whatsoever; he has forbidden Catholic policemen to arrest, Catholic judges to try, and
Catholic law-makers to make laws affecting any priest
of the Church of Rome. And of course we know, upon
the authority of a cardinal, that the Pope is "the sole,
last, supreme judge of what is right and wrong." He
has held that position for a thousand years and more;

and wherever you consult the police records throughout the thousand years, you find the same entries concerning Catholic ecclesiastics. I turn to Riley's "Illustrations of London Life from Original Documents," and I find in the year 1385 a certain chaplain, whose name is considerately suppressed, had a breviary stolen from him by a loose woman, because he has not given her any money, either on that night or the one previous. In 1320 John de Sloghtre, a priest, is put in the tower "for being found wandering about the city against the peace", and Richard Heyring, a priest, is indicted in the ward of Farringdon and in the ward of Crepelgate "as being a bruiser and nightwalker." That this has been going on for six hundred years is due, not to any special corruption of the Catholic heart, but to the practice of clerical celibacy, which is contrary to nature, a transgression of fundamental instinct. It should be noted that the purpose of this transgression, which pretends to be spiritual, is really economic; it was the means whereby the church machine built up its power through the Middle Ages. The priests had children then, as they have them today; but these children not being recognized, the church machine remained the sole heir of the property of its clergy.

The Church Militant

Knowing what we know today, we marvel that it was possible for Germany to prepare through so many years for her assault on civilization, and for England to have slept through it all. In exactly the same way, the historian of a generation from now will marvel that America should have slept, while the New Inquisition was planning to strangle her. For we are told with the

utmost explicitness precisely what is to be done. We
are to see wiped out these gains of civilization for which
our race has bled and agonized for many centuries; the
very gains are to serve as the means of their own destruction! Have we not heard Pope Leo tell his faithful
how to take advantage of what they find in America—
our easy-going trust, our quiet certainty of liberty, our
open-handed and open-homed and hail-fellow-well-met
democracy?

We see the army being organized and drilled under
our eyes; and we can read upon its banners its purpose
proclaimed. Just as the Prussian military caste had its
slogan "Deutschland ueber Alles!" so the Knights of
Slavery have their slogan: "Make America Catholic!"

Their attitude to democratic institutions is attested
by the fact that none of their conventions ever fails in
its resolutions to "deeply deplore the loss of the temporal power of Our Father, the Pope." Their subjection to priestly domination is indicated by such resolutions as this, bearing date of May 13th, 1914 :

> The Knights of Columbus of Texas in annual convention as-
> sembled, prostrate at the feet of Your Holiness, present filial
> regards with assurances of loyalty and obedience to the Holy
> See and request the Papal blessing.

On June 10th, 1912, one T. J. Carey of Palestine,
Texas, wrote to Archbishop Bonzano, the Apostolic Delegate: "Must I, as a Catholic, surrender my political
freedom to the Church? And by this I mean the right
to vote for the Democratic, Socialist, or Republican
parties when and where I please?" The answer was:
"You should submit to the decisions of the Church, even
at the cost of sacrificing political principles." And to

the same effect Mgr. Preston, in New York City, Jan. 1, 1888: "The man who says, 'I will take my faith from Peter, but I will not take my politics from Peter,' is not a true Catholic."

Such is the Papal machine; and not a day passes that it does not discover some new scheme to advance the Papal glory; a "Catholic battle-ship" in the United States navy; Catholic chaplains on all ships of the navy; Catholic holidays—such as Columbus Day—to be celebrated by all Protestants in America; thirty million dollars worth of church property exempted from taxation in New York City; mission bells to be set up at the expense of the state of California; state support for parish schools—or, if this cannot be had, exemption of Catholics from taxation for school purposes. So on through the list which might continue for pages.

More than anything else, of course, the Papal machine is concerned with education, or rather, with the preventing of education. It was in its childish days that the race fell under the spell of the Priestly Lie; it is in his childish days that the individual can be most safely snared. Suffer little children to come unto the Catholic priest, and he will make upon their sensitive minds an impression which nothing in after life can eradicate. So the mainstay of the New Inquisition is the parish-school, and its deadliest enemy is the American school system. Listen to the Rev. James Conway, of the Society of Jesus, in his book, "The Rights of Our Little Ones":

Catholic parents cannot, in conscience, send their children to

American public schools, except for very grave reasons approved by the ecclesiastical authorities.

While state education removes illiteracy and puts a limited amount of knowledge within the reach of all, it cannot be said to have a beneficial influence on civilization in general.

The state cannot justly enforce compulsory education, even in case of utter illiteracy, so long as the essential physical and moral education are sufficiently provided for.

And so, at all times and in all places, the Catholic Church is fighting the public school. Eternal vigilance is necessary; as "America", the organ of the Jesuits, explains:

> Sometimes it is a new building code, or an attempt at taxing the school buildings, which creates hardships to the parochial and other private schools. Now it is the free text book law that puts a double burden on the Catholics. Then again it is the unwise extension of the compulsory school age that forces children to be in school until they are 16 to 18 years old.

And if you wish to know the purpose of the Catholic schools, hear Archbishop Quigley of Chicago, speaking before the children of the Mary Sodality in the Holy Name Parish-School:

> Within twenty years this country is going to rule the world. Kings and emperors will pass away, and the democracy of the United States will take their place. The West will dominate the country, and what I have seen of the Western parochial schools has proved that the generation which follows us will be exclusively Catholic. When the United States rules the world the Catholic Church will rule the world.

The Church Triumphant

The question may be asked, What of it? What if the Church were to rule? There are not a few Americans who believe that there have to be rich and poor, and that rule by Roman Catholics might be preferable

to rule by Socialists. Before you decide, at least do not
fail to consider what history has to tell about priestly
government. We do not have to use our imaginations
in the matter, for there was once a Golden Age such
as Archbishop Quigley dreams of, when the power of
the church was complete, when emperors and princes
paid homage to her, and the civil authority made haste
to carry out her commands. What was the condition of
the people in those times? We are told by Lea, in his
"History of the Inquisition" that:

The moral condition of the laity was unutterably depraved.
Uniformity of faith had been enforced by the Inquisition and its
methods, and so long as faith was preserved, crime and sin was
comparatively unimportant except as a source of revenue to
those who sold absolution. As Theodoric Vrie tersely puts it,
hell and purgatory would be emptied if enough money could be
found. The artificial standard thus created is seen in a revelation of the Virgin to St. Birgitta, that a Pope who was free
from heresy, no matter how polluted by sin and vice, is not so
wicked but that he has the absolute power to bind and loose
souls. There are many wicked popes plunged in hell, but all
their lawful acts on earth are accepted and confirmed by God,
and all priests who are not heretics administer true sacraments,
no matter how depraved they may be. Correctness of belief was
thus the sole essential; virtue was a wholly subordinate consideration. How completely under such a system religion and morals
came to be dissociated is seen in the remarks of Pius II, that
the Franciscans were excellent theologians, but cared nothing
about virtue.

This, in fact, was the direct result of the system of persecution embodied in the Inquisition. Heretics who were admitted
to be patterns of virtue were ruthlessly exterminated in the
name of Christ, while in the same holy name the orthodox could
purchase absolution for the vilest of crimes for a few coins.
When the only unpardonable offence was persistence in some
trifling error of belief, such as the poverty of Christ; when men

had before them the example of their spiritual guides as leaders
in vice and debauchery and contempt of sacred things, all the
sanctions of morality were destroyed and the confusion between
right and wrong became hopeless. The world has probably never
seen a society more vile than that of Europe in the fourteenth
and fifteenth centuries. The brilliant pages of Froissart fasci-
nate us with their pictures of the artificial courtesies of chivalry; the mystic reveries of Rysbroek and of Tauler show us that
spiritual life survived in some rare souls, but the mass of the
population was plunged into the depths of sensuality and the
most brutal oblivion of the moral law. For this Alvaro Pelayo
tells us that the priesthood were accountable, and that, in com-
parison with them, the laity were holy. What was that state of
comparative holiness he proceeds to describe, blushing as he
writes, for the benefit of confessors, giving a terrible sketch
of universal immorality which nothing could purify but fire and
brimstone from heaven. The chroniclers do not often pause in
their narrations to dwell on the moral aspects of the times, but
Meyer, in his annals of Flanders, under date of 1379, tells us
that it would be impossible to describe the prevalence everywhere of perjuries, blasphemies, adulteries, hatreds, quarrels,
brawls, murder, rapine, thievery, robbery, gambling, whoredom,
debauchery, avarice, oppression of the poor, rape, drunkenness,
and similar vices, and he illustrates his statement with the fact
that in the territory of Ghent, within the space of ten months,
there occurred no less than fourteen hundred murders committed in the bagnios, brothels, gambling-houses, taverns, and
other similar places. When, in 1396, Jean sans Peur led his
Crusaders to destruction at Micopolis, their crimes and cynical
debauchery scandalized even the Turks, and led to the stern rebuke of Bajazet himself, who as the monk of St. Denis admits
was much better than his Christian foes. The same writer,
moralizing over the disaster at Agincourt, attributes it to the
general corruption of the nation. Sexual relations, he says, were
an alternation of disorderly lust and of incest; commerce was
nought but fraud and treachery; avarice withheld from the Church
her tithes, and ordinary conversation was a succession of blasphemies. The Church, set up by God as a model and protector
of the people, was false to all its obligations. The bishops,

THE PROFITS OF RELIGION

through the basest and most criminal of motives, were habitual
accepters of persons; they annointed themselves with the last
essence extracted from their flocks, and there was in them
nothing of holy, of pure, of wise, or even of decent.

God in the Schools

But that, you may say, was a long time ago. If so,
let us take a modern country in which the Catholic
Church has worked its will. Until recently, Spain was
such a country. Now the people are turning against the
clerical machine; and if you ask why, turn to Rafael
Shaw's "Spain From Within":

> On every side the people see the baleful hand of the Church,
> interfering or trying to interfere in their domestic life, ordering
> the conditions of employment, draining them of their hard-won
> livelihood by trusts and monopolies established and maintained in
> the interest of the Religious Orders, placing obstacles in the way
> of their children's education, hindering them in the exercise of
> their constitutional rights, and deliberately ruining those of
> them who are bold enough to run counter to priestly dictation.
> Riots suddenly break out in Barcelona; they are instigated by
> the Jesuits. The country goes to war in Morocco; it is dragged
> into it solely in defense of the mines owned, actually, if not
> ostensibly, by the Jesuits. The consumos cannot be abolished
> because the Jesuits are financially interested in their continu-
> ance.

We have read the statement of a Jesuit father, that
"the state cannot justly enforce compulsory education,
even in case of utter illiteracy." How has that doctrine
worked out in Spain? There was an official investigation of school conditions, the report appearing in the
"Heraldo de Madrid" for November, 1909. In 1857
there had been passed a law requiring a certain number of schools in each of the 79 provinces: this re-
quirement being below the very low standards prevail-

ing at that time in other European countries. Yet in 1909 it was found that only four provinces had the required number of elementary schools, and at the rate of increase then prevailing it would have taken 150 years to catch up. Seventy-five per cent of the population were wholly illiterate, and 30,000 towns and villages had no government schools at all. The government owed nearly a million and a half dollars in unpaid salaries to the teachers. The private schools were nearly all "nuns' schools", which taught only needle-work and catechism; the punishments prevailing in them were "cruel and disgusting."

As to the location of the schools, a report of the Minister of Education to the Cortes, the Parliament of Spain, sets forth as follows:

More than 10,000 schools are on hired premises, and many of these are absolutely destitute of hygienic conditions. There are schools mixed up with hospitals, with cemeteries, with slaughter houses, with stables. One school forms the entrance to a cemetery, and the corpses are placed on the master's table while the last responses are being said. There is a school into which the children cannot enter until the animals have been sent out to pasture. Some are so small that as soon as the warm weather begins the boys faint for want of air and ventilation. One school is a manure-heap in process of fermentation, and one of the local authorities has said that in this way the children are warmer in winter. One school in Cataluna adjoins the prison. Another, in Andalusia, is turned into an enclosure for the bulls when there is a bull-fight in the town.

These conditions excited the indignation of a Spanish educator by the name of Francesco Ferrer. He founded what he called a "modern school", in which the pupils should be taught science and common sense. He drew, of course, the bitter hatred of the Catholic hier-

archy, which saw in the spread of his principles the
end of their mastery of the people. When the Barce-
lona insurrection took place, they had Ferrer seized
upon a charge of having been its instigator; they had
him tried in secret before a military tribunal, convicted
upon forged documents, and shot beneath the walls of
the fortress of Montjuich. The case was thoroughly in-
vestigated by William Archer, one of England's leading
critics, a man of scrupulous rectitude of mind. His conclusion is that Ferrer was absolutely innocent of the
charges against him, and that his execution was the
result of a clerical plot. Of Ferrer's character Archer
writes:

> Fragmentary though they be, the utterances which I have
> quoted form a pretty complete revelation. From first to last we
> see in him an ardent, uncompromising, incorruptible idealist.
> His ideals are narrow, and his devotion to them fanatical; but
> it is devoid, if not of egoism, at any rate of self-interest and
> self-seeking. As he shrank from applying the money entrusted
> him to ends of personal luxury, so also he shrank from making
> his ideas and convictions subserve any personal ambition or
> vanity.

The Menace

There are, of course, many people in America who
will not rest idle while their country falls into the condition of Spain. There are anti-Catholic propaganda
societies, which send out lecturers to discuss the Church
and its records; and this is exasperating to devout believers, who regard the Church as holy, and any criticism of it as blasphemy. So we have opportunity to
observe the working out of the doctrine that the Church
is superior to the civil law.

On June 12th, 1913, there came to the little town of

Oelwein, Iowa, a former priest of the Catholic Church, named Jeremiah J. Crowley, to deliver a lecture exposing the Papal propaganda. The Catholics of the town made efforts to intimidate the owner of the place in which the lecture was to be given; the priest of the town, Father O'Connor, preached a sermon furiously denouncing the lecturer; and after the lecture the unfortunate Crowley was surrounded by a mob of men, women and boys, and although he was six feet three in size, he was beaten almost to death. At the trial which followed it developed that Father O'Connor and also his brother, a judge on the Superior Bench, were accessories before the fact.

Nor is this a solitary instance. The Catholic military societies, with their uniforms and their armories, are not maintained for nothing. As Archbishop Quigley declared before the German Catholic Central Verein:

> We have well ordered and efficient organizations, all at the beck and nod of the hierarchy and ready to do what the church authorities tell them to do. With these bodies of loyal Catholics ready to step into the breach at any time and present an unbroken front to the enemy we may feel secure.

And so, on the evening of April 15th, 1914, a group of Catholics entered the Pierce Hotel in Denver, Colorado, overpowered a police guard and seized the Rev. Otis L. Spurgeon, an anti-Catholic lecturer. They bound and gagged him, took him to a lonely woods, and beat him to insensibility. The same thing happened to the Rev. Augustus Barnett, at Buffalo; the Rev. William Black was killed at Marshall, Texas. In each case the assailants avowed themselves Knights of Columbus, and efforts to punish them failed, because no jury can be got to convict a Catholic, fighting for his Pope against a godless state. The most pious Leo XIII has laid down:

> It is an impious deed to break the laws of Jesus Christ for the purpose of obeying the magistrates, or to transgress the law of the Church under the pretext of observing the civil law.

There are papers published to warn Americans against the plotting of this political Church. One of them, "The Menace," has a circulation of more than a million; and naturally the Knights of Slavery do not enjoy reading it. Year after year they have marshalled their power to have this paper barred from the mails— so far, in vain. They caused an obscenity prosecution, which failed; so finally the press rooms of the paper were blown up with dynamite. At the present time there is a "Catholic Truth Society" with a publication called "Truth", to oppose the anti-Catholic campaign; and that is all right, of course—except when the agents who collect the two-dollar subscriptions to this publication make use of Untruth in their labors—promising absolution and salvation to the families, dead and living, of those who "come across" with subscriptions. In the "Bulletin of the American Federation of Catholic Societies" for September, 1915, I find a record of the ceaseless plotting to bar criticism of the Catholic Church from the mails. Fitzgerald, a Tammany Catholic congressman, proposes a bill in Washington; and Judge St. Paul, of New Orleans, a member of the Federation's "law committee", points out the difficulties in the way of such legislation. You cannot pass a law against ridiculing religion, because the Catholics want to ridicule Christian Science, Mormonism, and the

"Holy Ghost and Us" Society! The Judge thinks the purpose of the Papal plotters will be accomplished if they can slip into the present law the words "scurrilous and slanderous"; he hopes that this much can be done without the American people catching on!

You read these things for the first time, perhaps, and you want to start an American "Kultur-kampf." I make haste, therefore, to restate the main thesis of this book. It is not the New Inquisition which is our enemy today; it is hereditary Privilege. It is not Superstition, but Big Business which makes use of Superstition as a wolf makes use of sheep's clothing.

You remember how, when Americans first awakened to the universal corruption of our politics, we used to attribute it to the "ignorant foreign vote." Turn to Lecky's "Democracy and Liberty" and you will see how reformers twenty years ago explained our political depravity. But we probed deeper, and discovered that the purely American communities, such as Rhode Island, were the most corrupt of all. It dawned upon us that wherever there was a political boss paying bribes on election day, there was a captain of industry furnishing the money for the bribes, and taking some public privilege in return. So we came to realize that political corruption is merely a by-product of Big Business.

And when we come to probe this problem of the spread of Supersition in America, this amazing renascence of Romanism in a democracy, we find precisely the same phenomenon. It is not the poor foreigner who troubles us. Our human magic would win him—our easy-going trust, our quiet certainty of liberty, our open-handed and open-homed and hail-fellow-well-met

democracy. We should break down the Catholic machine, and not all the priests in the hierarchy could stop
us—were it not for the Steel Trust and the Coal Trust
and the Beef Trust, the Liquor Trust and the Traction
Trust and the Money Trust—those masters of America
who do not want citizens, free and intelligent and self-
governing, but who want the slave-hordes as they come,
ignorant, inert, physically, mentally and morally helpless!

No, do not let yourself be lured into a Kultur-kampf.
It is not the pennies of the servant-girls which build
the towering cathedrals; it is not the two-dollar contributions for the salvation of souls which support the
Catholic Truth Society and the Knights of Columbus
and the Holy Name Society and the Mary Sodality and
the National Shrine of the Immaculate Conception and
all the rest of the machinery of the Papal propaganda.
These help, of course; but the main sources of growth
are, first, the subsidies of industrial exploiters, the majority of whom are non-Catholic, and second, the privilege of public plunder granted as payment for votes
by politicians who are creatures and puppets of Big
Business.

King Coal

The proof of these statements is written all over
the industrial life of America. I will stop long enough
to present an account of one industry, asking the reader to accept my statement that if space permitted I
could present the same sort of proof for a dozen other
industries which I have studied—the steel-mills of
Western Pennsylvania, the meat-factories of Chicago,
the glass-works of Southern Jersey, the silk-mills of

Paterson, the cotton-mills of North Carolina, the woolen-mills of Massachusetts, the lumber-camps of Louisiana, the copper-mines of Michigan, the sweat-shops of New York.

In a lonely part of the Rocky Mountains lies a group of enormously valuable coal-mines owned by the Rockefellers and other Protestant exploiters. The men who work these mines, some twelve or fifteen thousand in number, come from all the nations of Europe and Asia, and their fate is that of the average wage-slave. I do not ask anyone to take my word, but present sworn testimony, taken by the United States Commission on Industrial Relations in 1914. Here is the way the Italian miners live, as described in a doctor's report:

> Houses up the canyon, so-called, of which eight are habitable, and forty-six simply awful; they are disreputably disgraceful. I have had to remove a mother in labor from one part of the shack to another to keep dry.

And here is the testimony of the Rev. Eugene S. Gaddis, former superintendent of the Sociological Department of the Colorado Fuel and Iron Company:

> The C. F. & I. Company now own and rent hovels, shacks and dug-outs that are unfit for the habitation of human beings and are little removed from the pig-sty make of dwellings. And the people in them live on the very level of a pig-sty. Frequently the population is so congested that whole families are crowded into one room; eight persons in one small room was reported during the year.

And here is what this same clergyman has to say about the bosses whom the Rockefellers employ:

> The camp superintendents as a whole impressed me as most uncouth, ignorant, immoral, and in many instances, the most brutal set of men that I have ever met. Blasphemous bullies.

Sometimes the miner grows tired of being robbed of his weights, and applies for the protection which the law of the state allows him. What happens then?

"When a man asked for a checkweighman, in the language of the super he was getting too smart."

"And he got what?"

"He got it in the neck, generally."

And when these wage-slaves, goaded beyond endurance, went on strike, in the words of the Commission's report:

Five strikers, one boy, and thirteen women and children in the strikers' tent colony were shot to death by militiamen and guards employed by the coal companies, or suffocated and burned to death when these militiamen and guards set fire to the tents in which they made their homes.

And now, what is the position of education in such camps? The Rev. James McDonald, a Methodist preacher, testified that the school building was dilapidated and unfit. One year there were four teachers, the next three, and the next only two. The teacher of the primary grade had a hundred and twenty children enrolled, ninety per cent of whom could not speak a word of English.

Every little bench was seated with two or three. It was overcrowded entirely, and she could hardly get walking room around there.

And as to the political use made of this deliberately cultivated ignorance, former United States Senator Patterson testified that the companies controlled all elections and all nominations:

Election returns from the two or three counties in which the large companies operate show that in the precincts in which the mining camps are located the returns are nearly unanimous in favor of the men or measures approved by the companies, regardless of party.

And now comes the all-important question. What of the Catholic Church and these evils? The majority of these mine-slaves are Catholics, it is this Church which is charged with their protection. There are priests in every town, and in nearly every camp. And do we find them lifting their voices in behalf of the miners, protesting against the starving and torturing of thirty or forty thousand human beings? Do we find Catholic papers printing accounts of the Ludlow massacre? Do we find Catholic journalists on the scene reporting it, Catholic lawyers defending the strikers, Catholic novelists writing books about their troubles? We do not!

Through the long agony of the fourteen months strike, I know of just one Catholic priest, Father Le Fevre, who had a word to say for the strikers. One of the first stories I heard when I reached the strike-field was of a priest who had preached on the text that "Idleness is the root of all evil," and had been reported as a "scab" and made to shut up. "Who made him?" I asked, naively, thinking of his church superiors. My informant, a union miner, laughed. "We made him!" he said.

I talked with another priest who was prudently saving souls and could not be interested in questions of worldly greed. Max Eastman, reporting the strike in the "Masses", tells of an interview with a Catholic sister.

"Has the Church done anything to try to help these people, or to bring about peace?" we asked. "I consider it the most useless thing in the world to attempt it," she replied.

The investigating committee of Congress came to the scene, and several clergymen of the Protestant Church appeared and bore testimony to the outrages which were being committed against the strikers; but of all the Catholic priests in the district not one appeared—not one! Several Protestant clergymen testified that they had been driven from the coal-camps— not because they favored the unions, but because the companies objected to having their workers educated at all; but no one ever heard of the Catholic Church having trouble with the operators. To make sure on this point I wrote to a former clergyman of Trinidad who watched the whole strike, and is now a first lieutenant in the First New Mexico Infantry. He answered:

The Catholic Church seemed to get along with the companies very cordially. The Church was permitted in all the camps. The impression was abroad that this was due to favoritism. I honor what good the Church does, but I know of no instance, during the Colorado coal-strike or at any other time or place, when the Catholic Church has taken any special interest in the cause of the laboring men. Many Catholics, especially the men, quit the church during the coal-strike.

The Unholy Alliance

Everywhere throughout America today the ultimate source of all power, political, social, and religious, is economic exploitation. To all other powers and all other organizations it speaks in these words: "Help us, and you will thrive; oppose us, and you will be destroyed." It has spoken to the Catholic Church, for sixteen hundred years the friend and servant of every ruling class; and the Church has hastened to fit itself into the situation, continuing its pastoral role as shepherd to the wage-slave vote.

In New York and Boston and Chicago the Church is "Democratic"; so in the Blaine campaign it was possible for a Republican clergyman to describe the issue as "Rum, Romanism and Rebellion." But the Holy Office was shrewd and socially ambitious, and the Grand Old Party was desperately in need of votes, so under the regimé of Mark Hanna, the President-maker, there began a rapprochment between Big Business and the New Inquisition. Under Hanna the Catholic Church got representation in the Cabinet; under him the Cardinal's Mass became a government institution, a Catholic College came to the fore in Washington, and Catholic prelates were introduced in the role of eminent publicists, their reactionary opinions on important questions being quoted with grave solemnity by a prostitute press. It was Mark Hanna himself who founded the National Civic Federation, upon whose executive committee Catholic cardinals and archbishops might work hand in glove with Catholic labor-leaders for the chloroforming of the American working-class. Hanna's biographer naively calls attention to the President-maker's popularity among Catholics, high and low, and the support they gave him. "Archbishop Ireland was in frequent correspondence with him, and used his influence in Mr. Hanna's behalf."

And this tradition, begun under Hanna, was continued under Roosevelt, and reached its finest flower in the days of Taft, the most pliant tool of the forces of evil who has occupied the White House since the days of the Slave Power. President Taft was himself a Unitarian; yet it was under his administration that the Catholic Church achieved one of its dearest ambitions, and broke into the Supreme Court. Why not? We can imagine the powers of the time in conference. It is desired to pack the Court against the possibility of progress; it is desired to find men who will stand like a rock against change—and who better than those who have been trained from childhood in the idea of a divine sanction for doctrine and morals? After all, what is it that Hereditary Privilege wants in America? A Roman Catholic code of property rights, with a supreme tribunal to play the part of an infallible Pope!

Under this Taft administration the country was governed by the strangest legislative alliance our history ever saw; a combination of the Old Guard of the Republican Party with the leaders of the Tammany Democracy of New York. "Bloody shirt" Foraker, senator from Ohio, voting with the sons of those Irish Catholic mob-leaders whom the Federal troops shot down in the draft-riots! By this unholy combination a pledge to reduce the tariff was carried out by a bill which greatly increased its burdens; by this combination the public lands and resources of the country were fed to a gang of vultures by a thievish Secretary of the Interior. And of course under such an administration the cause of "Religion" made tremendous strides. Catholic officials were appointed to public office, Catholic ecclesiastics were accorded public honors, and Catholic favor became a means to political advancement. You might see a hard-swearing old political pirate like "Uncle Joe" Cannon, taking his cigar out of the corner of his blasphemous mouth and betaking himself to the "Cardinal's Day Mass", to bend his stiff knees and bow his hoary unrepentant head before a jeweled prelate on a throne. You might see an emissary of the United States government proceeding to Rome, prostrating himself before the Pope, and paying over seven million dollars of our taxes for lands which the filthy and sensual friars of the Philippine Islands had filched from the wretched serfs of that country and which the wretched serfs had won back by their blood in a revolution.

Secret Service

This Taft administration, urged on by the Catholic intrigue, made the most determined efforts to prevent the spread of radical thought. Because the popular magazines were opposing the plundering of the country, a bill was introduced into Congress to put them out of business by a prohibitive postal tax; the President himself devoted all his power to forcing the passage of this bill. At the same time the Socialist press was handicapped by every sort of persecution. I was at that time in intimate touch with the "Appeal to Reason", and I know that scarcely a month passed that the Post Office Department did not invent some new "regulation" especially designed to limit its circulation. I recall one occasion when I met the editor on his way to Washington with a trunkful of letters from subscribers who complained that their postmasters refused to deliver the paper to them; and later on this same editor was prosecuted by a Catholic Attorney General and sentenced to prison for seeking to awaken the pepole concerning the Moyer-Haywood case.

From my personal knowledge I can say that under the administration of President Taft the Roman Catholic Church and the Secret Service of the Federal Gov-

ernment worked hand in hand for the undermining of
the radical movement in America. Catholic lecturers
toured the country, pouring into the ears of the public
vile slanders about the private morality of Socialists;
while at the same time government detectives, paid
out of public funds, spent their time seeking evidence
for these Catholic lecturers to use. I know one man, a
radical labor-leader, whose morals happened to approach those of the average capitalist politician, and
who was prevented by threats of exposure and scandal
from accepting the Socialist nomination for President.
I know a dozen others who were shadowed and spied
upon; I know one case—myself—a man who was asking
a divorce from his wife, and whose mail was opened
for months.

This subject is one on which I naturally speak with
extreme reluctance. I will only say that my opponent
in the suit made no charge of misconduct against me;
but those in control of our political police evidently
thought it likely that a man who was not living with
his wife might have something to hide; so for months
my every move was watched and all my mail inter-
cepted. In such a case one might at first suspect one's
private opponent; but it soon became evident that this
net was cast too wide for any private agency. Not
merely was my own mail opened, but the mail of all
my relatives and friends—people residing in places as
far apart as California and Florida. I recall the bland
smile of a government official to whom I complained
about this matter: "If you have nothing to hide you
have nothing to fear." My answer was that a study of
many labor cases had taught me the methods of the

agent provocateur. He is quite willing to take real evidence if he can find it; but if not, he has familiarized himself with the affairs of his victim, and can make evidence which will be convincing when exploited by the yellow press. In my own case, the matter was not brought to a test, for I went abroad to live; when I made my next attack on Big Business, the Taft administration had been repudiated at the polls, and the Secret Service of the government was no longer at the disposal of the Catholic machine.

Tax Exemption

Today the Catholic Church is firmly established and everywhere recognized as one of the main pillars of American capitalism. It has some fifteen thousand churches, fourteen million communicants, and property valued at half a billion dollars. Upon this property it pays no taxes, municipal, state or national; which means, quite obviously, that you and I, who do not go to church, but who **do** pay taxes, furnish the public costs of Catholicism. We pay to have streets paved and lighted and cleaned in front of Catholic churches; we pay to have thieves kept away from them, fires put out in them, records preserved for them—all the services of civilization given to them gratis, and this in a land whose constitution provides that Congress (which includes all state and municipal legislative bodies) "shall make no law respecting a religious establishment." When war is declared, and our sons are drafted to defend the country, all Catholic monks and friars, priests and dignitaries are exempted. They are "ministers of religion"; whereas we Socialists may not even

have the status of "conscientious objectors." We do
not teach "religion"; we only teach justice and humanity, decency and truth.

In defense of this tax-exemption graft, the stock
answer is that the property is being used for purposes
of "education" or "charity". It is a school, in which
children are being taught that "liberty of conscience is
a most pestiferous error, from which arises revolution,
corruption, contempt of sacred things, holy institutions,
and laws." (Pius IX). It is a "House of Refuge", to
which wayward girls are committed by Catholic magistrates, and in which they are worked twelve hours a
day in a laundry or a clothing sweat-shop. Or it is a
"parish-house", in which a celibate priest lives under
the care of an attractive young "house-keeper". Or it
is a nunnery, in which young girls are held against
their will and fed upon the scraps from their sisters'
plates to teach them humility, and taught to lie before
the altar, prostrate in the form of a cross, while their
"Superiors" walk upon their bodies to impress the religious virtues. "I was a teacher in the Catholic schools
up to a very recent period," writes the woman friend
who tells me of these customs, "and I know about the
whole awful system which endeavors to throttle every
genuine impulse of the human will."

Concerning a large part of this church property,
the claim of "religious" use has not even the shadow of
justification. In every large city of America you will
find acres of land owned by the Catholic machine, and
supposed to be the future site of some institution; but
as time goes on and property values increase, the
church decides to build on a cheaper site, and proceeds

to cash in the profits of its investment, precisely as does any other real estate speculator. Everywhere you turn in the history of Romanism you find it at this same game, doing business under the cloak of philanthropy and in the holy name of Christ. Read the letter which the Catholic Bishop of Mexico sent to the Pope in 1647, complaining of the Jesuit fathers and their boundless graft. In McCabe's "Candid History of the Jesuits" appears a summary:

A remarkable account is given of the worldly property of the fathers. They hold, it seems, the greater part of the wealth of Mexico. Two of their colleges own 300,000 sheep, besides cattle and other property. They own six large sugar refineries, worth from half a million to a million crowns each, and making an annual profit of 100,000 crowns each, while all the other monks and clergy of Mexico together own only three small refineries. They have immense farms, rich silver mines, large shops and butcheries, and do a vast trade. Yet they continually intrigue for legacies—a woman has recently left them 70,000 crowns—and they refuse to pay the appointed tithe on them. It is piquant to add to this authoritative description that the Jesuit congregation at Rome were still periodically forbidding the fathers to engage in commerce, and Jesuit writers still gravely maintain that the society never engaged in commerce. It should be added that the missionaries were still heavily subsidized by the King of Spain, that there were (the Bishop says) only five or six Jesuits to each of their establishments, and that they conducted only ten colleges.

"Holy History"

And if you think this tax-exemption privilege should be taken away from the church grafters, let me suggest a course of procedure. Write a letter about it to your daily newspaper; and if the letter is not published, go and see the editor and ask why; so you will

learn something about the partnership between Supersition and Big Business!

It is not too much to say that today no daily newspaper in any large American city dares to attack the
emoluments of the Catholic Church, or to advocate re-
strictions upon the ecclesiastical machine. As I write,
they are making a new Catholic bishop in Los Angeles,
and all the newspapers of that graft-ridden city herald
it as an important social event. Each paper has the
picture of the new prelate, with his shepherd's crook
upraised, his empty face crowned with a rhomboidal
fool's cap, and enough upholstery on him to outfit a
grand opera company. The Los Angeles "Examiner",
the only paper in the city with a pretense to radicalism,
turns loose its star-writer—one of those journalist
virtuosos who will describe you a Wild West "rodeo"
one day, and a society elopement the next, and a G. O.
P. convention the next; and always with his picture, one
inch square, at the head of his effusion. He takes in
the Catholic festivity; and does it phaze him? It does
not! He is a newspaper man, and if his city editor sent
him to hell, he would take the assignment and write
like the devil. To read him now you might think he
had been reared in a convent; his soul is uplifted, and
he bursts forth in pure spontaneous ecstacy:

Solemnly magnificent, every brilliant detail symbolically
picturing the holy history of the Roman Catholic Church in the
inexorable progress of its immense structure, which rises from
the rock of Peter, with its beacons of faith and devotion pierc-
ing the fog of doubt and fear which surround the world and the
worldly, was the ceremony yesterday at the Cathedral of St.
Vibiana, whereby Bishop John J. Cantwell was installed in his
diocese of Monterey and Los Angeles.

And then, a month later, comes another occasion of state—the Twenty-third Annual Banquet of the Merchants' and Manufacturers' Association of Los Angeles. I should have to write a little essay to make clear the sociological significance of that function; explaining first, a nation-wide organization which has been proven by congressional investigation and by the publication of its secret documents to be a machine for the corruption of our political life; and then exhibiting our "City of the Angels", from which all Angels have long since fled; a city in the first crude stage of land speculation, without order, dignity or charm; a city of real estate agents, who exist by selling climate to new arrivals from the East; a city whose intellectual life is "boosting", whose standards of truth are those of the horse-trade. Its newspapers publish a table of temperatures, showing the daily contrast between Southern California and the East. This device is effective in the winter-time; but last June, when for five days and nights the temperature was over 110, and several times 114—the Los Angeles space was left empty!

In the same way, there is a rule that our earthquake shocks are never mentioned, unless they destroy whole towns. On the afternoon of Jan. 26th, 1918, a cyclone hit Pasadena, of violence sufficient to lift a barn over a church-steeple and deposit it in the pastor's front yard. That evening a friend of mine in Los Angeles called up the office of the "Times" to make inquiry; and although they are only thirteen miles away, and have a branch office and a special correspondent in Pasadena, the answer was that they had heard nothing about the cyclone! And next morning I made a careful

search of their columns. On the front page I read:
"Fourth Blizzard of Season Raging in East"; also:
"Another Earthquake in Guatemala". But not a line
about the Pasadena cyclone! That there was plenty of
space in that issue, you may judge from the fact that
there were twenty headlines like the following—many
of them representing full page and half page illustrated
"write-ups":

Where Spring is January; Wealth Waits in California; The
Bright Side of Sunshine Land; Come to California: Southland's
Arms Outstretched in Cordial Invitation to the East; Flower
Stands Make Gay City Streets; Southland Climate Big Manu-
facturing Factor; Joy of Life Demonstrated in Los Angeles'
Beautiful Homes; Nymphs Knit and Bathe at Ocean's Sunny
Beach; etc.

Now we are in the War and our business is booming,
we are making money hand over fist. It is all the more
delightful, because we are putting our souls into it, we
are lending our money to the government and saving
the world for Democracy! Our labor unionists have
been driven to other cities, and our Mexican agitators
and I. W. W.'s are in jail; so, in the gilt ball-room of
our palatial six-dollar-a-day hotel the four hundred
masters of our prosperity meet to pat themselves on the
back, and they invite the new Catholic bishop to come
and confer the grace of God upon their eating.

The Bishop comes; and I take up the "Times"—the
labor-hating, labor-baiting, fire-and-slaughter-breath-
ing "Times"—and here is the episcopal picture on the
front page, the arms stretched four columns wide in
oratorical beneficence. How the shepherd of Jesus does
love the Merchants and Manufacturers! How his eloquence is poured out upon them! "You represent, gent-

lemen, the largest and the most civilizing secular body
in the country. You are the pioneers of American civilization.....I am glad to be among you; glad that my
lines have fallen in this glorious land by the sunset sea,
and honored to meet in intimate acquaintance the big
men who have raised here in a few years a city of metropolitan proportions."

And then, bearing in mind his responsibilities as
guardian of Exploitation, the Bishop goes on to tell
them about the coming class-war. "On the one side a
statesman preaching patience and respect for vested
rights, strict observance of public faith; on the other
a demagog speaking about the tyranny of capitalists
and usurers." And then, of course, the inevitable religious tag: "How will men obey you, if they believe
not in God, who is the author of all authority?" At
which, according to the "Times", "prolonged applause
and cheers" from the Merchants and Manufacturers!
The editor of the "Times" goes back to his office, and
inspired by this episcopal eloquence writes a "leader"
with the statement that: **We have no proletariat in
America!"**

Das Centrum

In order to see clearly the ultimate purpose of this
Unholy Alliance, this union of Superstitition and the
Merchants' and Manufacturers' Association, we have to
go to Europe, where the arrangement has been working
for a thousand years. In Europe to-day we see the whole
world in conflict with a band of criminals who have been
able to master the minds and lives of a hundred million
highly civilized people. As I write, the Junker aristocracy
is at bay, and soon to have its throat cut; but there comes

a Holy Father to its rescue, with the cross of Jesus uplifted, and a series of pleas for mercy, written in Vienna,
edited in Berlin, and sent out from Rome. The Holy
Father loves all mankind with a tender and touching
love; his heart bleeds at the sight of bloodshed and suffering, and he pleads the sacred cause of peace on earth
and good-will toward men.

But what was the Holy Father doing through the
forty-three years that the Potsdam gang were preparing
for their assault on the world? How was the Holy
Father manifesting his love of peace and good will? He
is, you understand, the "sole, last, supreme judge of what
is right and wrong," and his followers obey him with the
utmost promptness and devotion—they express themselves as "prostrate at his feet." And when the masters
of Prussia came to him and said: "Give us the power to
turn this nation into the world's greatest military empire"—what did the Roman Church answer? Did it speak
boldly for the gentle Jesus, and the cause of peace on
earth and good-will towards men? No, it did not. To
Bismarck in Germany it said, precisely as it said to Mark
Hanna in America: "Give us honors and prestige; give
us power over the minds of the young, so that we may
plunder the poor and build our cathedrals and feed fat
our greed; and in return we will furnish you with votes,
so that you may rule the state and do what you will."

You think there is exaggeration in that statement?
Why, we know the very names of the prelates with whom
the master-cynic of the Junkerthum made his "deal." He
had tried the method of the Kultur-kampf, and had failed;
but before he repealed the anti-Catholic laws, he made
sure that the Church had learned its lesson, and would

nevermore oppose the Prussian ruling caste. We know
how this bargain was carried out; we have the record of
the Centrum, the Catholic party of Germany, whose hundred deputies were the solid rock upon which the military regime of Prussia was erected. Not a battle-ship
nor a Zeppelin was built for which the Black Terror did
not vote the funds; not a school-child was beaten in
Posen or Alsace that the New Inquisition did not shout
its "Hoch!" The writer sat in the visitors' gallery of the
Reichstag when the Socialists were protesting against
the torturing of miserable Herreros in Africa, and he
heard the deputies of the Holy Father's political party
screaming their rage like jaguars in a jungle night. All
over Europe the Catholic Church organized fake labor
unions, the "yellows," as they were called, to scab upon
the workers and undermine the revolutionary movement.
The Holy Father himself issued precise instructions for
the management of these agencies of betrayal. Hear the
most pious and benevolent Leo XIII:

"They must pay special and principal attention to
piety and morality, and their internal discipline must be
directed precisely by these considerations; otherwise
they entirely lose their special character, and come to be
very little better than those societies which take no
account of Religion at all."

It is so hard, you see, to keep a man thinking about
piety and morality while he is starving! I am quoting
from the Encyclical Letter on "The Condition of Labor,"
issued in 1891, and addressed "to our Venerable Brethren,
all Patriarchs, Primates, Archbishops and Bishops of the
Catholic World in Grace and Communion with the Apos-

tolic See." The purpose of the letter is "to refute false teaching," and the substance of its message is:

This great labor question cannot be solved except by assuming as a principle that private property must be held sacred and inviolable.

And again, the purpose of churches proclaimed in language as frank as any used in the present book:

The chief thing to be secured is the safe-guarding, by legal enactment and policy, of private property. Most of all it is essential in these times of covetous greed, to keep the multitude within the line of duty; for if all may justly strive to benefit their condition, yet neither justice nor the common good allows any one to seize that which belongs to another, or, under the pretext of futile and ridiculous equality, to lay hands on other peoples' fortunes.

And this, you understand, in lands where rapine and conquest, class-tyranny and priestly domination have been the custom since the dawn of history; in which no property-right can possibly trace back to any other basis than force. In Austria, for example—Austria, the leader and guardian of the Holy Alliance—Austria, which had no Reformation, no Revolution, no Kultur-kampf—Austria, in which the income of the Catholic Primate is $625,000 a year! In other words, Austria is still to a large extent a "Priestly Empire;" and it was Austria which began the war—began it in a religious quarrel, with a Slav people which does not acknowledge the Holy Father as the ruler of the world, but persists in adhering to the Eastern Church. So of course to-day, when Austria is learning the bitter lesson that they who draw the sword shall perish by the sword, the heart of the Holy Father is wrung with grief, and he sends out these eloquent peace-notes, written in Vienna and edited in Ber-

lin. And at the same time his private chaplain is convicted and sentenced to prison for life as Austria's Mas-
ter-Spy in Rome!

It is a curious thing to observe—the natural instinct
which, all over the world, draws Superstition and Exploitation together. This war, which is hailed as a war
against autocracy, might almost as accurately be described as a war against the clerical system. Wherever
in the world you find the Papal power strong, there you
find sympathy with the Prussian infamy and there you
find German intrigue. In Spain, for example; in Ireland
and Quebec, and in the Argentine. The treatment of
Belgium was a little too raw—too many priests were
shot at the outset, and so Cardinal Mercier denounces the
Germans; but you notice that he pleads in vain with the
Vatican, which stands firm by its beloved Austria, and
against the godless kingdom of Italy. The Kaiser allows the hope of restoration of the temporal power at
the peace settlement; and meantime the law forbidding
the presence of the Jesuits in Germany has been repealed,
and all over the world the propagandists of this order are
working for the Kaiser. Sir Roger Casement was raised
a Catholic, and so also "Jim" Larkin, the Irish labor-
leader who is touring America denouncing the Allies.
The Catholic Bishop of Melbourne opposed and beat con-
scription in Australia, and it was Catholic propaganda of
treachery among the ignorant peasant-soldiers from
Sicily which caused the breaking of the Italian line at
Tolmino. So deeply has this instinct worked that, in the
fall of 1917 while the Socialist party in New York was
campaigning for immediate peace, the Catholic Irish suddenly forgot their ancient horrors. The Catholic "Free-

man's Journal" published nine articles favoring Socialism in a single issue; while even "The Tablet," the diocesan paper, began to discover that the Socialists were not such bad fellows after all. The same "Tablet" which a few years ago allowed Father Belford to declare that Socialists were mad dogs who should be "stopped with a bullet"!

Note to second edition: Since the above was written, the war fervor has swept America, including even the rank and file of the Catholics, and what has here been said might seem unfair to persons who have forgotten the attitude of the Church during the early part of the conflict, and the struggle it cost to bring the hierarchy into line. It is one of the ironies of history that the most reactionary organization in the world should be lending its aid to the destruction of the second most reactionary. When the Catholic Church marches forth to war for Democracy, it is not drawing America down into the pit, but is letting America pull it out of the pit—at least for a time, and the spectacle is one in which all lovers of progress will rejoice.

BOOK FOUR

The Church of the Slavers

See, underneath the Crown of Thorn,
  The eye-balls fierce, the features grim!
And merrily from night to morn
  We chaunt his praise and worship him—
Great Christus-Jingo, at whose feet
Christian and Jew and Atheist meet!

A wondrous god! most fit for those
  Who cheat on 'Change, then creep to prayer;
Blood on his heavenly altar flows,
  Hell's burning incense fills the air,
And Death attests in street and lane
The hideous glory of his reign.

—Buchanan

Face of Caesar

The thesis of this book is the effect of fixed dogma in producing mental paralysis, and the use of this mental paralysis by Economic Exploitation. From that standpoint the various Protestant sects are better than the Catholic, but not much better. The Catholics stand upon Tradition, the Protestants upon an Inspired Word; but since this Word is the entire literary product, history and biography, science and legislation, poetry, drama and fiction of a whole people for something like a thousand years, it is possible by judicious selection of texts to prove anything you wish to prove and to justify anything you wish to do. The "Holy Book" being full of polygamy, slavery, rape and wholesale murder, committed by priests and rulers under the direct orders of God, it was a very simple matter for the Protestant Slavers to construct a Bible defense of their system.

They get poor Jesus because he was given to irony, that most dangerous form of utterance. If he could come back to life, and see what men have done with his little joke about the face of Caesar on the Roman coin, I think he would drop dead. As for Paul, he was a Roman bureaucrat, with no nonsense in his make-up; when he ordered, "Servants obey your masters," he meant exactly what he said. The Roman official stamp which he put upon the gospel of Jesus has been the salvation of the Slavers from the Reformation on.

In the time of Martin Luther, the peasants of Germany were suffering the most atrocious and awful misery; Luther himself knew about it, he had denounced the princely robbers and the priestly land-exploiters with that picturesque violence of which he was a master. But nothing had been done about it, nothing ever is done about it—until at last the miserable peasants attempted to organize and win their own rights. Their demands do not seem to us so very criminal as we read them today; the privilege of electing their own pastors, the abolition of villeinage, the right to hunt and fish and cut wood in the forest, the reduction of exorbitant rents, extra payment for extra labor, and—that universal cry of peasant communes whether in Russia, England, Mexico or sixteenth century Germany—the restoration to the village of lands taken by fraud. But Luther would hear nothing of slaves asserting their own rights, and took refuge in the Pauline sociology: If they really wished to follow Christ, they would drop the sword and resort to prayer; the gospel has to do with spiritual, not temporal, affairs; earthly society cannot exist without inequalities, etc.

And when the peasants went on in spite of this, he turned upon them and denounced them to the princes; he issued proclamations which might have been the instructions of Mr. John Wanamaker to the police-force of his "City of Brotherly Love": "One cannot answer a rebel with reason, but the best answer is to hit him with the fist until blood flows from the nose." He issued a letter: "Against the Murderous and Thieving Mob of Peasants," which might have come from the Reverend Woelfkin, Fifth Avenue Pastor of Standard Oil: "The ass needs to be beaten, and the populace needs to be controlled with a strong hand. God knew this well, and therefore he gave the rulers, not a fox's tail, but a sword." He implored these rulers, after the fashion of Methodist Chancellor Day of the University of Syracuse: "Do not be troubled about the severity of their repression, for it will save many souls." With such pious exhortations in their ears the princes set to work, and slaughtered a hundred thousand of the miserable wretches; they completely aborted the social hopes of the Reformation, and cast humanity into the pit of wage-slavery and militarism for four centuries. As a church scholar, Prof. Rauschenbusch, puts it:

> The glorious years of the Lutheran Reformation were from 1517 to 1525, when the whole nation was in commotion, and a great revolutionary tidal wave seemed to be sweeping every class and every higher interest one step nearer to its ideal of life. . . . . The Lutheran Reformation had been most truly religious and creative when it embraced the whole of human life and enlisted the enthusiasm of all ideal men and movements. When it became "religious" in the narrow sense, it grew scholastic and spiny, quarrelsome, and impotent to awaken high enthusiasm and noble life.

Deutschland ueber Alles

As a result of Luther's treason to humanity, his church became the state church of Prussia, and Bibleworship and Devil-terror played their part, along with the Mass and the Confessional, in building up the Junker dream. A court official—the Oberhofprediger—was set up, and from that time on the Hohenzollerns were the most pious criminals in Europe. Frederick the Great, the ancestral genius, was an atheist and a scoffer, but he believed devoutly in religion for his subjects. He said: "If my soldiers were to begin to think, not one would remain in the ranks." And Carlyle, instinctive friend of autocrats, tells with jocular approval how he kept them from thinking:

> He recognizes the uses of Religion; takes a good deal of pains with his Preaching Clergy; will suggest texts to them; and

for the rest expects to be obeyed by them, as by his Sergeants and Corporals. Indeed, the reverend men feel themselves to be a body of Spiritual Sergeants, Corporals, and Captains, to whom obedience is the rule, and discontent a thing not to be indulged in by any means.

So the soldiers stayed in the ranks, and Frederick raided Silesia and Poland. His successors ordered all the Protestant sects into one, so that they might be more easily controlled; from which time the Lutheran Church has been a department of the Prussian state, in some cases a branch of the municipal authority.

In 1848, when the people of various German states demanded their liberty, it was an ultra-pious king of Prussia who sent his troops and shot them down—precisely as Luther had advised to shoot down the peasants. At this time the future maker of the German Empire rose in the Landtag and made his bow before the world; a young Prussian land-magnate, Otto von Bismarck by name, he shook his fist in the face of the new German liberalism, and incidentally of the new German infidelity:

Christianity is the solid basis of Prussia; and no state erected upon any other foundation can permanently exist.

The present Hohenzollern has diligently maintained this tradition of his line. It was his custom to tour the Empire in a train of blue and white cars, carrying as many costumes as any stage favorite, most of them military; with him on the train went the Prussian god, and there was scarcely a performance at which this god did not appear, also in military costume. After the failure of the "Kultur-kampf," the official Lutheran religion was ordered to make friends with its ancient enemy, the Catholic Church. Said the Kaiser:

I make no difference between the adherents of the Catholic and Protestant creeds. Let them both stand upon the foundation of Christianity, and they are both bound to be true citizens and obedient subjects. Then the German people will be the rock of granite upon which our Lord God can build and complete his work of Kultur in the world.

And here is the oath required of the Catholic clergy, upon their admission to equality of trustworthiness with their Protestant confreres:

I will be submissive, faithful and obedient to his Royal Majesty,—and his lawful successors in the government,—as my most gracious King and Sovereign; promote his welfare according to my ability; prevent injury and detriment to him; and particularly endeavor carefully to cultivate in the minds of the people under my care a sense of reverence and fidelity towards the King, love for the Fatherland, obedience to the laws, and all those virtues which in a Christian denote a good citizen; and I will not suffer any man to teach or act in a contrary spirit. In particular I vow that I will not support any society or association, either at home or abroad, which might endanger the public security, and will inform His Majesty of any proposal made, either in my diocese or elsewhere, which might prove injurious to the State.

And later on this heaven-guided ruler conceived the scheme of a Berlin-Bagdad railway, for which he needed one religion more; he paid a visit to Constantinople, and made another **debut** and produced another god—with the result that millions of Turks are fighting under the belief that the Kaiser is a convert to the faith of Mohammed!

Der Tag.

All this was, of course, in preparation for the great event to which all good Germans looked forward—to which all German officers drank their toasts at banquets—the Day.

This glorious day came, and the field-gray armies marched forth, and the Pauline-Lutheran God marched with them. The Kaiser, as usual, acted as spokesman:

Remember that the German people are the chosen of God. On me, the German emperor, the spirit of God has descended. I am His sword, His weapon and His viceregent. Woe to the disobedient and death to cowards and unbelievers.

As to the Prussian state religion, its attitude to the war is set forth in a little book written by a high clerical personage, the Herr Consistorialrat Dietrich Vorwerk, containing prayers and hymns for the soldiers, and for the congregations at home. Here is an appeal to the Lord God of Battles:

Though the warrior's bread be scanty, do Thou work daily death and tenfold woe unto the enemy. Forgive in merciful long-suffering each bullet and each blow which misses its mark. Lead us not into the temptation of letting our wrath be too tame in carrying out Thy divine judgment. Deliver us and our ally from the Infernal Enemy and his servants on earth. Thine is the kingdom, the German land; may we, by the aid of Thy steel-clad hand, achieve the fame and the glory.

It is this Herr Consistorialrat who has perpetrated the great masterpiece of humor of the war—the hymn in which he appeals to that God who keeps guard over Cherubim, Seraphim, and Zeppelins. You have to say over the German form of these words in order to get the effect of their delicious melody—"Cherubinen, Seraphinen, Zeppelinen!" And lest you think that this too-musical clergyman is a rara avis, turn to the little book which has been published in English under the same title as Herr Vorwerk's "Hurrah and Hallelujah." Here is the Reverend S. Lehmann:

Germany is the center of God's plans for the world. Germany's fight against the whole world is in reality the battle of the spirit against the whole world's infamy, falsehood and devilish cunning.

And here is Pastor K. Koenig:

It was God's will that we should will the war.

And Pastor J. Rump:

Our defeat would mean the defeat of His Son in humanity. We fight for the cause of Jesus within mankind.

And here is an eminent theological professor:

The deepest and most thought-inspiring result of the war is the German God. Not the national God such as the lower nations worship, but "our God," who is not ashamed of belonging to us, the peculiar acquirement of our heart.

King Cotton

It is a cheap way to gain applause in these days, to denounce the Prussian system; my only purpose is to show that Bible-worship, precisely as saint-worship or totem-worship, delivers the worshipper up to the Slavers. This truth has held in America, precisely as in Prussia. During the middle of the last century there was fought out a mighty issue in our free republic; and what was the part played in this struggle by the Bible-cults? Hear the testimony of William Lloyd Garrison: "American Christianity is the main pillar of American slavery." Hear Parker Pillsbury: "We had almost to abolish the Church before we could reach the dreadful institution at all."

In the year 1818 the Presbyterian General Assembly, which represented the churches of the South as well as of the North, passed by a **unanimous** vote a resolution to the effect that "Slavery is utterly inconsistent with the law of God, which requires us to love our neighbor as ourselves." But in a generation the views of the entire South, including the Presbyterian Church, had changed entirely. What was the reason? Had the "law of God" been altered? Had some new "revelation" been handed down? Nothing of the kind; it was merely that a Yankee by the name of Eli Whitney had perfected a machine to take the seeds out of short staple cotton. The cotton crop of the South increased from four thousand bales in 1791 to four hundred and fifty thousand in 1820 and five million, four hundred thousand in 1860.

There was a new monarch, King Cotton, and his empire depended upon slaves. According to the custom of monarchs since the dawn of history, he hired the ministers of God to teach that what he wanted was right and holy. From one end of the South to the other the pulpits rang with the text: "Cursed be Canaan; a servant to servants shall he be to his brethren." The learned Bishop Hopkins, in his "Bible View of Slavery", gave the standard interpretation of this text:

> The Almighty, forseeing the total degredation of the Negro race, ordained them to servitude or slavery under the descendants of Shem and Japheth, doubtless because he judged it to be their fittest condition.

I might fill the balance of this volume with citations from defenses of the "peculiar institution" in the name of Jesus Christ—and not only from the South, but from the North. For it must be understood that leading families of Massachusetts and New York owed their power to Slavery; their fathers had brought molasses from New Orleans and made it into rum, and taken it to the coast of Africa to be exchanged for slaves for the Southern planters. And after this trade was outlawed, the slave-grown cotton had still to be shipped to the North and spun; so the traders of the North must have divine sanction for the Fugitive Slave law. Here is the Bishop of Vermont declaring: "The slavery of the negro race appears to me to be fully authorized both in the Old and New Testaments." Here in the "True Presbyterian", of New York, giving the decision of a clerical man of the world: "There is no debasement in it. It might have existed in Paradise, and it may continue through the Millenium."

And when the slave-holding oligarchy of the South rose in arms against those who presumed to interfere with this divine institution, the men of God of the South called down blessings upon their armies in words which, with the proper change of names, might have been spoken in Berlin in August, 1914. Thus Dr. Thornwell, one of the leading Presbyterian divines of the South: "The triumph of Lincoln's principles is the death-knell of slavery......Let us crush the serpent in the egg." And the Reverend Dr. Smythe of Charleston: "The war is a war against slavery, and is therefore treasonable rebellion against the Word, Providence and Government of God." I read in the papers, as I am writing, how the clergy of Germany are thundering against President Wilson's declaration that that country must become democratic. Here is a manifesto of the German Evangelical League, made public on the four hundredth anniversary of the Reformation:

We especially warn against the heresy, promulgated from America, that Christianity enjoins democratic institutions, and that they are an essential condition of the kingdom of God on earth.

In exactly the same way the religious bodies of the entire South united in an address to Christians throughout the world, early in the year 1863:

The recent proclamation of the President of the United States, seeking the emancipation of the slaves of the South, is in our judgment occasion of solemn protest on the part of the people of God.

Witches and Women

To whatever part of the world you travel, to whatever page of history you turn, you find the endowed and established clergy using the word of God in defense of whatever form of slave-driving may then be popular and profitable. Two or three hundred years ago it was the custom of Protestant divines in England and America to burn poor old women as witches; only a hundred and fifty years ago we find John Wesley, founder of Methodism, declaring that "the giving up of witchcraft is in effect the giving up of the Bible." And if you investigate this witch-burning, you will find that it is only one aspect of a blot upon civilization, the Christian Mysogyny. You see, there were two Hebrew legends—one that woman was made out of a man's rib, and the other that she ate an apple; therefore in modern England a wife must be content with a legal status lower than a domestic servant.

Perhaps the most comical of the clerical claims is this—that Christianity has promoted chivalry and respect for womanhood. In ancient Greece and Rome the woman was the equal and helpmate of man; we read in Tacitus about the splendid women of the Germans, who took part in public councils, and even fought in battles. Two thousand years before the Christian era

we are told by Maspero that the Egyptian woman was
the mistress of her house; she could inherit equally
with her brothers, and had full control of her property.
We are told by Paturet that she was "juridically the
equal of man, having the same rights and being treated
in the same fashion." But in present-day England, under the common law, woman can hold no office of trust
or power, and her husband has the sole custody of her
person, and of her children while minors. He can steal
her children, rob her of her clothing, and beat her with
a stick provided it is no thicker than his thumb. While
I was in London the highest court handed down a decision on the law which does not permit a woman to
divorce her husband for infidelity, unless it has been
accompanied by cruelty; a man had brought his mistress into his home and compelled his wife to work for
and wait upon her, and the decision was that this was
not cruelty in the meaning of the law!

And if you say that this enslavement of Woman has
nothing to do with religion—that ancient Hebrew
fables do not control modern English customs—then
listen to the Vicar of Crantock, preaching at St. Crantock's, London, Aug. 27th, 1905, and explaining why
women must cover their heads in church:

(1) Man's priority of creation. Adam was first formed,
then Eve.

(2) The manner of creation. The man is not of the woman,
but the woman of the man.

(3) The purport of creation. The man was not created for
the woman, but the woman for the man.

(4) Results in creation. The man is the image of the glory
of God, but woman is the glory of man.

(5) Woman's priority in the fall. Adam was not deceived;
but the woman, being deceived, was in the transgression.

(6) The marriage relation. As the Church is subject to Christ, so let the wives be to their husbands.

(7) The headship of man and woman. The head of every man is Christ, but the head of the woman is man.

I say there is no modern evil which cannot be justified by these ancient texts; and there is nowhere in Christendom a clergy which cannot be persuaded to cite them at the demand of ruling classes. In the city where I write, three clergymen are being sent to jail for six months for protesting against the use of the name of Jesus in the wholesale slaughter of men. Now, I am backing this war. I know that it has to be fought, and I want to see it fought as hard as possible; but I want to leave Jesus out of it, for I know that Jesus did not believe in war, and never could have been brought to support a war. I object to clerical cant on the subject; and I note that an eminent theological authority, "Billy" Sunday, appears to agree with me; for I find him on the front page of my morning paper, assailing the three pacifist clergymen, and making his appeal not to Jesus, but to the blood-thirsty tribal diety of the ancient Hebrews:

I suppose they think they know more than God Almighty, who commanded the sun to stand still while Joshua won the battle for the Lord; more than the God who made Samson strong so he could slay thousands of his nation's enemies in a righteous cause.

Right you are, Billy! And if the capitalist system continues to develop unchecked, we shall some day see it dawn upon the masters of the world how wasteful it is to permit the superannuated workers to perish by slow starvation. So much more sensible to make use of them! So we shall have a Bible defense of cannibalism;

we shall hear our evangelists quoting Leviticus: "**They shall eat the flesh of their own sons and daughters.**" Or perhaps some of our leisure-class ladies might make the discovery that the flesh of working-class babies is relished by pomeranians and poodles. If so, the Billy Sundays of the twenty-first century may discover the text: "**Happy shall be he that taketh and dasheth thy little ones against the stones.**"

Moth and Rust

It is especially interesting to notice what happens when the Bible texts work **against** the interests of the Slavers and their clerical retainers. Then they are null and void—and no matter how precise and explicit and unmistakable they may be! Take for example the Sabbath injunction: "Six days shalt thou labor and do all that thou hast to do." Karl Marx records of the pious England of his time that

Occasionally in rural districts a day-labourer is condemned to imprisonment for desecrating the Sabbath by working in his front garden. The same labourer is punished for breach of contract if he remains away from his metal, paper or glass works on the Sunday, even if it be from a religious whim. The orthodox Parliament will hear nothing of Sabbath-breaking if it occurs in the process of expanding capital.

Or consider the attitude of the Church in the matter of usury. Throughout ancient Hebrew history the money-lender was an outcast; both the law and the prophets denounced him without mercy, and it was made perfectly clear that what was meant was, not the taking of high interest, but the taking of any interest whatsoever. The early church fathers were explicit, and the Catholic Church for a thousand years consigned money-lenders unhesitatingly to hell. But then came the modern commercial system, and the money-lenders became the masters of the world! There is no more amusing illustration of the perversion of human thought than the efforts of the Jesuit casuists to escape from the dilemma into which their Heavenly Guides had trapped them.

Here, for example is Alphonso Ligouri, a Spanish Jesuit of the eighteenth century, a doctor of the Church, now worshipped as St. Alphonsus, presenting a long and elaborate theory of "mental usury"; concluding that, if the borrower pay interest of his own free will, the lender may keep it. In answer to the question whether the lender may keep what the borrower pays, not out of gratitude, but out of fear that otherwise loans will be refused to him in future, Ligouri says that "to be usury, it must be paid by reason of a contract, or as justly due; payment by reason of such a fear does not cause interest to be paid as an actual price." Again the great saint and doctor tells us that "it is not usury to exact something in return for the danger and expense of regaining the principal!" Could the house of J. P. Morgan and Company ask more of their ecclesiastical department?

The reader may think that such sophistications are now out of date; but he will find precisely the same knavery in the efforts of present-day Slavers to fit Jesus Christ into the system of competitive commercialism. Jesus, as we have pointed out, was a carpenter's son, a thoroughly class-conscious proletarian. He denounced the exploiters of his own time with ferocious bitterness, he drove the money-changers out of the

temple with whips, and he finally died the death of a
common criminal. If he had forseen the whole modern
cycle of capitalism and wage-slavery, he could hardly
have been more precise in his exortations to his followers to stand apart from it. But did all this avail him?
Not in the least!

I place upon the witness-stand an exponent of Bible-
Christianity whom all readers of our newspapers know
well: a scholar of learning, a publicist of renown; once
pastor of the most famous church in Brooklyn; now editor of our most influential religious weekly; a liberal
both in theology and politics; a modernist, an advocate
of what he calls industrial democracy. His name is Lyman Abbott, and he is writing under his own signature
in his own magazine, his subject being "The Ethical
Teachings of Jesus". Several times I have tried to persuade people that the words I am about to quote were
actually written and published by this eminent doctor
of divinity, and people have almost refused to believe
me. Therefore I specify that the article may be found
in the "Outlook", the bound volumes of which are in all
large libraries: volume 94, page 576. The words are
as follows, the bold face being Dr. Abbott's, not mine:

My radical friend declares that the teachings of Jesus are
not practicable, that we cannot carry them out in life, and that
we do not pretend to do so. Jesus, he reminds us, said, 'Lay not
up for yourself treasures upon earth;' and Christians do universally lay up for themselves treasures upon earth; every man
that owns a house and lot, or a share of stock in a corporation,
or a life insurance policy, or money in a savings bank, has laid
up for himself treasure upon earth. But Jesus did not say, "Lay
not up for yourselves treasures upon earth." He said, "Lay not
up for yourselves treasures upon earth **where moth and rust doth
corrupt and where thieves break through and steal.**" And no

sensible American does. Moth and rust do not get at **Mr. Rocke-feller's** oil wells, nor at the Sugar Trust's sugar, and thieves do not often break through and steal a railway or an insurance company or a savings bank. What Jesus condemned was hoarding wealth.

Strange as it may sound to some of the readers of this book, I count myself among the followers of Jesus of Nazareth. His example has meant more to me than that of any other man, and all the experiences of my revolutionary life have brought me nearer to him. Living in the great Metropolis of Mammon, I have felt the power of Privilege, its scourge upon my back, its crown of thorns upon my head. When I read that article in the "Outlook", I felt just as Jesus himself would have felt; and I sat down and wrote a letter—

To Lyman Abbott

This discovery of a new method of interpreting the Bible is one of such very great interest and importance that I cannot forbear to ask space to comment upon it. May I suggest that Dr. Abbott elaborate this exceedingly fruitful idea, and write us another article upon the extent to which the teachings of the Inspired Word are modified by modern conditions, by the progress of invention and the scientific arts? The point of view which Dr. Abbott takes is one which had never occurred to me before, and I had therefore been completely mistaken as to the attitude of Jesus on the question. Also I have, like Dr. Abbott, many radical friends who are still laboring under error.

Jesus goes on to bid his hearers: "Consider the lilies of the field, how they grow; they toil not, neither do they spin." What an apt simile is this for the "great mass of American wealth," in Dr. Abbott's portrayal of it! "It is serving the community," he tells us; "it is building a railway to open a new country to settlement by the homeless; it is operating a railway to carry grain from the harvests of the West to the unfed millions of the East," etc. Incidentally, it is piling up dividends for its pious owners; and so everybody is happy —and Jesus, if he should come back to earth, could never know that he had left the abodes of bliss above.

Truly, there should be a new school of Bible interpretation founded upon this brilliant idea. Jesus says, "Therefore when thou doest thine alms, do not sound a trumpet before thee, as the hypocrites do in the synagogues and in the streets, that they may have glory of men." Verily not; for of what avail are trumpets, compared with the millions of copies of newspapers which daily go forth to tell of Mr. Rockefeller's benefactions? How transitory are they, compared with the graven marble or granite which Mr. Carnegie sets upon the front of each of his libraries!

There is the paragraph, "Neither shalt thou swear by thy head, because thou canst not make one hair white or black." I have several among my friends who are Quakers; presumably Dr. Abbott has also; and he should not fail to point out to them the changes which scientific discovery has wrought in the significance of this command against swearing. We can now make our hair either white or black, or a combination of both. We can make it a brilliant peroxide golden; we could, if pushed to an extreme, make it purple or green. So we are clearly entitled to swear all we please by our head.

Nor should we forget to examine other portions of the Bible according to this method. "Look not upon the wine when it is red," we are told. Thanks to the activities of that Capitalism which Dr. Abbott praises so eloquently, we now make our beverages in the chemical laboratory, and their color is a matter of choice. Also, it should be pointed out that we have a number of pleasant drinks which are not wine at all—"high-balls" and "gin rickeys" and "peppered punches"; also **vermouthe** and **creme de menthe** and **absinthe**, which I believe, are green in hue, and therefore entirely safe.

Then there are the Ten Commandments. "Thou shalt not make unto thee any graven image." See how completely our understanding of this command is changed, so soon as we realize that we are free to make images of molten metal! And that we may with impunity bow down to them and worship them and serve them—even, for instance, a Golden Calf!

"The seventh day is the sabbath of the Lord thy God; in it thou shalt not do any work, thou, nor thy son, nor thy daughter, thy manservant, nor thy maidservant, nor thy cattle, nor the stranger that is within thy gates." This, again, it will be noted, is open to new interpretations. It specifies maidservants, but does not prevent one's employing as many married women as he pleases. It also says nothing about the various kinds of labor-saving machinery which we have now taught to work for us—sail-boats, naptha launches, yachts, automobiles, and private cars—all of which may be busily occupied during the seventh day of the week. The men who run these machines—the guides, boatmen, stokers, pilots, chauffeurs, and engineers—would all indignantly resent being regarded as "servants", and so they do not come under the prohibition any more than the machines.

"Thou shalt not covet thy neighbor's house, thou shalt not covet thy neighbor's wife, nor his manservant, nor his maidservant, nor his ox, nor his ass, nor anything that is thy neighbor's." I read this paragraph over for the first time in quite a while, and I came with a jolt to its last words. I had been intending to point out that it said nothing about a neighbor's automobile, nor a neighbor's oil wells, sugar trusts, insurance companies and savings banks. The last words, however, stop one off abruptly. One is almost tempted to imagine that the Divine Intelligence must have foreseen Dr. Abbott's ingenious method of interpretation, and taken this precaution against him. And this was a great surprise to me—for, truly, I had not supposed it possible that such an interpretation could have been foreseen, even by Omniscience itself. I will conclude this communication by venturing the assertion that it could not have been foreseen by any other person or thing, in the heavens above, on the earth beneath, or the waters under the earth. Dr. Abbott may accept my congratulations upon having achieved the most ingenious and masterful exhibition of casuistical legerdemain that it has ever been my fortune to encounter in my readings in the literatures of some thirty centuries and seven different languages.

And I will also add that I respectfully challenge Dr. Abbott to publish this letter. And I announce to him in advance that if he refuses to publish it, I will cause it to be published upon the first page of the "Appeal to

Reason", where it will be read by some five hundred thousand Socialists, and by them set before several million followers of Jesus Christ, the world's first and greatest revolutionist, whom Dr. Lyman Abbott has traduced and betrayed by the most amazing piece of theological knavery that it has ever been my fortune to encounter.

The Octopus

Dr. Lyman Abbott published this letter! In his editorial comment thereon he said that he did not know which of two biblical injunctions to follow: "Answer not a fool according to his folly, lest thou be thought like unto him"; or "Answer a fool according to his folly, lest he be wise in his own conceit". I replied by pointing out a third text which the Reverend Doctor had possibly overlooked: "He that calleth his neighbor a fool shall be in danger of hell-fire." But the Reverend Doctor took refuge in his dignity, and I bided my time and waited for that revenge which comes sooner or later to us muck-rakers. In this case it came speedily. The story is such a perfect illustration of the functions of religion as oil to the machinery of graft that I ask the reader's permission to recite it at length.

For a couple of decades the political and financial life of New England has been dominated by a gigantic aggregation of capital, the New York, New Haven and Hartford Railroad. It is a "Morgan" concern; its popular name, "The New Haven", stands for all the railroads of six states, nearly all the trolley-lines and steamship-lines, and a group of the most powerful banks of Boston and New York. It is controlled by a little group of insiders, who followed the custom of railroad-wrecking familiar to students of American industrial life: buying up new lines, capitalizing them at fabulous sums, and unloading them on the investing public; paying dividends out of capital, "passing" dividends as a means of stock manipulation, accumulating surpluses and cutting "melons" for the insiders, while at the same time crushing labor unions, squeezing wages, and permitting rolling-stock and equipment to go to wreck.

All these facts were perfectly well known in Wall Street, and could not have escaped the knowledge of any magazine editor dealing with current events. In eight years the "New Haven" had increased its capitalization 1501 per cent; and what that meant, any office boy in "the Street" could have told. What attitude should a magazine editor take to the matter?

At that time there were still two or three free magazines in America. One of them was Hampton's, and the story of its wrecking by the New Haven criminals will some day serve in school text-books as the classic illustration of that financial piracy which brought on the American social revolution. Ben Hampton had bought the old derelict "Broadway Magazine", with twelve thousand subscribers, and in four years, by the simple process of straight truth-telling, had built up for it a circulation of 440,000. In two years more he would have had a million; but in May, 1911, he announced a series of articles dealing with the New Haven management.

The articles, written by Charles Edward Russell, were so exact that they read today like the reports of the Interstate Commerce Commission, dated three years later. A representative of the New Haven called upon the editor of Hampton's with a proof of the first article—obtained from the printer by bribery—and was invited to specify the statements to which he took exception; in the presence of witnesses he went over the article line by line, and specified two minor errors, which were at once corrected. At the end of the conference he announced that if the articles were published, Hampton's Magazine would be "on the rocks in ninety days."

Which threat was carried out to the letter. First came a campaign among the advertisers of the magazine, which lost an income of thousands of dollars a month, almost over night. And then came a campaign among the banks—the magazine could not get credit. Anyone familiar with the publishing business will understand that a magazine which is growing rapidly has to have advances to meet each month's business. Hampton undertook to raise the money by selling stock; whereupon a spy was introduced into his office as bookkeeper, his list of subscribers was stolen, and a campaign was begun to destroy their confidence.

It happened that I was in Hampton's office in the summer of 1911, when the crisis came. Money had to be had to pay for a huge new edition; and upon a property worth two millions of dollars, with endorsements worth as much again, it was impossible to borrow thirty thousand dollars in the city of New York. Bankers, personal friends of the publisher, stated quite openly that word had gone out that any one who loaned money to him would be "broken". I myself sent telegrams to everyone I knew who might by any chance be able to

help; but there was no help, and Hampton retired
without a dollar to his name, and the magazine was sold
under the hammer to a concern which immediately
wrecked it and discontinued publication.

The Industrial Shelley

Such was the fate of an editor who opposed the
"New Haven". And now, what of those editors who
supported it? Turn to "The Outlook, a Weekly Journal
of Current Events," edited by Lyman Abbott—the
issue of Dec. 25th, nineteen hundred and nine years
after Christ came down to bring peace on earth and
good-will toward Wall Street. You will there find an
article by Sylvester Baxter entitled "The Upbuilding of
a Great Railroad." It is the familiar "slush" article
which we professional writers learn to know at a glance.
"Prodigious", Mr. Baxter tells us, has been the progress
of the New Haven; this was "a masterstroke", that was
"characteristically sagacious". The road had made
"prodigious expenditures", and to a noble end: "Transportation efficiency epitomizes the broad aim that ani-
mated these expenditures and other constructive activities." There are photographs of bridges and sta-
tions—"vast terminal improvements", "a masterpiece
of modern engineering", "the highest, greatest and
most architectural of bridges". Of the official under
whom these miracles were being wrought—President
Mellen—we read: "Nervously organized, of delicate
sensibility, impulsive in utterance, yet with an extraordinarily convincing power for vividly logical presen-
tation." An industrial Shelley, or a Milton, you perceive; and all this prodigious genius poured out for the
general welfare! "To study out the sort of transpor-

tation service best adapted to these ends, and then to provide it in the most efficient form possible, that is the life-task that President Mellen has set himself."

There was no less than sixteen pages of these raptures—quite a section of a small magazine like the "Outlook". "The New Haven ramifies to every spot where industry flourishes, where business thrives." "As a purveyor of transportation it supplies the public with just the sort desired." "Here we have the new efficiency in a nutshell." In short, here we have what Dr. Lyman Abbott means when he glorifies "the great mass of American wealth". "It is serving the community; it is building a railway to open a new country to settlement by the homeless; it is operating a railway to carry grain from the harvests of the West to the unfed millions of the East," etc. The unfed millions—my typewriter started to write "underfed millions"—are humbly grateful for these services, and hasten to buy copies of the pious weekly which tells about them.

The "Outlook" runs a column of "current events" in which it tells what is happening in the world; and sometimes it is compelled to tell of happenings against the interests of "the great mass of American wealth". The cynical reader will find amusement in following its narrative of the affairs of the New Haven during the five years subsequent to the publication of the Baxter article.

First came the collapse of the road's service; a series of accidents so frightful that they roused even clergymen and chambers of commerce to protest. A number of the "Outlook's" subscribers are New Haven "commuters", and the magazine could not fail to refer to their troubles. In the issue of Jan. 4th, 1913, three years and ten days after the Baxter rhapsody, we read:

The most numerous accidents on a single road since the last fiscal year have been, we believe, those on the New Haven. In the opinion of the Connecticut Commission, the Westport wreck would not have occurred if the railway company had followed the recommendation of the Chief Inspector of Safety Appliances of the Interstate Commerce Commission in its report on a similar accident at Bridgeport a year ago.

And by June 28th, matters had gone farther yet; we find the "Outlook" reporting:

Within a few hours of the collision at Stamford, the wrecked Pullman car was taken away and burned. Is this criminal destruction of evidence?

This collapse of the railroad service started a clamor for investigation by the Interstate Commerce Commission, which of course brought terror to the bosoms of the plunderers. On Dec. 20, 1913, we find the "Outlook" "putting the soft pedal" on the public indignation. "It must not be forgotten that such a road as the New Haven is, in fact if not in terms, a National possession, and as it goes down or up, public interests go down or up with it." But in spite of all pious admonitions, the Interstate Commerce Commission yielded to the public clamor, and an investigation was made—revealing such conditions of rottenness as to shock even the clerical retainers of Privilege. "Securities were inflated, debt was heaped upon debt", reports the horrified "Outlook"; and when its hero, Mr. Mellen—its industrial Shelley, "nervously organized, of delicate sensibility"—admitted that he had no authority as to the finances of the road and no understanding of them, but had taken all his

orders from Morgan, the "Outlook" remarks, deeply
wounded: "A pitiable position for the president of a
great railway to assume." A little later, when things
got hotter yet, we read:

In the search for truth the Commissioners had to overcome
many obstacles, such as the burning of books, letters and documents, and the obstinacy of witnesses, who declined to testify
until criminal proceedings were begun. The New Haven system
has more than three hundred subsidiary corporations in a web
of entangling alliances, many of which were seemingly planned,
created and manipulated by lawyers expressly retained for the
purpose of concealment or deception.

But do you imagine even that would sicken the
pious jackals of their offal? If so, you do not know
the sturdiness of the pious stomach. A compromise
was patched up between the government and the
thieves who were too big to be prosecuted; this bargain
was not kept by the thieves, and President Wilson declared in a public statement that the New Haven administration had "broken an agreement deliberately
and solemnly entered into," in a manner to the President "inexplicable and entirely without justification."
Which, of course, seemed to the "Outlook" dreadfully
impolite language to be used concerning a "National
possession"; it hastened to rebuke President Wilson,
whose statement was "too severe and drastic."

A new compromise was made between the government and the thieves who were too big to be prosecuted,
and the stealing went on. Now, as I work over this
book, the President takes the railroads for war use,
and reads to Congress a message proposing that the
securities based upon the New Haven swindles, together with all the mass of other railroad swindles, shall

be sanctified and secured by dividends paid out of the public purse. New Haven securities take a big jump; and the "Outlook", needless to say, is enthusiastic for the President's policy. Here is a chance for the big thieves to baptize themselves—or shall we say to have the water in their stocks made "holy"? Says our pious editor, for the government to take property without full compensation "would be contrary to the whole spirit of America."

The Outlook for Graft

Anyone familiar with the magazine world will understand that such crooked work as this, continued over a long period, is not done for nothing. Any magazine writer would know, the instant he saw the Baxter article, that Baxter was paid by the New Haven, and that the "Outlook" also was paid by the New Haven. Generally he has no way of proving such facts, and has to sit in silence; but when his board bill falls due and his landlady is persistent, he experiences a direct and earnest hatred of the crooks of journalism who thrive at his expense. If he is a Socialist, he looks forward to the day when he may sit on a Publications' Graft Commission, with access to all magazine books which have not yet been burned!

In the case of the New Haven, we know a part of the price—thanks to the labors of the Interstate Commerce Commission. Needless to say, you will not find the facts recorded in the columns of the Outlook; you might have read it line by line from the palmy days of Mellen to our own, and you would have got no hint of what the Commission revealed about magazine and newspaper graft. Nor would you have got much more from the great metropolitan dailies, which systematically "played down" the expose, omitting all the really damaging details. You would have to go to the reports of the Commission—or to the files of "Pearson's Magazine", which is out of print and not found in libraries!

According to the New Haven's books, and by the admission of its own officials, the road was spending more than four hundred thousand dollars a year to influence newspapers and magazines in favor of its policies. (President Mellen stated that this was relatively less than any other railroad in the country was spending). There was a professor of the Harvard Law School, going about lecturing to boards of trade, urging in the name of economic science the repeal of laws against railroad monopolies—and being paid for his speeches out of railroad funds! There was a swarm of newspaper reporters, writing on railroad affairs for the leading papers of New England, and getting twenty-five dollars weekly, or two or three hundred on special occasions. Sums had been paid directly to more than a thousand newspapers—$3,000 to the Boston "Republic", and when the question was asked "Why?" the answer was, "That is Mayor Fitzgerald's paper." Even the ultra-respectable "Evening Transcript", organ of the Brahmins of culture, was down for $144 for typing, mimeographing and sending out "dope" to the country press. There was an item of $381 for 15,000 "Prayers"; and when asked about that President Mellen explained that it referred to a pamphlet called "Prayers from the Hills", embodying the yearnings of the back-country people for trolley-franchises to be issued to the New Haven. Asked why the pamphlet was called "Prayers", Mr. Mellen explained that "there was lots of biblical language in it."

And now we come to the "Outlook"; after five years of waiting, we catch our pious editors with the goods on them! There appears on the pay-roll of the New Haven, as one of its regular press-agents, getting sums like $500 now and then—would you think it possible?— Sylvester Baxter! And worse yet, there appears an item of $938.64 to the "Outlook", for a total of 9,716 copies of its issue of Dec. 25th, nineteen hundred and nine years after Christ came to bring peace on earth and good will towards Wall Street!

The writer makes a specialty of fair play, even when dealing with those who have never practiced it towards him. He wrote a letter to the editor of the "Outlook", asking what the magazine might have to say upon this matter. The reply, signed by Lawrence F. Abbott, President of the "Outlook" Company, was that the "Outlook" did not know that Mr. Baxter had any salaried connection with the New Haven, and that they had paid him for the article at the usual rates. Against this statement must be set one made under oath by the official of the New Haven who had the disbursing of the corruption fund—that the various papers which used the railroad material paid nothing for it, and "they all knew where it came from." Mr. Lawrence Abbott states that "the New Haven Railroad bought copies of the 'Outlook' without any previous understanding or arrangement as anybody is entitled to buy copies of the 'Outlook'." I might point out that this does not really say as much as it seems to; for the President of every magazine company in America knows without any previous understanding or arrangement that any time he cares to print an article such as Mr. Baxter's, dealing with the affairs of a great corporation, he can sell ten thousand copies to that corporation. The late unlamented Elbert Hubbard wrote a defense of the Rockefeller slaughter of coal-miners, published it in "The Fra," and came down to New York and unloaded several tons at 26 Broadway; he did the same thing in the case of the copper strike in Michigan, and again in the case of "The Jungle"—and all this without the slightest claim to divine inspiration or authority!

Mr. Abbott answers another question: "We certainly did not return the amount to the railroad company." Well, a sturdy conscience must be a comfort to its possessor. The President of the "Outlook" is in the position of a pawnbroker caught with stolen goods in his establishment. He had no idea they were stolen; and we might believe it, if the thief were obscure. But when the thief is the most notorious in the city—when his picture has been in the paper a thousand times? And when the thief swears that the broker knew him? And when the broker's shop is full of other suspicious goods? Why did the "Outlook" practically take back Mr. Spahr's revelations concerning the Powder barony of Delaware? Why did it support so vigorously the Standard Oil ticket for the control of the Mutual Life Insurance Company—and with James Stillman, one of the heads of Standard Oil, president of Standard Oil's big bank in New York, secretly one of its biggest stockholders!

Also, why does the magazine refuse to give its

readers a chance to judge its conduct? Why is it that
a search of its columns reveals no mention of the revelations concerning Mr. Baxter—not even any mention
of the $400,000 slush fund of its paragon of transporta-
tion virtues? I asked that question in my letter, and
the president of the "Outlook" Company for some reason failed to notice it. I wrote a second time, courteous-
ly reminding him of the omission; and also of another,
equally significant—he had not informed me whether
any of the editors of the "Outlook", or the officers or
directors of the Company, were stockholders in the
New Haven. His final reply was that the questions
seem to him "wholly unimportant"; he does not know
whether the "Outlook" published anything about the
Baxter revelations, nor does he know whether any of
the editors or officers or directors of the "Outlook"
Company are or ever have been stockholders of the
New York, New Haven and Hartford Railroad Company. The fact "would not in the slightest degree affect
either favorably or unfavorably our editorial treatment
of that corporation." Caesar's wife, it appears is above
suspicion—even when she is caught in a brothel!

Clerical Camouflage

I have seen a photograph from "Somewhere in
France", showing a wayside shrine with a statue of the
Virgin Mary, innocent and loving, with her babe in her
arms. If you were a hostile aviator, you might sail over
and take pictures to your heart's content, and you
would see nothing but a saintly image; you would have
to be on the enemy's side, and behind the lines, to make
the discovery that under the image had been dug a hole

for a machine-gun. When I saw that picture, I thought to myself—there is capitalist Religion!

You see, if cannon and machine-guns are out in the open, they are almost instantly spotted and put out of action; and so with magazines like "Leslie's Weekly", or "Munsey's", or the "North American Review", which are frankly and wholly in the interest of Big Business. If an editor wishes really to be effective in holding back progress, he must protect himself with a **camouflage** of piety and philanthropy, he must have at his tongue's end the phrases of brotherhood and justice, he must be liberal and progressive, going a certain cautious distance with the reformers, indulging in carefully measured fair play—giving a dime with one hand, while taking back a dollar with the other!

Let us have an illustration of this clerical **camouflage.** Here are the wives and children of the Colorado coal-miners being shot and burned in their beds by Rockefeller gun-men, and the press of the entire country in a conspiracy of silence concerning the matter. In the effort to break down this conspiracy, Bouck White, Congregational clergyman, author of "The Call of the Carpenter", goes to the Fifth Avenue Church of Standard Oil and makes a protest in the name of Jesus. I do not wish to make extreme statements, but I have read history pretty thoroughly, and I really do not know where in nineteen hundred years you can find an action more completely in the spirit and manner of Jesus than that of Bouck White. The only difference was that whereas Jesus took a real whip and lashed the money-changers, White politely asked the pastor to discuss with him the question whether or not Jesus condemned the

holding of wealth. He even took the precaution to write
a letter to the clergyman announcing in advance what
he intended to do! And how did the clergyman prepare
for him? With the sword of truth and the armor of the
spirit? No—but with two or three dozen strong-arm
men, who flung themselves upon the Socialist author
and hurled him out of the church. So violent were they
that several of White's friends, also one or two casual
spectators, were moved to protest; what happened
then, let us read in the New York "Sun", the most bitterly hostile to radicalism of all the metropolitan newspapers. Says the "Sun's' report:

A police billy came crunching against the bones of Lopez's
legs. It struck him as hard as a man could swing it eight times.
A fist planted on Lopez's jaw knocked out two teeth. His lip
was torn open. A blow in the eye made it swell and blacken
instantly. A minute later Lopez was leaning against the church
with blood running to the doorsill.

And now, what has the clerical **camouflage** to say on
this proceeding? Does it approve it? Oh no! It was "a
mistake", the "Outlook" protests; it intensifies the hatred which these extremists feel for the church. The
proper course would have been to turn the disturber
aside with a soft answer; to give him some place, say
in a park, where he could talk his head off to people of
his own sort, while good and decent Christians continued to worship by themselves in peace, and to have
the children of their mine-slaves shot and burned in
their beds. Says our pious editor:

The true way to repress cranks is not to suppress them; it
is to give them an opportunity to air their theories before any
who wish to learn, while forbidding them to compel those to
listen who do not wish to do so.

Or take another case. Twelve years ago the writer made an effort to interest the American people in the conditions of labor in their packing-plants. It happened that incidentally I gave some facts about the bedevilment of the public's meat-supply, and the public really did care about that. As I phrased it at the time, I aimed at the public's heart, and by accident I hit it in the stomach. There was a terrible clamor, and Congress was forced to pass a bill to remedy the evils. As a matter of fact this bill was a farce, but the public was satisfied, and soon forgot the matter entirely. The point to be noted here is that so far as concerned the atrocious miseries of the working-people, it was not necessary even to pretend to do anything. The slaves of Packingtown went on living and working as they were described as doing in "The Jungle", and nobody gave a further thought to them. Only the other day I read in my paper—while we are all making sacrifices in a "War for Democracy"—that Armour and Company had paid a dividend of twenty-one per cent, and Swift and Company a dividend of thirty-five per cent.

This prosperity they owe in good part to their clerical **camouflage.** Listen to our pious "Outlook", engaged in countermining "The Jungle". The "Outlook" has no doubt that there are genuine evils in the packing-plants; the conditions of the workers ought of course to be improved; BUT—

To disgust the reader by dragging him through every conceivable horror, physical and moral, to depict with lurid excitement and with offensive minuteness the life in jail and brothel—all this is to overreach the object....Even things actually terrible may become distorted when a writer screams them out in a sensational way and in a high pitched key......More convincing if it were less hysterical.

Don't you see what these clerical crooks are for?

The Jungle

A four years' war was fought in America, a million men were killed and half a continent was devastated, in order to abolish chattel slavery and put wage slavery in its place. I have made a thorough study of both these industrial systems, and I freely admit that there is one respect in which the lot of the wage slave is better than that of the chattel slave. The wage slave is free to think; and by squeezing a few drops of blood from his starving body, he may possess himself of machinery for the distribution of his ideas. Taking his chances of the policeman's club and the jail, he may found revolutionary organizations, and so he has the candle of hope to light him to his death-bed. But excepting this consideration, and taking the circumstances of the wage slave from the material point of view alone, I hold it beyond question that the average lot of the chattel slave of 1860 was preferable to that of the modern slave of the Beef Trust, the Steel Trust, or the Coal Trust. It was the Southern master's real concern, his business interest, that the chattel slave should be kept physically sound; but it is nobody's business to care anything about the wage slave. The children of the chattel slave were valuable property, and so they got plenty to eat, and a happy outdoor life, and medical attention if they fell ill. But the children of the sweat-shop or the cotton-mill or the canning-factory are raised in a city slum, and never know what it is to have enough to eat, never know a feeling of security or rest—

> We are weary in our cradles
>   From our mother's toil untold;
> We are born to hoarded weariness
>   As some to hoarded gold.

The system of competitive commercialism, of large-scale capitalist industry in its final flowering! I quote from "The Jungle":

Here in this city tonight, ten thousand women are shut up in foul pens, and driven by hunger to sell their bodies to live. Tonight in Chicago there are ten thousand men, homeless and wretched, willing to work and begging for a chance, yet starving, and fronting with terror the awful winter cold! Tonight in Chicago there are a hundred thousand children wearing out their strength and blasting their lives in the effort to earn their bread! There are a hundred thousand mothers who are living in misery and squalor, struggling to earn enough to feed their little ones! There are a hundred thousand old people, cast off and helpless, waiting for death to take them from their torments! There are a million people, men and women and children, who share the curse of the wage-slave; who toil every hour they can stand and see, for just enough to keep them alive; who are condemned till the end of their days to monotony and weariness, to hunger and misery, to heat and cold, to dirt and disease, to ignorance and drunkenness and vice! And then turn over the page with me, and gaze upon the other side of the picture. There are a thousand—ten thousand, maybe—who are the masters of these slaves, who own their toil. They do nothing to earn what they receive, they do not even have to ask for it—it comes to them of itself, their only care is to dispose of it. They live in palaces, they riot in luxury and extravagance—such as no words can describe, as makes the imagination reel and stagger, makes the soul grow sick and faint. They spend hundreds of dollars for a pair of shoes, a handkerchief, a garter; they spend millions for horses and automobiles and yachts, for palaces and banquets, for little shiny stones with which to deck their bodies. Their life is a contest among themselves for supremacy in ostentation and recklessness, in the destroying of useful and necessary things, in the wasting of the labor and the lives of their fellow-creatures, the toil and anguish of the nations, the sweat and tears and blood of the human race! It is all theirs—it comes to them; just as all the springs pour into streamlets, and the streamlets into rivers, and the rivers into the ocean—so, automatically and inevitably, all the wealth of society comes to them. The farmer tills the soil, the miner digs in the earth, the weaver tends the loom, the mason carves the stone; the clever man invents, the shrewd man directs, the wise man studies, the inspired man sings—and all the results, the products of the labor of brain and muscle, are gathered into one stupendous stream and poured into their laps!

This is the system. It is the crown and culmination of all the wrongs of the ages; and in proportion to the magnitude of its exploitation, is the hypocrisy and knavery of the clerical **camouflage** which has been organized in its behalf. Beyond all question, the supreme irony of history is the use which has been made of Jesus of Nazareth as the Head God of this blood-thirsty system; it is a cruelty beyond all language, a blasphemy beyond the power of art to express. Read the man's words, furious as those of any modern agitator that I have heard in twenty years of revolutionary experience: "Lay not up for yourselves treasures on earth! —Sell that ye have and give alms!—Blessed are ye poor, for yours is the kingdom of Heaven!—Woe unto you that are rich, for ye have received your consolation!—Verily, I say unto you, that a rich man shall hardly enter into the kingdom of Heaven!—Woe unto you also, you lawyers!—Ye serpents, ye generation of vipers, how can ye escape the damnation of hell?"

"And this man"—I quote from "The Jungle" again —"they have made into the high-priest of property and smug respectability, a divine sanction of all the horrors and abominations of modern commercial civilization!

Jewelled images are made of him, sensual priests burn insense to him, and modern pirates of industry bring their dollars, wrung from the toil of helpless women and children, and build temples to him, and sit in cushioned seats and listen to his teachings expounded by doctors of dusty divinity!"

BOOK FIVE

The Church of the Merchants

Mammon led them on—
Mammon, the least erected spirit that fell
From Heaven; for even in Heaven his looks and
    thoughts
Were always downward bent, admiring more
The riches of Heaven's pavement, trodden gold,
Than aught divine or holy else enjoyed
In vision beatific....Let none admire
That riches grow in Hell; that soil may best
Deserve the precious bane.

Milton.

The Head Merchant

Ours is the era of commerce, as its propagandists never weary of telling us. Business is the basis of our material lives, and consequently of our culture. Business men control our politics and dictate our laws; business men own our newspapers and direct their policy; business men sit on our school boards, and endow and manage our universities. The Reformation was a revolt of the newly-developing merchant classes against the tyrannies and abuses of feudal clericalism: so in all Protestant Christianity one finds the spirit, ideals, and language of Trade. We have shown how the symbolism of the Anglican Church is of the palace and the throne; in the same way that of the non-conformist sects may be shown to be of the counting-house. In the view of the middle-class Britisher, the nexus between man and man is cent per cent; and so in their Sunday services the worshippers sing such hymns as this:

> Whatever, Lord, we lend to Thee,
> Repaid a thousand fold shall be;
> Then gladly will we give to Thee,
> Who givest all.

The first duty of every man under the competitive system is to secure the survival of his own business; so on the Sabbath, when he comes to deal with eternity, he is practical and explicit:

> Nothing is worth a thought beneath
> But how I may escape the death
> That never, never dies;
> How make mine own election sure,
> And when I fail on earth secure
> A mansion in the skies.

Just as the priest of the aristocratic caste figures
God as a mighty Conqueror—

> Marching as to war
> With the cross of Jesus
> Going on before—

so the preacher to the trader figures the divinity as a
glorified Merchant keeping books. This Head Merchant
has a monopoly in His line; He knows all His rivals'
secrets, so there is no getting ahead of Him, and nothing to do but obey His Word, as revealed through His
clerical staff. The system is oily with protestations of
divine love; but when you read the comments of Luther
upon Calvin and of Calvin upon Luther, you understand
that this love is confined to the inside of each denomination. And even so restricted, there is not always enough
to go around. Recently I met a Presbyterian clergyman, to whom I remarked, "I see by the papers that you
have just finished a church building." "Yes," he answered; "and I have had three offers of a new church."
I did not see the connection, and asked, "Because you
were so successful with this one?" The reply was,
"They always take it for granted that you want to
change when you've finished a new building, because
you make so many enemies!"

The business man puts up the money to build the
church, he puts up the money to keep it going; and the
first rule of a business man is that when he puts up the
money for a thing he "runs" that thing. Of course he
sees that it spreads his own views of life, it helps to
maintain his tradition. In the days of Anu and Baal we
heard the proclamation of the divine right of Kings;
in these days of Mammon we hear the proclamation of

the divine right of Merchants. Some fifteen years ago the head of our Coal Trust announced during a great strike that the question would be settled "by the Christian men to whom God in His Infinite Wisdom has given control of the property interests of this country". And on that declaration all pious merchants stand; whatever their denominations, Catholic, Episcopalian, Baptist, Methodist, Presbyterian or Hebrew, their Sabbath doctrines are alike, as their week-day practices are alike; whether it is Rockefeller shooting his Bayonne oil-workers and burning alive the little children of his miners; or smooth John Wanamaker, paying starvation wages to department-store girls and driving them to the streets; or that clergyman who, at a gathering of society ladies, members of the "Law and Order League" of Denver, declared in my hearing that if he could have his way he would blow up the home of every coal-striker with dynamite; or the Rev. R. A. Torrey, Dean of the Bible institute of Los Angeles, who refused to employ union labor on the million dollar building of the Institute, declaring that "the Church cannot afford to have any dealings with a band of fire-bugs and murderers!"

"Herr Beeble"

The business of the Clerical Department of the Merchants' and Manufacturers' Association is to justify the processes of trade, and to preach to clerks and employees the slave-virtues of frugality, humility, and loyalty to the profit system. The depths of sociological depravity to which some of the agents of this Association have sunk is difficult of belief. Twelve years ago I was invited to address the book-sellers of New York, in company with a well-known clergyman of the city, the Reverend Madison C. Peters. This gentleman's address made such an impression upon me that I recall it even at this distance: a string of jokes spoken with an effect of rapid-fire smartness, and simply reeking with commercialism. I could not describe it better than to say that it was on the ethical level of the "Letters of a Self-Made Merchant to His Son". Again, I attended a debate on Socialism, in which the capitalist end was taken by another famous clergyman, pastor of the Metropolitan Temple, the Rev. J. Wesley Hill. He was so ignorant that when he wished to prove that Socialism means free love, he quoted a writer by the name of "Herr Beeble"; he was so dishonest that he garbled the writings of this "Herr Beeble", making him say something quite different from what he had meant to say. I could name several clergymen of various denominations who have stooped to that device against the Socialists; including the Catholic Father Belford, who says that we are mad dogs and should be stopped with bullets.

Or consider the Reverend Thomas Dixon. This gentleman's pulpit-slang used to be the talk of New York when I was a boy; and when I grew up, and came into the Socialist movement—behold, here he was, chief inquisitor of the capitalist Holy Office. I had a friend, a man who saved my life at a time when I was practically starving, and to whom therefore I owe my survival as a writer; this friend had been a clergyman in a Middle Western state, and had preached Jesus as he really was, and so was hated and feared like Jesus. It happened that he was unhappily married, and permitted his wife to divorce him so that he might marry the woman he loved; for which unheard of crime the organized hypocrisy of America fell upon him like a thousand devils with poisoned whips. The Reverend Dixon's holy rage was fired; he applied his imagination to my friend's story, producing a novel under the title of "The One Woman"; and it is as if you were reading the story of Jesus and the Magdalen transmitted through the personality of a he-goat. Of late years this clerical author has turned his energies to negrophobia and militarism, making millions out of motion-picture incitements to hatred and terror. The pictures were made here in Southern California, and friends in the business have described to me the pious propagandist in the position of St. Anthony surrounded by swarms of cute and playful little movie-girls.

Or take the Rev. James Roscoe Day, D. D., S. T. D., L. L. D., D. C. L., L. H. D., a leading light of the Methodist Episcopal Church, who offers himself as comic relief in our Clerical Vaudeville. Dr. Day is Chancellor of Syracuse University, a branch of the Mental Munitions Department of the Standard Oil Company; his function being to manufacture intellectual weapons and explosives to be used in defense of the Rockefeller fortune. It is generally not expected that the makers of ruling-class munitions should face the dirty and perilous work of the trenches; but ten years ago, during a raid by an active squad of muckrake-men, Chancellor Day astonished the world by rushing to the front with both arms full of star-shells and bombs. He afterwards put the history of this gallant action into a volume, "The Raid on Prosperity"; and if you want the real thrill of the class-war, here is where to get it!

The Chancellor is a quaint and touching figure; an enthusiast and dreamer, idealist and martyr, in whom the ordinary human virtues have been fused, absorbed, transformed and sublimated into a new supreme virtue of loyalty to Exploitation, patriotism for Profiteering. He began life as a working-man, he tells us, in the good old American fashion of hustle for yourself; but he differed from other Americans in that he had an instant, intuitive recognition of the intellectual and moral excellence of Plutocracy. The first time he met a rich man, he quivered with rapture, he burst into a hymn of appreciation. So very quickly he was recognized as a proper person to have charge of a Mental Munition Works; and the ruling classes proceeded to pin medals upon the bosom of his academic robes— D. D., S. T. D., L. L. D., D. C. L., L. H. D.

The Chancellor knows the masters of our Profit System, those "consummate geniuses of manufacture and trade by which the earth has yielded up her infinite treasures." And having been at the same time in intimate daily communion with the Almighty, he can tell us the Almighty's attitude towards these prodigies. "God has made the rich of this world to serve Him. . . . He has shown them a way to have this world's goods and to be rich towards God. . . . God wants the rich men . . . . Christ's doctrines have made the world rich, and provide adequate uses for its riches." Also the Chancellor knows our great corporations, and gives us the Almighty's views about them; they mean that "the forces with which God built the universe have been put into the hands of man." Likewise by divine authority we learn that "the sympathy given to Socialism is appalling. It is insanity." We learn that the income tax is "a doctrine suited to the dark ages, only no age ever has been dark enough." Somebody raises the issue of "tainted money", and the Chancellor disposes of this matter also. As a Deputy of Divinity, he settles it by Holy Writ: "Paul permitted meat offered to idols to be eaten in the fear of God." And then, to make assurance doubly sure, he settles it with plain human logic; and you are astonished to see how simple, under his handling, the complex problem becomes—how clear and clean-cut is the distinction he draws for you:

> Every boy knows that one cannot take stolen goods without being a partaker with the thief. But the proceeds of recognized business are quite a different thing.

Holy Oil

And here is Billy Sunday, most conspicuous phenomenon of Protestant Christianity at the beginning of the twentieth century. For the benefit of posterity I explain that "Billy" is a baseball player turned Evangelist, who has brought to the cause of God the crowds and uproar of the diamond; also the commercial spirit of America's most popular institution. He travels like a circus, with all the press-agent work and newspaper hurrah; he conducts what are called "revivals", in an enormous "tabernacle" built especially for him in each city. I cannot better describe the Billy Sunday circus than in the words of a certain Sidney C. Tapp, who brought suit against the evangelist for $100,000 damages for the theft of the ideas of a book. Says Mr. Tapp in his complaint:

> The so-called religious awakening or "trail-hitting" is produced by an appeal to the emotions and in stirring up the senses

by a combination of carrying the United States flag in one hand and the Bible in the other, singing, trumpeting, organ playing, garrulous and acrobatic feats of defendant, by defendant in his talk leaping from the rostrum to the top of the pulpit, lying prone on the floor of the rostrum on his stomach in the presence of the vast audience and from thence into a pit to shake hands with the so-called "trail-hitters" and the vulgar use of plaintiff's thoughts contained in said books. Said harangues and vulgarisms of said defendant and horns, drums, organs and singing by said choir and vast audience which are assembled by means of said newspaper advertisements for the purpose of inducing a habit of free and copious flow of money through religious and patriotic excitement produced by and through the vulgarisms, scurrility, buffoonery, obscenity and profanity of defendant pretending to be in the interest of the cause of religion through what he denominates "hitting the trail", the real object being to induce a religious frenzy and enthusiasm which he announces in advance is to result in large audiences composed of thousands of people generously contributing vast sums of money on the last day and night of the so-called revival which is invariably appropriated by the defendant and through which scheme and device defendant has become enormously wealthy.

As I write, the evangelist is in Los Angeles, and twice each day he holds forth to a crowd of ten or fifteen thousand; in addition the newspapers print literally pages of his utterances. The entire Protestant clergy for a score of miles around has been hitched to his triumphal chariot, and driven captive through the streets. Here in this dignified city of Pasadena, home of millionaire brewers and chewing-gum kings, all the churches have been plastered for weeks with cloth signs: "This Church is Cooperating in the Sunday Campaign." To give a sample of the intellectual level of the performance, here is what Billy has to say about modern thought:

All this blasphemy against God and Jesus Christ, all this

sneering, highbrow, rotten, loathesome, higher criticism, wrig-
gling its dirty, filthy, stinking carcass out of a beer-mug in
Leipzig or Heidelberg!

Whether willingly or reluctantly, the preachers sit
upon the platform and smile while Billy thus slangs the
devil; and being themselves, poor fellows, at their wits
end to draw the crowd, they watch and see how he does
it, and then return to their own churches and try the
same stunt; so the manners of the baseball diamond
spread like a contagion. I open my morning paper, and
find a picture of an intense-looking clerical gentleman,
the Rev. J. Whitcomb Brougher, pastor of the Baptist
Temple. He is discussing certain slanderous rumors
which he has heard about Billy Sunday, and he offers
ten thousand dollars reward to anyone who can prove
these things; though, as he says,

The dirty, low-down, contemptible, weazen-brained, impure-
hearted, shrivelled-souled, gossipping devils do not deserve to
be noticed.....Scandal-mongers, gossip-lovers, reputation-de-
stroyers, hypocritical, black-hearted, green-eyed slanderers.....
Corrupt, devil-possessed, vile debauchés.....Immoral, sin-loving,
vice-practicing, underhanded sneaks.....Carrion-loving buzzards
and foul-smelling skunks.

You will be prepared after this to hear that when
the Socialists were near to carrying Los Angeles, this
clergyman preached a sermon in support of the candidate of "Booze, Gas and Railroads".

In so far as Billy Sunday is trying to keep the neglected youth of our streets from drinking, gambling and
whoring, no one could wish him anything but success;
but his besotted ignorance, his childish crudity of
mind, make it impossible that he could have any success
except of a delusive nature. He is utterly devoid of a

social sense; utterly unaware of the existence of the forces of capitalism which are causing depravity ten times as fast as all the evangelists in creation can remedy it. So he is precisely like the Catholics ith their "charity", cleaning up loathsome and unsightly messes for a thousand years, and never stopping to ask why such messes continue to come into existence.

More than that, I question whether the spirit of commercialism which he fosters does not help the development of evil more than his preaching hinders it. The newspapers always report the cost of the tabernacle, and of the "free-will offering", which amounts to hundreds of thousands of dollars in each "campaign". In each city the expenses are guaranteed by men who are generally the most sinister exploiting forces of the community ; they welcome and fete him, and he visits their homes, and is in every way one of the crowd. After the big silk strike in Paterson, N. J., the employers, Jews and Catholics included, all subscribed a fund to bring Billy Sunday to that city; and it was freely proclaimed that the purpose was to undermine the radical union movement. This was never denied by Sunday himself, and his whole campaign was conducted on that basis.

Later Billy came to New York, where he met a certain rich young man, perhaps a thousand times as rich as any that lived in Palestine. This young man came to Billy and said: "What shall I do to inherit eternal life?" And Billy told him to keep the commandments— "Do not commit adultery, Do not kill, Do not steal, Do not bear false witness, Honor thy father and thy mother." The young man answered: "All these have I kept from my youth up." And Billy said: "Yet lackest thou one thing; sell all that thou hast and distribute unto the poor, and thou shalt have treasure in heaven; and come follow me." And when he heard this he was very sorrowful, for he was very rich.

—No, I have got the story mixed up. That is what happened in Palestine. What happened in New York is that Billy said, "I am delighted to meet you, Mr. Rockefeller." And Mr. Rockefeller said, "Come be my guest at my palace in the Pocantico Hills; and then we will go together and you may preach submission to my wage-slaves in the oil-factories at Bayonne and elsewhere." And Billy went to the palace, and went and preached to the wage-slaves, telling them to beware the 'stinking Socialists", and to concentrate their attention on the saving of their souls; so the rich young man was delighted, and he sent for all the newspaper reporters to come to his office at 26 Broadway, and told them what a great and useful man Billy Sunday is. As the New York "Times" tells about it:

Mr. Rockefeller seldom gives interviews and certainly he has never been charged with having an excess of verbally expressed enthusiasm on any subject. But he talked for an hour and a half about the evangelist. He was full of the subject of Billy Sunday. "Billy did New York a lot of good," he said. He went on to tell of 187 meetings held in 100 different factories, attended by 50,000 men. "That's good work." And he expressed his satisfaction with Sunday's theology: "He believes the Bible from cover to cover and that is good enough for me." The Sunday campaign had cost $200,000, and "If it had stopped here, if it was not kept up, it would be poor business; a poor dividend on the $200,000 and the work invested. But we expect to get dividends in the next year."

Again you note the symbolism of the counting-house!

Rhetorical Black-hanging

It is the duty of the clergy, not merely to defend large-scale merchants while they live, but to bury them when they die, and to place the seal of sanctity upon their careers. Concerning this aspect of Bootstrap-lifting I quote the opinion of an earnest hater of shams, William Makepeace Thackeray:

> I think the part which pulpits play in the death of kings is the most ghastly of all the ceremonial: the lying eulogies, the blinking of disagreeable truths, the sickening flatteries, the simulated grief, the falsehood and sycophancies—all uttered in the name of Heaven in our State churches: these monstrous Threnodies which have been sung from time immemorial over kings and queens, good, bad, wicked, licentious. The State parson must bring out his commonplaces; his apparatus of rhetorical black-hanging......

And this, of course, applies not merely to kings of England, but to kings of Steel, kings of Coal, kings of Oil, kings of Wall Street. When a certain king of Western railroads died, a Methodist clergyman, afterwards Bishop, likened his heir to the boy Christ; a statement which requires for its appreciation a mention of the fact that this heir died of syphilis. In the year 1904 there passed from his earthly reward in Pennsylvania a United States senator who had been throughout his lifetime a notorious and unblushing corruptionist. Matthew Stanley Quay was his name, and the New York "Nation", having no clerical connections, was free to state the facts about him:

> He bought the organization, bribed or intimidated the press, got his grip on the public service, including even the courts; imposed his will on Congress and Cabinet, and upon the last three Presidents—making the latter provide for the offal of his political machine, which even Pennsylvania could no longer stom-

ach—and all without identifying his name with a single measure of public good, without making a speech or uttering a party watchword, without even pretending to be honest, but solely because, like Judas, he carried the bag and could buy whom he would.

Such was the lay opinion; and now for the clerical. It was expressed by a Presbyterian divine, the Reverend Dr. J. S. Ramsey, who stood over the coffin of "Matt", and without cracking a smile declared that he had been "a statesman who was always on the right side of every moral question!"

In that same year of 1904 died the high priest of our political corruption, Mark Hanna. He had belonged to no church, but had backed them all, understanding the main thesis of this book as clearly as the writer of it. In his home city of Cleveland the eulogy upon him was pronounced by Bishop Leonard, in St. Paul's Episcopal Church; while in the United States Senate the service was performed by the Chaplain, the Rev. Edward Everett Hale. This is a name well-known in American letters, as in American religious life; it was borne by a benevolent old gentleman, a Unitarian and a liberal, who organized "Lend-a-Hand Clubs" and such like amiabilities. "Do You Love This Old Man?" the signs in the street-cars used to ask when I was a boy; and I promptly answered "Yes"—for my mother took the "Ladies' Home Journal", and I swallowed the sentimental dish-water set out for me. But when I read the Rev. Edward's funeral oration over the Irrev. Mark, I loved neither of them any longer. "This whole-souled child of God," cried the Rev. Edward, "who believed in success, and knew how to succeed by using the infinite powers!" You perceive that the Chaplain of the Millionaires' Club agrees with this book, that the "infinite powers" in America are the powers that prey!

The Great American Fraud

Among the most loathesome products of our native commercial greed is the patent medicine industry, "The Great American Fraud," as its historian has called it. In 1907 this historian wrote:

Gullible America will spend this year some seventy-five millions of dollars in the purchase of patent medicines. In consideration of this sum it will swallow huge quantities of alcohol, an appalling amount of opiates and narcotics, a wide assortment of varied drugs ranging from powerful and dangerous heart depressants to insidious liver stimulants; and, far in excess of all other ingredients, undiluted fraud. For fraud, exploited by the skillfullest of advertising bunco men, is the basis of the trade.

One by one Mr. Adams tells about these medical fakes: habit-forming laxatives, head-ache powders full of acetanilid, soothing-syrups and catarrh-cures full of opium and cocaine, cock-tails subtly disguised as "bitters", "sarsaparillas", and "tonics". He shows how the fake testimonials are made up and exploited; how the confidential letters, telling the secret troubles of men and women, are collected by tens and hundreds of thousands and advertised and sold—so that the victim, as he begins to lose faith in one fake, finds another at hand, fully informed as to his weakness. He quotes the amazing "Red Clause" in the contracts which the patent-medicine makers have with thousands of daily and weekly papers, whereby the makers are able to control the press of the country and prevent legislation against the "Great American Fraud."

There are a thousand religious papers in America,

weekly and monthly; and what is their attitude on this question? Mr. Adams tells us:

Whether because church-going people are more trusting, and therefore more easily befooled than others, or from some more obscure reason, many of the religious papers fairly reek with patent medicine fakes.

He gives us many pages of specific instances:

Dr. Smith belongs to the brood of cancer vampires. He is a patron and prop of religious journalism. It is his theory that the easiest prey is to be found among readers of church papers. Moreover he has learned from his father-in-law (who built a small church out of blood-money) to capitalize his own sectarian associations, and when confronted recently with a formal accusation he replied, with an air of injured innocence, that he was a regular attendant at church, and could produce an endorsement from his minister.

And here is the "Church Advocate", of Harrisburg, Pa., which publishes quack advertisements disguised as editorials. One of them Mr. Adams paraphrases:

As Dr. Smith is, on the face of his own statements, a self-branded swindler and rascal, you run no risk in assuming that the Rev. C. H. Forney, D. D., L. L. D., in acting as his journalistic supporter for pay, is just such another as himself!

And again:

Will the editor of the "Baptist Watchman" of Boston explain by what phenomenon of logic or elasticity of ethics he accepts the lucubrations of Dr. Bye, of Oren Oneal, of Liquozone, of Actina, that marvelous two-ended mechanical appliance which "cures" deafness at one terminus and blindness at the other, and all with a little oil of mustard?

And again:

The "Christian Observer" of Louisville replied to a protesting subscriber, suggesting that the "Collier" articles were written in a spirit of revenge, because "Collier's" could not get pat-

ent medicine advertising. When I asked the Rev. F. Bartlett
Converse for his foundation for the charge, he said that one
of the typewriters must have written the letter! Doubtless also
the same highly responsible typewriter imitated the signature
with startling fidelity to Dr. Converse's handwriting!

And here is—would you think it possible?—our
"Church of Good Society"! It has an organ in Chicago
called the "Living Church", most dignified and decorous. You have to study quite a while to ascertain what
denomination it belongs to; it will not tell you directly,
for the Anglician pose is that it is **the** church

> Elect from every nation,
>   Yet one o'er all the earth,
> Her charter of salvation,
>   One Lord, one Faith, one Birth;
> One holy name she blesses,
>   Partakes one holy food,
> And toward one Hope she presses,
>   With every grace endued.

And this one holy institution was found setting at its
peak the black flag of the trader, the "Jolly Roger" of
the modern commercial pirate—"Caveat emptor!" To
quote the precise words:

The editors and publishers of the "Living Church" assume
no responsibility for the assertions of advertisers.

And so it threw open its columns to the claims of
America's champion labor-baiter, the late C. W. Post,
that his "Grapenuts" would prevent appendicitis, and
obviate the need of operations in such cases!

And here is the "Christian Endeavor World", organ
of one of the most powerful non-sectarian religious
bodies in the country. Some one wrote complaining of
its medical advertising, and the answer was:

To the best of our knowledge and belief, we are not publishing any fraudulent or unworthy medical advertising......
Trusting that you will be able to understand that we are acting
according to our best and sincerest judgment, I remain, yours
very truly, The Golden Rule Company, George W. Coleman,
Business Manager.

Whereupon the historian of "The Great American
Fraud" remarks:

Assuming that the business management of the "Christian
Endeavor World" represents normal intelligence, I would like
to ask whether it accepts the statement that a pair of "magic
foot drafts" applied to the soles of the feet will cure any and
every kind of rheumatism in any part of the body? Further, if
the advertising department is genuinely interested in declining
"fraudulent and unworthy" copy, I would call their attention to
the ridiculous claims of Dr. Shoop's medicines, which "cure" almost every disease; to two hair removers, one an "Indian Secret", the other an "accidental discovery", both either fakes or
dangerous; to the lying claims of Hall's Catarrh Cure, that it
is "a positive cure for catarrh", in all its stages; to "Syrup of
Figs", which is not a fig syrup, but a preparation of senna; to
Dr. Kilmer's Swamp Root, of which the principal medical con-
stituent is alcohol; and, finally, to Dr. Bye's Oil Cure for cancer,
a particularly cruel swindle on unfortunates suffering from an
incurable malady. All of these, with other matter, which for
the sake of decency I do not care to detail in these columns,
appear in recent issues of the "Christian Endeavor World".

Riches in Glory

There came recently to Los Angeles a "world-
famous evangelist", known as "Gipsy" Smith. There
was a shirt-waist strike at the time, and the girls were
starving, and they sent a delegation to this evangelist
to ask for help. They told him how they were mis-
treated, exposed to insults, driven to sell their virtue because their wage would not support life; and to their

plea he made answer: "Get Jesus in your hearts, and these questions will take care of themselves!"

So we see the most important of the many services which the churches perform for the merchants—taking the revolutionary hope of Jesus, for a kingdom of heaven upon earth, and perverting it into a dream of a golden harp in an uncertain future. To appreciate the fullness of this betrayal, take the prayer which Jesus dictated—so simple, direct and practical: "Give us this day our daily bread", and put it beside the hymns which the slave-congregations are trained to sing. In my neighborhood is a one-roomed building with a plate glass front, upon which I observe a painter inscribing in red, white and blue letters the sign "Glory Mission". I approach him, and he drops his work and welcomes me with eager cordiality. Am I "living in grace"? I answer that I am. I have to shout the good tidings into his ear, as he is very deaf. He presents me with his card, which shows that he bears the title of "Reverend", also the sobriquet of "Mountain Missionary". I ask him to permit me to examine the hymn-book which he uses in his work, and with touching eagerness he presses upon me a well-worn volume bearing the title "Waves of Glory". I seat myself and note down a few of the baits it sets out for hungry wage-slaves:

> O, there's a plenty, O, there's a plenty,
> There's a plenty in my Father's bank above!
>
> Riches in glory, riches in glory,
> Royal supply our wants exceed!
>
> Feasting, I'm feasting,
> I'm feasting with my Lord!

Beautiful robes, beautiful robes,
Beautiful robes we then shall wear!

Jerusalem the golden,
With milk and honey blest!

Yes, I'll meet you in the city of the New Jerusalem,
I'll be there, I'll be there!

Blest Canaan land, bright Canaan land,
I love to be in Canaan land!

Oh, Beulah land, sweet Beulah land,
As on the highest mount I stand,
I look away across the sea,
Where mansions are prepared for me!

In the sweet bye and bye
We shall meet on that beautiful shore—

I stopped there, being reminded of Joe Hill, poet of the I. W. W. who was hanged three or four years ago in Utah, and who used this tune in his little red book of revolutionary chants:

You will eat, bye and bye,
In the glorious land above the sky;
Work and pray, live on hay,
You'll get pie in the sky when you die!

Captivating Ideals

In one of the writer's earlier novels, "Prince Hagen", the hero is a Nibelung out of Wagner's "Rheingold", who leaves his diggings in the bowels of the earth, and comes up to look into our superior civilization. The thing that impresses him most is what he calls "the immortality idea". The person who got that up was a world-genius, he exclaims. "If you can once get a man to believing in immortality, there is no more

left for you to desire; you can take everything he owns
—you can skin him alive if it pleases you—and he will
bear it all with perfect good humor."

And is that merely the spiritual deficiency of a Nibelung—or the effort of a young author to be smart?
Would you like to hear that view of the most vital of
Christian doctrines set forth in the language of scholarship and culture? Would you like to know how an
ecclesiastical authority, equipped with every tool of
modern learning, would set about voicing the idea that
the function of the teaching of Heaven is to chloroform
the poor, so that the rich may continue to rob them in
security?

Here under my hand is a volume in the newest dress
of scholarship, dated 1912, and written by Professor
Georges Chatterton-Hill, of the University of Geneva.
Its title is "The Sociological Value of Christianity", and
from cover to cover it is a warning to the rich of the
danger they run in giving up their religion and ceasing
to support its priests. It explains how "the genius of
Christianity has succeeded in making the individual
suffering, the individual sacrifices, which are indispensible for the welfare of the collectivity, appear as
indispensible for the individual welfare." The learned
professor makes plain just what he means by "individual suffering, individual sacrifices"; he means all the
horrors of capitalism; and the advantage of Christianity is that it makes you think that by submitting to
these horrors, you are profiting your own soul. "By
making individual salvation depend on the acceptance
of suffering, on the voluntary sacrifice of egotistical
interests, Christianity adapts the individual to society".

And this, as the professor explains, is not an easy thing to do, in a world in which so many people are thinking for themselves. "The only means of causing the rationalized individual to consent to the sacrifice......is to captivate him with a sufficiently powerful ideal" And the professor shows how beautifully Jesus can be used for this purpose. "Jesus, the so-called humanitarian, never ceased to insist on the necessity of suffering, the desirableness of suffering—of that suffering which a weak and sickly humanitarianism would fain suppress if it could."

You get this, you "blanket-stiff", you "husky", or "wop", or whatever you are—you disinherited of the earth, you proletarians who have only your labor-power to sell, you weak and sickly ones who are condemned to elimination? There has come, let us say, a period of "overproduction"; you have raised too much food, and therefore you are starving, you have woven too much cloth, and therefore you are naked, you have finished the world for your masters, and it is time for you to move out of the way. As the sociologist from Geneva phrases it, "Your suppression imposes itself as an imperious necessity." And the function of the Christian religion is to make you enjoy the process, by "captivating you with a sufficiently powerful ideal"! The priest will fill your nostrils with incense, your eyes with candle-lights and images, your ears with sweet music and soothing words; and so you will perish without raising a finger! "Here," reflects the professor, "we see how magnificently the teaching of Jesus applies to all classes of society!"

Somebody has evidently put up to our Christian

sociologist the embarrassing fact that so many of those who survive under the capitalist system are godless scoundrels. But do you think that troubles him? Not for long. Like all religious thinkers, he carries with his scholar's equipment a pair of metaphysical wings, wherewith at any moment he may soar into the empyrean, out of reach of vulgar materialists, like you and me. "Inequality signifies inequality of capacity," he explains; but the standard whereby we judge this capacity "cannot be the standard of the moral law."

The laws which govern the biological evolution of man are known, but those which govern his moral nature cannot be known; the moral nature appertains to the Absolute, and hence is not subject to the law of inequality!

As an exhibition of metaphysical wing-power, that is almost as wonderful as the flight of Cardinal Newman when confronted with the fact that his divinely guided church had burned men for teaching the Copernican view of the universe; that infallible popes had again and again condemned this heresy **ex cathedra.** Said the eloquent cardinal:

Scripture says that the sun moves and the earth is stationary, and science that the earth moves and the sun is comparatively at rest. How can we determine which of these opposite statements is the very truth till we know what motion is?

Spook Hunting

Do not imagine that it is only in Geneva that Christian professors realize this peril from the loss of faith. It is never far from the thoughts of any of them—for, of course, no man can look at the present system and not wonder how the poor stand it, and more especially why they stand it. There have been many

thinking men who have given up the miracle-business
quite cheerfully, but have stood appalled at the idea of
letting the lower classes find out the truth. You note
that idea continually in the writings of Professor Gold-
win Smith, who was a free-thinker, but also a
bourgeois publicist, with a deep sense of responsibility
to the money-masters of the world. He was about as
honest a man as ѣhe capitalist system can produce; he
was the **beau ideal** of the New York "Evening Post",
which indicates his point of view. He wrote:

It can hardly be doubted that hope of compensation in a future state, for a short measure of happiness here, has materially
helped to reconcile the less favored members of the community
to the inequalities of the existing order of things.

When I was a student in Columbia University, I took
a course called "Practical Ethics", under a professor
by the name of Hyslop. The course differed from most
of the forty that I tried, in that it gave evidence that
the professor was accustomed to read the morning
paper. He had learned that American politics were
rotten; his idea of "Practical Ethics" was to outline in
elaborate detail a complete scheme of constitutional
changes which would make it impossible for the "boss"
to control the government. I think I must have been
born with a charm against **bourgeois** thought, for the
good professor never fooled me an instant; I remember
I used to smile at the idea of how quickly the "boss"
would brush through his constitutional cobwebs. The
reforms required an elaborate campaign of publicity—
and of course long before they could be put into practice, the politicians would be ready with devices to make
them of no effect.

Soon after this, my ethical professor resigned and went to hunting spooks. I don't want to be unfair to him; I know that he is a determined and courageous man, and it seems possible that he may really have bagged some spooks. All I wish to point out here is the method he uses in seeking to persuade the heedless rich to support the spook-hunting industry. The very same argument as we got from the University of Geneva and the University of Toronto! Says our head spook-hunter:

There has been no belief that exercised so much power upon the poor as that in a future life. The politicians, men of the world, have known this so well as to postpone the day of political judgment by it for many years.

And again:

The Church, having lost all its battles with science, and having abandoned a strenuous intellectual defense of its fundamental beliefs, has lost its power over the poor and the laboring classes.....The spiritual ideal of life has gone out of the masses as well as the classes, and nothing is left but a venture on a struggle with wealth.

And again, more menacingly yet:

The rich will learn in the dangers of a social revolution that the poor will not sacrifice both wealth and immortality.

What is to be done about this? The question answers itself: Step up, ladies and gentlemen, and empty your purses into the Psychical Research hat! So that we may accumulate statistics as to the cost of milk and honey in Jerusalem the Golden!

You read what I had to say about Bootstrap-lifters, and the Wholesale Pickpockets' Association making use of their incantations. You admired my ability to sling language, but not my taste; and you certainly did not

think that I would back my rhetoric with facts. But
what do these quotations mean, unless they mean what
I have said? Are not these three professors men of culture? Are they not as "spiritual" as any men of learning you can find in our present-day society?

And now stop for a moment and put yourself in
the position of the young student of the working-class,
who goes to these books and discovers that truth is
not truth, but only a bait for a snare. Who discovers
that professors of ethics, practical or impractical, are
not interested in justice among men, but only in col-
lecting funds for their specialty; that in order to get
funds, they are willing to teach the rich how to para-
lyze the minds of the poor! Do you wonder that such
young students conclude that **bourgeois** thinkers do not
know what honesty is, but are prostitutes, retainers
and lackeys, to be kicked out of the temple of truth?

Running the Rapids

And now, can you form to yourselves a clear concept
of what it means to society that practically all its moral
teaching should be in the hands of men who are incapable
of clean, straight thinking? That all the intellectual
prestige of the Church should be lent to the support of
vagueness, futility, and deliberate evasion? Here we are,
all of us, caught in the most terrific social crisis of history; I search for a metaphor to picture our position, and
I recall a canoe-trip in the wilds of Ontario, hundreds of
miles down a long swift river. You sit in the bow of the
canoe, your partner in the stern, watching ahead; and
there comes a slide of smooth green water, and you go
over it, and into a torrent of foaming white, which seizes
you and rushes you along with the speed of a race-horse.

With every sense alert, you watch for the rocks, and when you see one, you dip your paddle on one side or the other and with a quick motion draw the canoe clear of the danger. If by any chance you fail to do it, over you go, and your partner with you, and all your belongings go down-stream, and maybe you are sucked into a whirlpool, and not seen for several hours afterwards. Precisely like this is the voyage of life, for the whole of society and for every individual. The paddle which would save us from the rocks is experimental science; but in most of our canoes we put a man who has no paddle, but a Holy Book; and he casts up his eyes and murmurs words in ancient Greek and Hebrew, and now and then, when he sees an especially formidable obstruction—a war, or the gonococcus, or the I. W. W.—he casts a holy wafer upon the foaming torrent.

And mind you, it isn't as if I could save myself and you could save yourself; we are all in the same canoe, and we all go overboard together. You, perhaps, have a son who is drafted into the trenches in winter-time, and drowned in blood and mud, because in Europe the Catholic party supported militarism, and kept aristocratic criminals in control of states. Or you find yourself involved in a marital tragedy, and in order to free yourself from unendurable misery, you are obliged to go to law-courts dominated by the tradition of Paul, the Roman bureaucrat, who despised women, and regarded marriage as a means of gratifying an unclean animal desire. "It is better to marry than to burn," he said, with unmatchable brutality; and so of course those who think him a voice of God can form no conception of the dignity and grace of love, and if you want sound and wholesome sex-

conventions, you will be as apt to find them among the
Ashantees or the Kamchadals as among the followers of
the Apostle to the Gentiles.

You go to a so-called "divorce-court," which is dominated by this Christian taboo, and exists for the purpose
of barring you from a second chance at the gratification
of your unclean animal desire. You are not permitted to
tell your own story, for that would be "collusion;" you
listen while your intimate friends recite the pitiful and
shameful details of your domestic misfortune, under the
cross-questioning of lawyers who have suppressed for the
time whatever decent instincts they may possess, and
follow blindly the details of a prescribed procedure, at
the cost of all sincerity, humanity and truth. The next
morning you find that the privacy guaranteed you by law
has been taken from you by corrupt court officials, who
have sold copies of the testimony to the newspapers, so
that all the intimate details of where you slept and where
your wife slept and what you saw your wife doing have
been thrown out to journalistic jackals, who scream with
glee as they rend the carcass of your dead love. And in
the end, perhaps, you find that you have gone through
this horror for nothing—the august court with its Roman
Catholic judge throws out your petition, its suspicions
having been excited by the fact that when you discovered
your domestic tragedy, you sought to behave like a
civilized person, with pity and self-restraint, instead of
like a sultan in Turkey, or a basso in an Italian grand
opera.

Birth Control

I assert that the control of our thinking on ethical
questions by minds enslaved to tradition and priestcraft

is an unmitigated curse to the race. The armory of science is full of weapons which might be used to slay the monsters of disease and vice—but these weapons are not allowed to be employed, sometimes not even to be mentioned. Consider the misery which is piling itself up in the slums of our great cities—the degenerate, the defective, the insane, who are multiplying as never before in history. There exists a perfectly harmless and painless method of sterilizing the hopelessly unfit, so that they can not reproduce their hopeless unfitness; but religion objects to this operation, and so the law does not make use of this knowledge. There exists a simple, entirely harmless, and practically costless method of preventing conception, which would enable us to check the blind and futile fecundity of Nature, and to multiply as gods instead of as animals. Consider the festering mass of misery in the slums of our great cities; consider the millions of terrified, poverty-hounded women, bearing one half-nurtured infant after another, struggling desperately to feed and care for them, and seeing them drop into the grave as fast as they are born—until finally the mother, worn out with the Sisyphean labor, gives up and follows her misbegotten offspring. Consider how many women, in their agony and despair, make use of the methods of the primitive savage, to escape from Nature's curse of fecundity. Dr. Wm. J. Robinson has estimated that in the United States alone there are a million abortions every year; and consider that all this hideous mass of suffering—a bloody European war going on continually, unheeded by any newspaper correspondent—might be avoided by the use of a simple sterilizing formula, which we are not permitted to give! The Federation of Catholic

Societies have placed a law upon the statute-books of the nation, and of all the states as well; the whole power of police and courts and jails is at the service of religious bigots, and a young girl is sent to prison and forcibly fed with a tube through the nose for telling poverty-ridden slum-women how to keep from becoming pregnant!

And go among the sleek, cynical men of the world, the judges and district attorneys, the commissioners of correction and doctors who perpetrated this infamy under a so-called "reform" administration in New York City— and what do you find? The first thing you find is that they themselves, one and all, practice birth-control with their wives or their mistresses. The second thing you find is that the statute-books are crowded with other laws which they make no pretense of enforcing; for example, the law which forbids the saloons to be open on Sunday—which law they take the liberty of understanding to mean that the saloons shall not have their front doors open on Sunday. You will find that they are not at all afraid of the religious taboos; they are afraid of the religious vote—and even more they are afraid of the campaign contributions of sweat-shop manufacturers and landlords, who cannot see what would become of prosperity if the women of the slums were to cease to breed. So once more we discover the wolf in sheep's clothing, the trader, making use of Tradition-worship; hiding behind the skirts of devout old maiden aunts and grandmothers, who repeat the instructions which God gave to Adam and Eve, "Be fruitful and multiply and replenish the earth." As if God were as blind as a Fifth Avenue preacher, and could see no difference between the Garden of Eden, full of all fruits that grow and all creatures that

run and fly and swim, and a modern East Side tenement-
room, with an oil stove and no windows and no water-
closet, and the price of cabbage seven cents a pound!

Sheep

There are more than a hundred thousand Protestant
churches in America. They own more than a billion dollars' worth of property, and in the West and South they
dominate the intellectual life of the country. I do not
wish to be unfair in what I say of them. They are far
more democratic than the Catholic Church; they fight
valiantly against the liquor traffic and those forms of
graft which are obvious, or directly derived from vice.
There are among their clergy many men who are honestly
seeking light, and trying to make their institutions a
factor for progress. But they are caught in the spirit
Lutheran scholasticism, narrow and ignorant, dogmatic
and jealous; and they cannot help it, because they are
pledged by their creeds and foundations to Tradition-
worship; they have to believe certain things because
their ancestors believed them, they have to act in certain
ways, because of certain facts which existed in the world
three thousand years ago, but which now are known only
to historians.

You are familiar with the habit of a herd of sheep to
follow the example of their leader; if this leader leaps
over a stick, all the rest will leap when they come to that
spot, even though the stick may have been taken away in
the meantime. The scientist explains this seeming-
foolishness by the fact that sheep once lived in high
mountains, and fled from their enemies in swiftly rushing
herds; when the leader leaped across an abyss, the others
had to leap, without waiting to see in the dust and con-

fusion. Now there are no mountains and no enemies, but
the sheep still jump. And in exactly the same way the
tailor still sews buttons at the back of your dress-coat,
because a couple of hundred years ago all gentlemen wore
swords; in the same way our railroad builders make cars
narrow and uncomfortable and liable to overturn, because
a hundred years ago all cars were hauled by mules. In
the same way the Orthodox Hebrew will eat no pork, in
spite of the fact that the microscope affords him complete
protection against disease; the orthodox Catholic will not
eat meat on Friday, because he thinks Jesus was crucified
on that day; the orthodox Anglican will not marry his
deceased wife's sister, because of something he reads in
Leviticus; the orthodox Baptist requires total immersion
in a climate quite different from that of Palestine; the
orthodox Methodist refuses to enjoy fresh air and exercise on the Sabbath.

In ancient Judea, you see, the people lived an open-air
life, tending sheep and working the fields; so it was an
excellent thing for them to rest from labor one day of
the week, and to gather in temples to hear the reading
of the best literature of their time. But nowadays the city
slave spends his week-days shut up in an office, poring
over a ledger, or in a sweat-shop, chained to a sewing-
machine. Obviously, therefore, the thing to do on the
seventh day is to lure him into the open air, and persuade
him to run and play. But do we do that, we human sheep?
We write ancient Hebrew laws upon our modern statute-
books, and if the city slave goes into a vacant lot and tries
to play base-ball, we send a policeman and take him to
jail, and next morning he is fined five dollars, and probably loses his job.

In the city where I live, a city supposed to be free and enlightened, but in reality heavily burdened with churches, there are tennis courts built and paid for out of public funds, my own included; yet I cannot use these tennis courts on Sunday, because of the ancient Hebrew taboo. My mail is not delivered to me, the swimming pool in the park is closed to me, the library is closed nearly all day. If I enquire about it, I am told that it is desirable that city employees should have one day's rest a week; but when I ask why it might not be possible to relay the employees, so that they might all have one, or even two days' rest a week, and still give the public their rights on Sunday, there is no answer. But I know the answer, having probed our politics of hypocrisy. There is a "church vote" at which all politicians tremble; there are clergymen, humanly jealous when their peculiar graft is threatened, and hoping that if the law enforces a general boredom, the public may be more disposed to endure the boredom of sermons.

In New York City the theaters are closed on Sunday; but moving pictures having come into being since the days of Puritan rule, the picture-shows are free to keep open. The law permits "sacred concerts"—which, under the benevolent sway of Tammany, has come to mean any sort of vaudeville; so what we have is a free rein to the imbecilities of "Mutt & Jeff" and the obscenities of Anna Held and Gaby Deslys—while we bar the greatest moralists of our times, such as Ibsen and Brieux.

I speak with some crossness of this Sabbath taboo, because of an experience which once befell me. In the second decade of this century of enlightenment and progress, in our free American democracy, whose constitution proclaims religious toleration, and forbids the establishment by the state of any form of worship, I was made to serve a sentence of eighteen hours in the state prison of Delaware for playing a game of tennis on the Sabbath. I was duly arrested upon a warrant, duly sentenced by a magistrate, duly clad in a prison costume, duly set to work upon a stone-pile, duly locked up over night in a steel-barred cell full of vermin—in a building housing some five hundred wretches, black and white, thirty of them serving life-terms under circumstances which never permitted them a breath of fresh air nor a glimpse of the sunshine or the sky. They had no exercise court to their prison, and the inmates were not permitted to speak to one another, but ate their meals in dead silence, and walked back to their cells with folded arms, and had their only occupation working for a sweat-shop contractor; this on the outskirts of the capital city of Wilmington, with no less than ninety-one churches! The writer was informed that he would return to this institution regularly every week unless he abandoned his godless habit of playing tennis on a private club court on Sunday; he only escaped the painful punishment by making the discovery that at the Wilmington Country Club it was the custom of the leading officials of the city and state to play golf every Sunday, and by threatening to employ detectives and have these mighty ones arrested and sent to their own prison. Which shows again the importance of understanding the relationship of Superstition and Big Business!

BOOK SIX

The Church of the Quacks

They may talk as they please about what they call pelf,
And how one ought never to think of one's self,
And how pleasures of thought surpass eating and
           drinking—
My pleasure of thought is the pleasure of thinking
      How pleasant it is to have money, heigh ho!
      How pleasant it is to have money.

Clough.

Tabula Rasa

Nature has given us a virgin continent, a clean slate upon which to write what we will. And what are we writing? What is our intellectual life? I came to the far West, which I had been taught by novelists and poets to think of as a place of freedom. I came, because I like freedom; I am staying because I like the climate. I find that what freedom means in the West is the ability of ignorant and fanatical persons to start some new, fantastical quirk of scriptural interpretation, to build a new cult around it, and earn a living out of it.

My first contact with that sort of thing was when I went to the Battle Creek Sanitarium to investigate hydrotherapy, and found myself in a nest of Seventh-day Adventists. Three generations or so ago some odd character hit upon the discovery that the Christian churches had let the devil snare them into resting on the first day of the week, whereas the Bible states distinctly that the Lord "rested on the seventh day". So here is a million dollar establishment, with a thousand or two patients and employees, and on Friday at sundown the silence of death settles upon the place, and stays settled until sundown of Saturday, when everything comes suddenly to life again, and there is a little celebration, like Easter or New Year's, with what I used to call "sterilized dancing"—the men pairing with men and the women with women.

They are decent and kindly people, and you learn to put up with their eccentricities; it is really convenient in some ways, because, as not all the city shares their delusions, there are some stores open every day of the week. But then you discover that the Sanitarium is training "medical missionaries" to send to Africa, and is teaching these supposed-to-be-scientists that evolution is a doctrine of the devil, and not proven anyhow!

You get the shrewd little doctor who is running this establishment alone in his office, and he will smile and admit that of course it is not necessary to take all Bible phrases literally; but you know how it is—there are different levels of intelligence, and so on. Yes, I know how it is. You have an institution founded upon a certain dogma, and run by means of that dogma, and it is hard to change without smashing things. It is especially convenient when servants and nurses have a religious upbringing, and do not steal the pocket-books of the patients. People will come from all over the country, and pay high prices to stay in such a sanitarium; you can make vegetarians of them, which you think more important than teaching abstract notions about their being descended from monkeys. Also you can manufacture vegetarian foods for them, and build up an enormous business—so obtaining that Power which is the thing desired of men.

This is but one illustration of a sort of thing of which I could cite a hundred. The city in which I live is headquarters of another sect, the "Pentecostal Church of the Nazarene"; primitive Methodists, Bible-worshippers not content with the King James version, but going back to the Sinaitic MS. They have a "University", located in one of the most beautiful spots that Nature ever made; an institution with seventy-five students. A couple of years ago I happened to meet the "president," who was a preacher with grease on the ample expanse of his black broadcloth waistcoat, and a speech full of the commonest grammatical errors, such as "you was" and "I seen". The past year witnessed a split, and the founding of a brand new church and "University"—because one of the preachers insisted upon preaching so much that the students got no chance to study; also because he sent home a rich man's daughter whose shirt-waists revealed too much of her fleshly nature.

And there is an even stranger phenomenon in the locality, taking you back to the Libyan desert and the time of Thais. A lady friend of mine, generously blessed with this world's goods, asks me have I seen the hermit. "Hermit?" I say, and she replies, "Didn't you know there was a hermit? He lives on a mountain, in a cave, and never has anything to do with the world. He has no books; he contemplates spiritually." I picture my friend with her large limousine, a rolling palace full of ladies, drawing up at the door of this hermit's cave. "He received you?" I ask. "Yes, he was quite polite." "And what was your impression of him?" "Oh, how he **stank**!" I answer that this is the odor of sanctity, and my friend thinks that I am enormously witty; I have to explain to her that I am not jesting, but that there are definite physiological phenomena incidental to the ecstatic life.

The Book of Mormon

Or let us take a trip to Salt Lake City, the headquarters of a still stranger cult.

On the morning of the 22nd of September, 1827, the Angel of the Lord delivered unto Joseph Smith, Jr.,

an ignorant farmer-youth in a "backwoods" part of
New York State, some plates which had "the appearance of gold". As we know from the scriptures, it is
the habit of the Angel of the Lord to appear in unex-
pected places and to make miraculous revelations to
men in humble walks of life; so, as devout believers, we
hold ourselves in readiness. In this case the plates
were written in "reformed Egyptian"; but the Angel
thoughtfully provided Joseph Smith, Jr., with Urim and
Thummim, two magic stones with which to read the
records. They proved to deal with a mystery which
has haunted the minds of Bible students for centuries
—the fate of the "lost ten tribes of Israel", who were
now revealed to have been the ancestors of the American Indians. The Angel told Smith to found a new religion, and gave him prophecies concerning things in
general; so, on the 6th of April, 1830, in the town of
Manchester, N. Y., there was formally launched the
"Church of the Latter Day Saints." Smith turned over
to his followers his translation of the miraculous plates,
called "The Book of Mormon"; obviously genuine, for
it read precisely like the books which we already know
are the revealed word of God. But, on chance that this
might not be sufficient, we were offered in the preface
two documents, the "Testimony of Three Witnesses",
and the "Further Testimony of Eight Witnesses". The
latter being the shorter, may be quoted:

Be it known unto all nations, kindreds, tongues and people,
unto whom this work shall come: That Joseph Smith Jr., the
translator of this work, has shewn unto us the plates of which
hath been spoken, which have the appearance of gold; and as
many of the leaves as the said Smith hath translated, we did
handle with our hands; and we also saw the engravings there-

on, all of which has the appearance of ancient work and of curious workmanship. And this we bear record with words of soberness, that the said Smith has shewn unto us, for we have seen and hefted, and know of a surety that the said Smith hath got the plates of which we have spoken. And we give our names unto the world, to witness that which we have seen, and we lie not, God bearing witness of it.

> Christian Whitmer
> Jacob Whitmer
> Peter Whitmer, Jr.
> John Whitmer
> Hiram Page
> Joseph Smith, Sr.
> Hyrum Smith
> Saml. H. Smith

The subsequent career of the Church of the Latter Day Saints bore out the Angel's prophesies and proved conclusively its divine origin; it was persecuted as the saints of old were persecuted, and its followers proceeded to massacre the nearby unbelieving populations, just as the divinely guided Hebrews had done. Driven from place to place, they built at Nauvoo, Ill., a beautiful temple, according to plans revealed in a vision, exactly like Solomon. Finally they settled in Utah, where they have a magnificent marble tabernacle, and some 300,000 followers. The United States government, not being entirely Biblical, objected to their practice of allowing the patriarchs of the tribe to have as many wives as they could support; the government confiscated the church's property, and forced it to conceal the practice of polygamy, as is done by elderly church members in other parts of the country. Recently the head of the church, who bears the title of "Prophet, Seer and Revelator", was persuaded to permit an examination of one of its secret plates, the "Book of Abraham", by egyptologists, who found that it was ordinary Egyptian hieroglyphics, not "reformed", but containing prayers to the sun-god. But this will of course make no difference to the devout followers of Joseph—any more than it has made to devout Catholics and Episcopalians that German scholars have proven that the Bible legends and ritual have come from the Babylonians, and that the four gospels date from the second and third centuries after Christ.

Holy Rolling

All over America you will find these weird Bible-cults, some of them pathetic, some of them dangerous, some of them merely grotesque. Thus, for example, there was John Alexander Dowie, who founded the "Christian Catholic Church in Zion" and dressed himself up in scarlet and purple robes with stars on. Through his Zion City Bank and Zion City Realty Company he became enormously wealthy; he finally announced himself as "Elijah the Restorer." I remember as a boy how he brought his gospel to New York, and P. T. Barnum with Tom Thumb and the white elephant never made such a sensation. The ridicule of the metropolis overwhelmed the old prophet, and he died and passed on his robes and his tabernacle and his bank to his son; straightway, according to the rule of all religions, the followers fell to quarrelling and splitting up, and suing one another in the law-courts.

Also there are the "Holy Rollers" and "Holy Jumpers", ghastly sects which cultivate the religious hysterias, and have spread like a plague among the women of our lonely prairie farms and desert ranches. The "Holy Rollers", who call themselves the "Apostolic Church", have a meeting place here in Pasadena, and any Sunday evening at nine o'clock you may see the Spirit of the Lord taking possession of the worshippers, causing moans and shrieks and convulsions; you may see a woman holding her hands aloft for seventeen minutes by the watch, making chattering sounds like an ape. This is called "talking in tongues" and is a sign of the presence of the Holy Spirit. If you come back at eleven in the evening, you will find the entire congregation, men and women, prostrate on the floor, or hanging over the benches; and maybe a child moaning in terror, having a devil cast out.

You may be interested, perhaps, to know how to throw yourself into these convulsions. Here is a paper called "Trust", which is "published Monthly (D. V.) in the interests of Elim Faith Work and Bible Training School." Elizabeth Sisson writes on "The Pentecostal Baptism", and tells the story of her experiences. She "camped on the Word of God," she declares.

I went up to Calgary in Canada, and the leader of the mission told me, "You can go down to the mission and stay there all day. There is plenty of wood, and you can stay there all night." I went down, and there was plenty of "let go" in me. I cried, and prayed all I knew, and got wonderfully loosed.....

Then the Lord said to me, "Now, no more praying!" God told me it was mine. What was there left for me to pray about. He spoiled my praying and I took up praising. I praised God that He who worked in the Upper Room was working the same in me. I praised, and I praised, and I praised. The devil said to me, "That's mechanical." I said, "I'll praise You Lord, and if You want real praise, You'll have to put the wind in the sails."

That's the way I came through. One morning I was just

getting out of bed, "this gibberish, this jargon" as the enemy likes to call it, began to come. The Lord said, "Let it babble!" I let. The babble increased, and by night I was up to my neck. I let. I still let. That's all. Someone else does the work, and it does not tire you.

And here is another paper. "Meat in Due Season: published monthly, or as often as the Lord leads." The editor quotes the Bible, "Call upon the name of the Lord," and explains that "Call means **call**." The word appears to have a special meaning to these pentecostal persons—it means working yourself into a frenzy of agitation; as the editor puts it, "you must **lay** hold of the **horns** of the **altar**." He goes on to exhort—the bold face being his:

Pray as if your very life depended upon it! The first few minutes seemingly all the powers of hell will contend every word, the next few, relief in a measure will come, more liberty in calling. In a very little while you will be **dead to the room, dead to the chair,** dead to everyone around you, dead to all and tremendously alive to your desperate need and emptyness; this conviction will grow as you increase calling upon Him. It maybe you'll weep, it maybe you'll perspire, it maybe your clothing will be deranged, it maybe your throat will get sore. Never for a moment let your mind rest on the condition of your person. Open your mouth and God has promised to fill it. Ask persistently until the very floor seems to sink beneath you and the fountains of the deep, of your heart let loose. Like David, "pour out your soul" like one would pour water out of a bucket. I have seen hundreds get through right at this point. When self-**thought, reticence, decorum, reserve, propriety and dignity** had all been thrown to the four winds of heaven. Self was then obliterated and consciousness of person gone. Draw near to God and He will draw near to you saith the scripture, but you must draw near to Him first.

These enthusiasts derive their practices from the **Shakers,** a sect which originated in England, but was driven by persecution to the New World. The Shakers call themselves the "United Society of True Believers in Christ's Second Coming," and were founded by Ann Lee, who variously termed herself the "Female Christ", the "Holy Comforter", and the "God-anointed Woman". They might be termed the suffragettes of religion, for they pray always to "Our Father and Mother, which are in heaven." They were taught the convenient doctrine that their Founder had "spiritual illumination", so that any evidence of the senses used against her might deceive. She governed through terror, holding that by her mental powers she could inflict torment upon any of her followers. Fortunately she taught absolute celibacy, and so there are now only about a thousand of her disciples.

Bible Prophecy

This far western country swarms with those fanatics who await the return of Christ, and find in Bible chronology positive evidence that he is coming on a specified day. Seldom do I give a lecture on Socialism that some eager old lady does not come up to me and point out how futile are my hopes, because the Millenium will come before the Revolution. Several times I have come on an item in the newspapers, telling of a group of people, sometimes whole villages, selling their goods and going out into the fields to shout and sing and pray, expecting the vision of the Lord and His Angels in the skies. I have in my hand a pamphlet entitled "Shekineh: The Glory of God in Israel, Facts Mathematically Foretold, of the Soon Coming of Our Blessed Lord." It is earnestly, yearningly written, in that spirit of feeble-minded affectionateness which the Bible-sects seem to encourage:

Now dear reader you see that these problems tell a wonderful story which I know are the Eternal Truths of God. Jesus is soon coming. I believe that from now on we can say, next week perhaps our blessed Lord will return. Yet the time may not end till the close of the A. M. year, which will be March 20th, 1897. But let us take up the sickle of God, etc. Oh, my Christian friends, live near the Blessed Christ, and gain eternal life through Jesus Our Lord!

In the public library I find another pamphlet, entitled "The Our Race," which proves that the "lost ten tribes of Israel" are not the American Indians, but the Irish! And here is a publication of the "Watch Tower Bible and Tract Society," declaring:

The great pyramid in Egypt is a witness to all the events of the ages and of our day. The pyramid's downward passage under "a Draconis" symbolizes the course of Sin. Its first ascending passage symbolizes the Jewish Age. Its Grand Gallery symbolizes the Gospel Age. Its upper step symbolizes the approaching period of tribulation and anarchy, "Judgment" upon Christendom.

It is a Sunday morning, and I sit in the California sunshine revising this manuscript, when a decorous-looking young man approaches, having a sack over his shoulder. "From the Bible-students," he says politely, and hands me a little paper, "The Bible Students' Monthly: an Independent, Unsectarian Religious Newspaper, Specially devoted to the Forwarding of the Laymen's Home Missionary Movement for the Glory of God and Good of Humanity." The leading article is headed "The Fall of Babylon: Ancient Babylon a Type—Mystic Babylon the Antitype: Why Christendom must Suffer—the Final Outcome." A note explains:

The following article is extracted from Pastor Russell's posthumous volume entitled "The Finished Mystery," the 7th in the series of his Studies in the Scriptures and published subsequent to his death. Pastor Russell held the distinction of being the most fearless and powerful writer of modern times on ecclesiastical subjects. In this posthumous volume, which is called "his last legacy to the Christians on earth," is found a thorough exposition of every verse in the entire book of Revelation and also an elucidation of the obscure prophecy of Ezekiel. The book contains 608 pages, handsomely bound in embossed cloth.

Pastor Russell used to publish a two-column sermon in some hundreds of Sunday newspapers, together with a presentment of his features—solemn, stiff, white-whiskered, set off with a "choker" and a black broadcloth coat. There are five million such faces in America, but if you have an impulse to despair for your country, remember that it produced Mark Twain and Artemus Ward, as well as Pastor Russell and the Moody and Sankey hymn-book. I quote one passage from "The Finished Mystery", in order that the reader may know what it means to "hold the distinction of being the most fearless and powerful writer of modern times on ecclesiastical subjects." Pastor Russell does not approve of the Methodists, and he quotes twelve verses of Revelation, line by line and phrase by phrase, showing how the evil course and downfall of the Wesleyan system were divinely foretold. Thus:

"But that they should be tormented five months."—In symbolic time, 150 years—5 × 30 = 150. (Ezek. 4:6.) Wesley became the first Methodist in 1728. (Rev. 9:1.) When the Methodist denomination, with all the others, was cast off from favor in 1878 (Rev. 3:14) its powers to torment men by preaching what Presbyterians describe as "Conscious misery, eternal in duration" came to an end legally, and to a large extent actually.—Rev. 9:10.

P. S. A few months pass, and while this book is going to press, "The Finished Mystery" is suppressed by the government and several score "Bible Students" are landed in jail for sedition.

Koreshanity

Such are the beliefs built on the Bible. But there are other ancient writings with strange nomenclature and ritual and symbolism, calculated to impress the unlettered; also our prophets have imaginations of their own, and can invent nomenclature and ritual and symbolism never seen in heaven nor on earth before. Thus there is Dr. Newo Newi New, who called himself "Archbishop of the Newthot Church," and gathered about him a harem of devoted females in San Francisco, and was landed in jail for using the mails to defraud. Or there is "Oahspe, the Cosmic Bible," a work of brandnew revelation with a brand-new view of the universe and all things therein:

The reader soon discovers that he must radically revise not only his ideas of celestial Cosmogony, but the order and significance of names and titles commonly applied to the Transcendental Brethren. The great provinces of Etheria are presided over by chiefs, chosen for their superior development in wisdom and love. For our solar system to cross one of these provinces requires about 3,000 years, and between them are belts of high Etherian light which take several years to pass over. The passage of each province is a cycle of earthly history, and the crossings are called Dawns of Dan.

And here is Koreshanity, a revelation vouchsafed by the Lord to Dr. C. R. Teed of Chicago in the year 1889. This new seer took the name of Koresh, which is Hebrew for Cyrus, "the Shepherd from Joseph, the Stone of Israel, the Sun-Man; the illuminating center of the

Son of man", and went out on the streets of the city to preach that the earth is a hollow sphere with the stars inside. The street urchins of the pork-packing metropolis threw stones at him, and the irreverent newspapers took up his adventures, with the result that followers gathered, and now there is a flourishing colony in Florida, with a dignified magazine called "The Flaming Sword", and a collection of propaganda volumes: "The Cellular Cosmogony, an Exposition of Koreshan Universology and the New Geodesy"; "The Immortal Manhood, the Laws and Processes of its Attainment in the Flesh"; "The Great Red Dragon, by Lord Chester"; "The Coming of the Shepherd from Joseph, The Standing of the Great Ensign, by Koresh." The "Religio-science" of this Chicago revelator is based, first upon some precise measurements of the earth which prove that its surface is concave; and second upon some philological discoveries very much resembling puns. Thus the "cross of Christ" is explained in a sense of the word more common among horse-breeders than among theologians:

The highest characteristic of the alchemical law is the cross of Christ with sensual man. The cross means that the Lord God, in order to perpetuate his own being, descends into the race of sensuality.

And again, when someone asks about meteors:

The word Heaven means things heaved up, that is, heaved up from their material basis, the earth; thus, the meteors which fall to the earth are composed of metallic, mineral, and geological substances, being materialized or actually created in the atmosphere by an alchemico-organic process from zones or belts periodically open, which precipitate their contents in the form or shape of meteors."

And perhaps I ought also to quote the "Indicia of Human Progress", by "Berthaldine, Matrona". I don't know what a "Matrona" is—unless it is a female matron. This female matron tells me that now is the "Time of Restitution", and explains that "the prolification of the human race has reached a fruition of the adultery of the truth and good of the Lord with the fallacies and evils of the mortal hells"..... We have come, it seems, to the "age of Pisces", which is "one of the greatest radical prolification"; and what we now need is the "power of polarization", so that we may join the "White Horse Army of the Most High", which is the organization of the "Aquarian age", proclaimed by Koresh on January 15th, 1891.

Mazdaznan

And here is another and even more startling revelation from Chicago, given to a seer by the name of Dr. Otoman Prince of Adusht Ha'nish, prophet of the Sun God, Prince of Peace, Manthra Magi of Temple El Katman, Kalantar of Zoroastrian Breathing and Envoy of Mazdaznan living, Viceroy-Elect and International Head of Master-Thot. If you had happened to live near the town of Mendota, Illinois, and had known the German grocer-boy named Otto Hanisch, you might at first have trouble in recognizing him through this transmogrification. I have traced his career in the files of the Chicago newspapers, and find him herding sheep, setting type, preaching prestidigitation, mesmerism, and fake spiritualism, joining the Mormon Church, then the "Christian Catholic Church in Zion", and then the cult of Brighouse, who claimed to be Christ returned.

Finally he sets himself up in Chicago as a Persian Magi, teaching Yogi breathing exercises and occult sex-lore to the elegant society ladies of the pork-packing metropolis. The Sun God, worshipped for two score centuries in India, Egypt, Greece and Rome, has a new shrine on Lake Park Avenue, and the prophet gives tea-parties at which his disciples are fed on lilac-blossoms—"the white and pinkish for males, the blue-tinted for females". He wears a long flowing robe of pale grey cashmere, faced with white, and flexible white kid shoes, and he sells his lady adorers a book called "Inner Studies", price five dollars per volume, with information on such subjects as:

The Immaculate Conception and its Repetition; The Secrets of Lovers Unveiled; Our Ideals and Soul Mates; Magnetic Attraction and Electric Mating.

A Grand Jury intervenes, and the Prophet goes to jail for six months; but that does not harm his cult, which now has a temple in Chicago, presided over by a lady called Kalantress and Evangelist; also a "Northern Stronghold" in Montreal, an "Embassy" in London, an "International Aryana" in Switzerland, and "Centers" all over America. At the moment of going to press, the prophet himself is in flight, pursued by a warrant charging him with improper conduct with a number of young boys in a Los Angeles hotel.

I have dipped into Ha'nish's revelations, which are a farrago of every kind of ancient mysticism—paper and binding from the Bible, illustrations from the Egyptian, names from the Zoroastrian, health rules from the Hindoos, laws from the Confucians—price ten dollars per volume. Would you like to discover your

seventeen senses, to develop them according to the Ga-
Llama principle, and to share the "expansion of the
magnetic circles"? Here is the way to do it:

Inhale through nostrils for four seconds, and upon one exhalation, speak slowly:
Open, O thou world-sustaining Sun, the entrance unto Truth
hidden by the vase of dazzling light.
Again inhale for four seconds, and breathe out the following
sentence upon one exhalation as before:
Soften the radiation of Thy Illuminating Splendor, that I
may behold Thy True Being.

I have a clipping from a Los Angeles newspaper
telling of the prophet's arriving there. He takes the
front page with the captivating headline: "Women
Didn't Think Till They Put On Corsets". The interview
tells about his mysteriousness, his aloofness, his bird-
like-diet, and his personal beauty. "Despite his seventy-
three years, Ha'nish evidences no sign of age. His keen
blue eyes showed no sign of wavering. There were no
wrinkles on his face, and his walk was that of a man of
forty." The humor of this becomes apparent when we
mention that at Ha'nish's trial, three or four years ago,
he was proven to be thirty-five years old!

Being thus warned as to the accuracy of American
journalism, we shall not be taken in by the repeated
statements that the Mazdaznan prophet is a millionaire.
But there is no doubt that he is wealthy; and as all
Americans wish to be wealthy, I will quote his formula
of prosperity, his method of accomplishing what might
be called the Individual Revolution:

When hungry and you do not know where to get your next
piece of bread, do not despair. Thy Father, all-loving, has provided you with everything that will meet all cases of emergency.

Place your teeth tightly together, with tongue pressing against the lower teeth and lips parted. Breathe in, close lips immediately, exhaling through the nostrils. Breathe again; if saliva forms in your mouth, hold your breath so you can swallow it first before you exhale. You thus take out of the air the metal-substance contained therein; you can even taste the iron which you convert into substance required for making the blood. Should you feel that, although you have sufficient iron in the blood, there is a lack of copper and zinc and silver, place upper teeth over lower, keep lower lip tightly to lower teeth, now breathe and you can even taste the metals named. Then should you feel you need more gold element for your brain functions, place your back teeth together just as if you were to grind the back teeth, taking short breaths only. You will then learn to know that there is gold and silver all around us. That our bodies are filled with quite a quantity of gold.

Black Magic

What all this means is that we have a continent, with a hundred million half-educated people, materially prosperous, but spiritually starving; so any man who possesses personality, who looks in any way strange and impressive, or has hunted up old books in a library, and can pronounce mysterious words in a thrilling voice —such a man can find followers. Anybody can do it with any doctrine, from anywhere, Persia or Patagonia, Pekin or Pompei. I would be willing to wager that if I cared to come out and announce that I had had a visit from God last night, and to devote such literary and emotional power as I possess to communicating a new revelation, I could have a temple, a university, and a million dollars within five years at the outside. And if at the end of five years I were to announce that I had played a joke on the world, some one of my followers would convince the faithful that I had been an

agent of God without knowing it, and that the leader-
ship had now been turned over to him.

I would not be understood as believing that all our
cults are undiluted fakery, for that would be doing injustice to some earnest people. There are, in this country, many followers of the Persian reformer, Abbas
Effendi, who call themselves Babists, and who have
what I am inclined to think is the purest and most dignified religion in existence. There was a man named
Jacob Beilhardt, who founded a cult in Illinois with the
painful name of "Spirit Fruit Colony", who nevertheless was a man of spiritual insight, a true mystic; he
was honest, and so he failed, and died of a broken heart.
Also there are the Christian Scientists and the Theosophists, so exasperating that one would like to throw
them onto the rubbish-heap, who yet compel us to sift
over their mountains of chaff for the grains of truth
which will bear fruit in future.

While we western races have been exploring the
natural world and perfecting the mechanical arts, the
Hindoo students have been exploring the subconscious
and its strange powers. What Myers and Lodge and
Janet and Charcot and Freud and Jung are telling us
today they had hints of a long time ago; and doubtless
they have hints of other things, upon which our scientists have not yet come. I have friends, perfectly
sane and competent people, who tell me that they can
see auras, and use this ability as a means of judging
character. Shall I say that there are no auras, simply
because I do not happen to have this gift of seeing
them? In the same way, having read Gurney's "Phan-
tasms of the Living," I am not ready to ridicule the

claim of the Yogi adepts, that they are able to project some kind of astral body, and to communicate with one another from distant places. But granting such occult powers in a world of economic strife, what follows? Simply new floods of charlatanism, elaborate and complicated systems of ritual and metaphysic for the deluding and plundering of the credulous.

I have seen the thing working itself out in one case known to me. A young man had a gift of mental healing; I know, because I saw it work; but it did not always work, and that was annoying. He was penniless and had a taste for power, and to eke out his erratic endowment he got himself books of Eastern lore, and day by day as I watched him I could see him becoming more and more impressive, mysterious and forbidding. Today he is a full-fledged wonder-worker, with the language of a dozen mystic cults at his tongue's end, and the reverent regard of many wealthy ladies. I have never tried to break through his guard, but I feel certain that he is a deliberate charlatan.

This is an economic process, automatic and irresistible. Just as the manufacturer of honest foods is driven out by the adulterator, so the worker of miracles drives out the sincere investigator. As a result we have here in America a plague of Eastern cults, with "swamis" using soft yellow robes and soft brown eyes to win the souls of idle society ladies. These teachers of ancient Hindoo lore despise us as a race of barbarians; but they stay—whether because of love of man or woman, I do not pretend to say.

There are the Theosophists of many brands, with schools and institutes and temples and colonies, and a

doctrine as complex and detailed and fantastic as that
of the Roman Catholics. I have already referred to the
writings of Madame Blavatsky, a runaway Russian
army officer's daughter, whose career reads like a tale
out of the Arabian Nights. And there is Annie Besant,
who was once an ardent worker in the Social-demo-
cratic Federation; H. M. Hyndman tells of his dismay
when she went to India and walked in a procession between two white bulls! Here in California is Madame
Tingley, with a colony and a host of followers in a min-
ature paradise. Men work at money-lending or manu-
facturing sporting-goods, and when they get old and
tired they make the thrilling discovery that they have
souls; the theosophists cultivate these souls and they
leave their money to the soul-cause, and there are law-
suits and exposés in the newspapers. For, you see,
there is ferocious rivalry in the game of cultivating millionaire souls; there are slanders and feuds, just as in
soulless affairs. "Don't have anything to do with
Madame Tingley," whispers a Theosophist lady to my
wife; and when my wife in all innocence inquires, "Why
not?" the awe-stricken answer comes, "She practices
black magic!"

Let me add that I do not say that she practices black
magic. I do not believe that she **could** practice it, even
if she wanted to—I do not believe in black magic. My
purpose is merely to show how theosophists quarrel:
going back to the days of Anu and Baal and the bronze
image of the Babylonian fire-god:

Let them die, but let me live!
Let them be put under a ban, but let me **prosper!**
Let them perish, but let me increase!
Let them become weak, but let me wax strong!

Mental Malpractice

This is the other side of the fair shield of religious faith. Why, if there be a power which loves and can be persuaded to aid us, may there not also be a power which hates, and can be persuaded to destroy? No religion has ever been able to answer this, and therefore none has ever been able to escape from devil-terrors. Even Jesus was pursued by Satan, and the Holy Catholic Church has its ceremonies for the exorcising of demons, and a most frightful formula for cursing. And here are our friends the Christian Scientists, proclaiming the unreality of all evil, their ability to banish disease by convincing themselves that they are perfect in God—yet tormented by a squalid phobia called "Mental Malpractice", or "Malicious Animal Magnetism".

Christian Science is the most characteristic of American religious contributions. Just as Billy Sunday is the price we pay for failing to educate our base-ball players, so Mary Baker Glover Patterson Eddy is the price we pay for failing to educate our farmer's daughters.

That she had a power to cure disease I do not doubt, because I have a little of it myself. At first my opinion was that her "Science" made its way by curing the imaginary ailments of the idle rich. If a person has nothing to do but think that he is sick, you can work easy miracles by persuading him to think that he is well; and if he has nothing to do but think that he is well, he will help you to build marble churches and maintain propaganda societies. But recently I have experimented with mental healing—enough to satisfy myself that the subconscious mind which controls our physical functions can be powerfully influenced by the will.

I told the story of some of these experiments in Hearst's Magazine for April, 1914. Suffice it here to say that if you will lay your hands upon a sick person, forming a vivid mental picture of the bodily changes you desire, and concentrating the power of your will upon them, you may be surprised by the results, especially if you possess anything in the way of psychic gifts. You do not have to adopt any theories, you do not have to do it in the name of any divinity, ancient or modern; the only bearing of such ideas is that they serve to persuade people to make the experiment, and to make it with persistence and intensity. So it has come about that "miracles" of healing are associated with "faith"; and so it comes about that scientists are apt to flout the subject. But read of the work of Janet and Charcot and their followers at the Salpetriere; they have proven that all kinds of seeming-organic ailments may be entirely hysterical in nature, and may be cured by the simplest form of suggestion. Understanding this, you may find it more easy to credit the fact that cripples do sometimes throw away their crutches in the grotto of Lourdes. For my part, I can believe that Jesus performed all the miracles of healing attributed to him —including the raising up of people pronounced to be dead by the ignorance of that time. I am convinced that in the new science of psycho-analysis we have a universe as vast as the universe of the atom or of the stars.

The Christian Scientists have got hold of this power; they have mixed it up with metaphysic and divinity, and built some four or five hundred churches, and printed the Mother Church alone knows how many million pamphlets and books. I once invested three of my hard-earned dollars for a copy of the Eddy Bible, and let myself be stunned and blinded by the flapping of metaphysical wings. It is unadulterated moonshine —as the Platonist and Berkeleyan and Hegelian and other orthodox collegiate metaphysical magi can prove to you in one minute. What interests me about the phenomenon is not the slinging of tremendous words, but the strictly Yankee use which is made of them. There is no nonsense about saving your soul in Christian Science; what it is for is to remove your wen, to nail down your floating kidney, and to enable you to hustle and make money. We saw in our politics the growth of a Party of the Full Dinner-Pail; contemporaneous therewith, and corresponding thereto, we see in our religious life the development of a Church of the Full Pocket-Book.

It is a strict religion—strictly cash. The heads of the cult do not issue cheap editions of "Science and Health, With Key to the Scriptures", to relieve the suffering of the proletariat; no—the work is copyrighted, in all its varying and contradictory editions, and the price is from three to seven-fifty, according to binding. Treatments cost from three dollars to ten, whether you come and get them or take them over the telephone. And we have no nonsense about charity, we don't worry about the poor who fester in our city slums; because poverty is a product of Mortal Mind, and we offer to all men a way to get rich right off the bat. You may come to our marble churches and hear people testify

how through the power of Divine Mind they were enabled to anticipate a rise in the stock-market. If you
don't avail yourself of the opportunity, the fault is
yours, and yours also the punishment.

As to the management of the Church, the Roman
Catholic hierarchy is a Bolshevik democracy in compar-
ison. The Church is controlled by an absolutely irre-
sponsible self-perpetuating body of five men, who alone
dictate its policy. I have in my hand a letter from a
Christian Science healer who was listed as an "authorized practitioner", and who withdrew from the Church
because of its attitude on public questions. He sends me
a copy of his correspondence with the editors of the
"Christian Science Monitor", containing a detailed analysis of the position of that paper on such issues as the
Ballinger land-frauds. He writes:

> I am thoroughly convinced now that the policy of the Church
> is consciously plutocratic. The only recommendation I have
> heard of the latest appointee to the Board of Directors is that he
> is one of the richest men in the movement.

After the Titanic disaster, Senator La Follette
brought in a carefully drawn bill to compel steamship
companies to provide life-boats and trained crews. The
"Christian Science Monitor" opposed this bill; and
when my correspondent cited the fact, he brought out
a quaint bit of metaphysical logic, as follows:

> One would prefer to travel on a vessel without a single
> boat, rather than on some other vessels which were loaded down
> with life-boats, where the government of Mind was not under-
> stood!

Science and Wealth

The truth is that the brand of Mammon was on our Yankee religion from the day of its birth. In the first edition of her new Bible "Mother" Eddy dropped the hint to her readers: "Men of business have said this science was of great advantage from a secular point of view." And in her advertisements she threw aside all pretense, declaring that her work "Affords an opportunity to acquire a profession by which one can accumulate a fortune." When her pupils did accumulate, she boasted of their success; nor did she neglect her own accumulating.

It has been a dozen years since I looked into this cult; in order to be sure that it has not been purified in the interim, I proceed to a street corner in my home city, where is a stand with a sign: "Christian Science Literature." I take four sample copies of a magazine, the "Christian Science Sentinel", published by the Mother Church in Boston, and turn to the "Testimonials of Healing". In the issue of August 11, 1917, Mary C. Richards of St. Margarets-on-Thames, England, testifies: "Through a number of circumstances unnecessary to relate, but proving conclusively that the result came not from man but from God, employment was found." In the issue of December 2, 1916, Frances Tuttle of Jersey City, N. J., testifies how her sister was successfully treated for unemployment by a scientist practitioner. "Every condition was beautifully met." In the same issue Fred D. Miller of Los Angeles, Cal., testifies: "Soon after this wonderful truth came to me, Divine Love led me to a new position with a responsible firm. The work was new to me, but I have given entire satisfaction, and my salary has been advanced twice in less than a year." In the issue of January 27, 1917, Eliza Fryant of Agricola, Miss., testifies how she cured her little dog of snake-bite and removed two painful corns from her own foot. In the issue of August 4, 1917, Marcia E. Gaier, of Everett, Wash., testifies how it suddenly occurred to her that because God is All, she would drop her planning and outlining in regard to real estate properties, "upon which for nine months all available material methods were tried to no effect." The result was a triumph of "Principle".

> While working in the yard one morning and gratefully communing with God, the only power, I suddenly felt that I should stop working and prepare for visitors on their way to look at the property. I obeyed this very distinct command, and in about an hour I greeted two people who had searched almost the entire city for just what we had to offer. They had been directed to our place by what to material sense would seem an accident, but we know it was the divine law of harmony in its universal operation.

After this no one will wonder that John M. Tutt, in a Christian Science lecture at Kansas City, Mo., should proclaim:

> My friends, do you know that since the world began Christian Science is the only system which has intelligently related religion to business? Christian Science shows that since all ideas belong to Mind, God, therefore all real business belongs to Him.

As I said, these people have the new-old power of mental healing. They blunder along with it blindly, absurdly, sometimes with tragic consequences; but meantime the rank and file of the pill-doctors know nothing about this power, and regard it with contempt mingled with fear; so of course the hosts of sufferers whom the pill-doctors cannot help flock to the healers of the "Church of Christ, Scientist". According to the custom of those who are healed by "faith", they swallow line, hook, and sinker, creed, ritual, metaphysic and divinity. So we see in twentieth-century America precisely what we saw in B. C. twentieth-century Assyria—a host of worshippers, giving their worldly goods without stint, and a priesthood, made partly of fanatics and partly of charlatans, conducting a vast enterprise of graft, and harvesting that thing desired of all men, power over the lives and destinies of others.

And of course among themselves they quarrel; they murder one another's Mortal Minds, they drive one another out, they snarl over the spoils like a pack of hungry animals. Listen to the Mother, denouncing one of her students—a perfectly amiable and harmless youth whose only offense was that he had gone his own way and was healing the sick for the benefit of his own pocket-book:

Behold! thou criminal mental marauder, that would blot out the sunshine of earth, that would sever friends, destroy virtue, put out Truth, and murder in secret the innocent, befouling thy track with the trophies of thy guilt—I say, Behold the "cloud" no bigger than a man's hand already rising on the horizon of Truth, to pour down upon thy guilty head the hailstones of doom.

And again:

The Nero of today, regaling himself through a mental method with the torture of individuals, is repeating history, and will fall upon his own sword, and it shall pierce him through. Let him remember this when, in the dark recesses of thought, he is robbing, committing adultery and killing. When he is attempting to turn friend away from friend, ruthlessly stabbing the quivering heart; when he is clipping the thread of life and giving to the grave youth and its rainbow hues; when he is turning back the reviving sufferer to his bed of pain, clouding his first morning after years of night; and the Nemesis of that hour shall point to the tyrant's fate, who falls at length upon the sword of justice.

New Nonsense

In a certain city of America is a large building given up entirely to the whims of pretty ladies. Its floors are not floors but "Promenades", and have walls of glass, behind which, as you stroll, you see bonnets from Paris and opera cloaks from London, furs from Alaska and blankets from Arizona, diamonds from South Africa and beads from the Philippines, grapes from Spain and cherries from Japan, fortune-tellers from Arabia and dancing-masters from Petrograd and "naturopaths" from Vienna. There are seventy-three shops, by actual count, containing everything that could be imagined or desired by a pretty lady, whether for her body, or for that vague stream of emotion she calls her "soul". One of the seventy-three shops is a "Metaphysical Library", having broad windows, and walls in pastel tints, and pretty vases with pink flowers, and pretty gray wicker chairs in which the reader will please to be seated, while we probe the mysteries of an activity widely spread throughout America, called "New Thought."

We begin with a shelf of magazines having mystical titles: Azoth; Master Mind; Aletheian; Words of Power; Qabalah; Comforter; Adept; Nautilus; True Word; Astrological Bulletin; Unity; Uplift; **Now.** And then come shelves of pretty pamphlets, alluring to the eye and the purse; also shelves of imposing-looking volumes containing the lore and magic of a score of races and two score of centuries—together with the very newest manifestations of Yankee hustle and graft.

As in the case of Christian Science, these New Thoughters have a fundamental truth, which I would by no means wish to depreciate. It is a fact that the mysterious Source of our being is infinite, and that we are only at the beginning of our thinking about it. It is a fact that by appeal to it we can perform seeming miracles of mental and moral regeneration; we can stimulate the flow of nervous energy and of the blood, thus furthering the processes of bodily healing. But the fact that God is Infinite and Omnipotent does not bar the fact that He has certain ways of working, which He does not vary; and that it is our business to explore and understand these ways, instead of setting our fancies to work imagining other ways more agreeable to our sentimentality.

Thus, for example, if we want bread, it is God's decree that we shall plant wheat and harvest it, and grind and bake and distribute it. Under conditions prevailing at the moment, it appears to be His decree that we shall store the wheat in elevators, and ship it in freight cars, and buy it through a grain exchange, with capital borrowed from a national bank; in other words, that our daily bread shall be the plaything of exploiters and speculators, until such a time as we have the intelligence to form an effective political party and establish Industrial Democracy. But when you come to study the ways of God in the literature of the New Thought, do you find anything about the Millers' Trust and the

Bakers' Trust and how to expropriate these agencies of starvation? You do not!

What you find is Bootstrap-lifting; you find gentlemen and lady practitioners shutting their eyes and lifting their hands and pronouncing Incantations in awe-inspiring voices—or in Capital Letters and LARGE TYPE: "God is infinite, **God is All-Loving, GOD WILL PROVIDE.** Bread is coming to you! **Bread is coming to you!! BREAD IS COMING TO YOU!!!**"

You think this is exaggeration? If so, it is because you have never entered the building of the pretty ladies, and sat in the gray wicker chairs of the metaphysical library. One of the highest high-priestesses of the cults of New Nonsense is a lady named Elizabeth Towne, editor of "The Nautilus"; and Priestess Elizabeth tells you:

I believe the idea that money wants you will help you to the right mental condition. Be a pot of honey and let it come.

I look over this Priestess' magazine, and find it full of testimonials and advertisements for the conjuring of prosperity. "Are you in the success sphere?" asks one exhorter; the next tells you "How to enter the silence. How to manifest what you desire. The secret of advancement." Another tells: "How a Failure at Sixty Won Sudden Success; From Poverty to $40,000 a year —a Lesson for Old and Young Alike." The lesson, it appears, is to pay $3.00 for a book called "Power of Will." And here is another book:

Master Key: Which can unlock the Secret Chamber of Success, can throw wide the doors which seem to bar men from the Treasure House of Nature, and bids those enter and partake

who are Wise enough to Understand and broad enough to Weigh
the Evidence, firm enough to Follow their Own Judgment and
Strong enough to Make the Sacrifice Exacted.

"Dollars Want Me"

I turn to the shelves of pamphlets. Here is a pretty
one called "All Sufficiency in All Things," published by
the "Unity School of Christianity", in Kansas City; it
explains that God is God, not merely of the Soul, but
also of the Kansas City stockyards.

This divine Substance is ever abiding within us, and stands
ready to manifest itself in whatever form you and I need or wish,
just as it did in Elisha's time. It is the same yesterday, today
and forever. Abundant Supply by the manifestation of the Father within us, from within outward, is as much a legitimate outcome of the Christ life or spiritual understanding as is bodily
healing..... "Know that I am God—all of God, Good, all of
Good. I am Life. I am Health. I am Supply. I am the Substance."

And here is W. W. Atkinson of Chicago, author of a
work called "Mind Power". Would you like to be an
Impressive Personality? Mr. Atkinson will tell you exactly how to do it; he will give you the secret of the
Magnetic Handclasp, of the Intense, Straight-in-the-
eye Look; he will tell you what to say, he will write out
for you Incantations which you may pronounce to yourself, to convince yourself that you have **Power,** that the
INDWELLING PRESENCE with all its **MIGHT** is
yours. Mr. Atkinson rebukes mildly the tendency of
some of his fellow Bootstrap-lifters to employ these
arts for money-making; but you notice that his magazine, "Advanced Thought", does not decline the advertisements of such too-practical practitioners.

Next comes a gentleman with the musical name of
Wallace Wattles, who tells in one pamphlet "How to Be
a Genius", and in another pamphlet "How to Get What
you Want". The thing for you to do is—

Saturate your mentality through and through with the
knowledge that YOU CAN DO WHAT YOU WANT TO DO.....
Look upon the peanut-stand merely as the beginning of the department store, and make it grow; you can.

And Mr. Wattles wattles on, in an ecstasy of ac-
quisitiveness:

Hold this consciousness and say with deep, earnest feeling: I
CAN succeed! All that is possible to any one is possible to me.
I AM success. I do succeed, for I am full of the Power of Suc-
cess.

Imagine, if you please, a poor devil chained in the
treadmill of the capitalist system—a "soda-jerker", a
"counter-jumper", a book-keeper for the Steel Trust.
His chances of rising in life are one in ten thousand;
but he comes to the Metaphysical Library, and pays the
price of his dinner for a pamphlet by Henry Harrison
Brown, who was first a Unitarian clergyman, and then
an extra-high Bootstrap-lifter in San Francisco,
an Honorary Vice-President of the International New
Nonsense Alliance. Mr. Brown will tell our soda-jerker
or counter-jumper exactly how to elevate himself by
mental machinery. All calculations of probabilities are
delusions of the senses; if you have faith, you can
move, not merely mountains, but Riker-Hegeman's,
Macy's, or the Steel Trust. "How to Promote Yourself"
is the title of one of Mr. Brown's pamphlets, in which
he explains that—

Your wants are impressed on the Divine Mind **only by your** faith. A doubt cuts the connection.

A second pamphlet, which we are told is now in its thirtieth edition, bears the thrilling title of **"Dollars Want Me!"** In it Mr. Brown lays claim to being a pioneer:

I believe that this little monograph is the first utterance of the thought that each individual has the ability so to radiate his mental forces that he can cause the Dollars to **feel** him, **love** him, **seek** him, and thus draw at will all things needed for his unfoldment from the universal supply.

"What are Dollars?" asks our author; and answers:

Dollars are manifestations of the One Infinite Substance as you are, but, unlike you, they are not Self-Conscious. They have no power till you give them power. Make them **feel** this through your thought-vibrations as you **feel** the importance of your work. They will then come to you to be used.

"What is Poverty?" Mr. Brown asks, and answers himself:

Poverty is a mental condition. It can be cured only by the Affirmation of Power to cure: I am a part of the One, and, in the One, I possess all! Affirm this and patiently wait for the manifestation. You have sown the thought seed.

And our author goes on to hand out packages of these thought-seeds—"Affirmations" as they are called, in the jargon of the New Conjuring:

I desire a deep consciousness of financial freedom.
I desire that the flow of prosperity become equalized.
I desire a greater consciousness of my power to attract the dollar.
The Indwelling Power cares for my purse.
I own whatever I desire.

I can afford to use dollars for my happiness.
I always have a good bank account. I actually see it.
My one idea of the law is to use, use, USE.

Spiritual Financiering

If the symbolism of the Episcopal Church is of the palace, and that of the non-conformist sects of the counting-house, that of the International New Nonsense Alliance is of Wall Street and the "ticker". What is your rating in the Spiritual Bradstreet?" asks William Morris Nichols in the publication of the " 'Now' Folk", San Francisco:

Is it low or high? Is your credit with the Bank of the Universe good or poor? If you draw a spiritual draft are you sure of its being honored?

If you can answer that last question affirmatively, you are on the road to become a Master in Spiritual Financiering.

Have you an account with the First (and only) Bank of Spirit? If not, then you should at once open one therewith. For no one can afford to keep less than a large deposit of spiritual funds with that Bank.

And how do you proceed to open your account? It is very simple:

Intend the mind in the direction indicated by your desire. Seek for the Light and Guidance by which you may open up the way for your Spiritual Substance, which governs material supply, to reach you and make you as rich as you ought to be, in freedom and happiness. All this you can, and when in earnest, will do.

I turn over the advertisements of this publication of the " 'Now' Folk". One offers "The Business Side of New Thought." Another offers "The Books Without an If", with your money back IF you are not satisfied!

Another offers land in Bolivia for two dollars an acre. Another quotes Shakespeare: "'Tis the mind that makes the body rich." Another offers two copies of the "Phrenological Era" for ten cents.

There is apparently no delusion of any age or clime which cannot find dupes among the readers of this New Nonsense. One notice commands:

Stop! A Revelation! A Book has been written entitled "Strands of Gold" or "From Darkness into Light!"

Another announces:

The Most Wonderful Book of the Ages: The Acquarian Gospel of Jesus the Christ, Transcribed from the Book of God's Remembrance, the Akashic Records.

And here is an advertisement published in Mr. Atkinson's paper:

Numerology: the Universal Adjuster! Do you know: What you appear to be to others? What you really are? What you want to be? What would overcome your present and future difficulties? Write to X, Philosopher. You will receive full particulars of his personal work which is dedicated to your service. No problem is too big or too small for Numerology. Understanding awaits you.

And looking in the body of the magazine, you find this Philosopher imparting some of this Understanding. Would you like, for example, to understand why America entered the War? Nothing easier. The vowels of the Words United States of America are uieaeoaeia, which are numbered 2951561591, which added make 45, or 4 plus 5 equals 9. You might not at first see what that has to do with the War—until the Philosopher points out that "9 in the number of completion, indicating the end of a cosmic cycle." That, of course, explains everything.

And here is a work on what you perhaps thought to be a dead science, Astrology. It is called "Lucky Hours for Everybody: A True System of Planetary Hours by Prof. John B. Early. Price One Dollar." It teaches you things like this:

Saturn's negative hours are especially good for all matters relating to gold-mining.....The Sun negative rules the emerald, the musical note D sharp, and the number four. The lunar hours are a good time to deal in public commodities, and to hire servants of both sexes.....

A recent lady visitor informed me that she had made several vain attempts to transact important business in the hours ruled by Jupiter, usually held to be fortunate, while she was nearly always fortunate in what she began in the hours ruled by Saturn. Upon investigation I found her name was ruled by the Sun negative, and that she had Capricorn with Saturn therein as her ascendant at birth, which explains.

And finally, here is a London "scientist", reported in the "Weekly Unity" of Kansas City, who proves his mental power over two-horse power oil engines which fail to act. "Going a little apart, he came back in a few minutes and said: 'The engine is all right now and will work satisfactorily.' and without any further difficulty it did." We are told how Dr. Rawson gave a demonstration of his method to a newspaper reporter the other day. Fixing his gaze as though looking into space, he apparently became absorbed in deep contemplation and said aloud: "There is no danger; man is surrounded by divine love; there is no matter; all is spirit and manifestation of spirit."

You might at first find difficulty in believing what

can be accomplished by "demonstrations" such as this; not merely are two-horse power oil engines made to work, but the whole gigantic machine of Prussian militarism is prevented from working. You may recall how Arthur Machen's magazine story of the Angels of Mons was taken up and made into a Catholic legend over-night; now here is a New-Nonsense legend, complete and perfect, going the rounds of our Nonsense magazines:

London, Dec. 14.—Shell-proof and bullet-proof soldiers have been discovered on the European battle-fronts. Heroes with "charmed lives" are being made every day, according to Frederick L. Rawson, a London scientist, who insists he has found the miraculous way by which they are developed. He calls it "audible treatment". "Practical utilization of the powers of God by right thinking," is the agency through which Dr. Rawson declares he can so treat a man that he will not be harmed when hundreds of men are being shot dead beside him. This amazing treatment includes a new type of prayer. It is being administered to hundreds of men audibly, and to hundreds more by letter. Nothing since the war began has aroused so much talk of modern miracles as have many of the statements of Dr. Rawson.......

At the taking of a wood there were five hundred yards of "No Man's Land" to be crossed. Our troops could not get across. Then Capt. —————, who practices this method of prayer, treated them for an hour before they started, and not a man was knocked out. He was the only officer left out of eighty in his brigade. He simply held onto the fact that man is spiritual and perfect and could not be touched. A bullet fired from a revolver only five yards away hit him over the chest, tore his shirt and went out at the shoulder. But it never penetrated his chest. He was frequently in a hail of shells and bullets which did not touch him.

The Graft of Grace

All this is grotesque; but it is what happens to religions in a world of commercial competition. It happens not merely to Christian Science and New Thought religions, Mazdaznan and Zionist, Holy Roller and Mormon religions, but to Catholic and Episcopalian, Presbyterian and Methodist and Baptist religions. For you see, when you are with the wolves you must howl with them; when you are competing with fakirs you must fake. The ordinary Christian will read the claims of the New Thought fakers with contempt; but have I not shown the Catholic Church publishing long lists of money-miracles? Have I not shown the Church of Good Society, our exclusive and aristocratic Protestant Episcopal communion, pretending to call rain and to banish pestilence, to protect crops and win wars and heal those who are "sick in estate"—that is, who are in business trouble?

The reader will say that I am a cynic, despising my fellows; but that is not so. I am an economic scientist, analyzing the forces which operate in human societies. I blame the prophets and priests and healers for their fall from idealism; but I blame still more the competitive wage-system, which presents them with the alternative to swindle or to starve.

For, you see, the prophet has to have food. He has frequently got along with almost none, and with only a rag for clothing; in Palestine and India, where the climate is warm, a sincere faith has been possible for short periods. But the modern prophet who expects to influence the minds of men has to have books and newspapers; he will find a telephone and a typewriter and postage-stamps hardly to be dispensed with, also in Europe and America some sort of a roof over his meeting place. So the prophet is caught, like all the rest of us, in the net of the speculator and the landlord. He has to get money, and in order to get it he has to impress those who already have it—people whose minds and souls have been deformed by the system of parasitism and exploitation.

So the prophet becomes a charlatan; or, if he refuses, he becomes a martyr, and founds a church which becomes a church of charlatans. I care not how sincere, how passionately proletarian a religious prophet may be, that is the fate which sooner or later befalls him in a competitive society—to be the founder of an organization of fools, conducted by knaves, for the benefit of wolves. That fate befell Buddha and Jesus, it befell Ignatius Loyola and Francis of Assisi, John Fox and John Calvin and John Wesley.

A friend of mine who has made a study of "Spiritualism" describes to me the conditions in that field. The mediums are people, mostly women, with a peculiar gift; whether we believe in the survival of personality, or whether we call it telepathy, does not alter the fact that they have a rare and special sensitiveness, a new faculty which science must investigate. They come, poor people mostly—for the well-to-do will seldom give their time to exacting and wearisome experiments. They come, wearing frayed and thin clothing, shivering with cold, obviously undernourished; and their survival depends upon their producing "phenomena"— which phenomena are capricious, and will not come at call. So, what more natural than that mediums should resort to faking? That the whole field should be reeking with fraud, and science should be held back from understanding an extraordinary power of the subconscious mind?

Ever since we came to Pasadena, various ladies have been telling us about the wondrous powers of a mulatto-woman, a manicurist at the city's most fashionable hotel. The other day, out of curiosity, my wife and I went; the moment the "medium" opened her mouth my wife recognized her as the person who has been trying for several months to get me on the telephone to tell me how the spirit of Jack London is seeking to communicate with me! The séance was a public one, a gathering composed, half of wealthy and cultured society-women, and half of confederates, people with the dialect and manners of a vaudeville troupe. A megaphone was set in the middle of the floor, the room was made dark, a couple of hymns were sung, and then the spirit of Dr. Oliver Wendell Holmes spoke through the megaphone with a Bowery accent, and gave communications from relatives and friends of the various confederates. "Jesus is with us", said Dr. Holmes. "The spirit of Jesus bids you to study spiritualism." And then came the voice of a child: "Mamma! Mamma!" "It is little Georgie!" cried Dr. Holmes; and one of the society ladies started, and answered, and presently burst into tears. A marvelous piece of evidence—especially when you recall that the story of this mother's bereavement had been published in all the papers a couple of months before!

And this kind of swindling is going on every night in every city of America. It goes on wholesale for months every summer at Lily Dale, in New York State, where the spiritualists hold their combination of Chau-

tauqua and Coney Island. And the same thing is going
on in the field of mental healing, and of all other "occult" forces and powers, whether real or imaginary. It
is going on with new spiritual fervors, new moral ideal-
isms, new poetry, new music, new painting, new sculpture. The faker, the charlatan is everywhere—using
the mental and moral and artistic forces of life as a
means of delivering himself from economic servitude.
Everywhere I turn I see it—credulity being exploited,
and men of practical judgment, watching the game and
seeing through it, made hard in their attitude of materialism. How many men I know who sit by in sullen
protest while their wives drift from one new quackery
to another, wasting their income seeking health and
happiness in futile emotionalism! How many kind and
sensitive spirits I know—both men and women—who
pour their treasures of faith and admiration into the
laps of hierophants who began by fooling all mankind
and ended by fooling themselves!

In each one of the cults of what I have called the
"Church of the Quacks", there are thousands, perhaps
millions of entirely sincere, self-sacrificing people. They
will read this book—if anyone can persuade them to
read it—with pain and anger; thinking that I am mock-
ing at their faith, and have no appreciation of their devotion. All that I can say is that I am trying to show
them how they are being trapped, how their fine and
generous qualities are being used by exploiters of one
sort or another; and how this must continue, world
without end, until there is order in the material affairs
of the race, until justice has been established as the law
of man's dealing with his fellows.

BOOK SEVEN

The Church of the Social Revolution

They have taken the tomb of our Comrade Christ—
    Infidel hordes that believe not in man;
Stable and stall for his birth sufficed,
    But his tomb is built on a kingly plan.
They have hedged him round with pomp and parade,
    They have buried him deep under steel and stone—
But we come leading the great Crusade
    To give our Comrade back to his own.

Waddell.

Christ and Caesar

In the most deeply significant of the legends concerning Jesus, we are told how the devil took him up
into a high mountain and showed him all the kingdoms
of the world in a moment of time; and the devil said
unto him: "All this power will I give unto thee, and
the glory of them, for that is delivered unto me, and to
whomsoever I will, I give it. If thou, therefore, wilt
worship me, all shall be thine." Jesus, as we know, answered and said "Get thee behind me, Satan!" And he
really meant it; he would have nothing to do with
worldly glory, with "temporal power;" he chose the
career of a revolutionary agitator, and died the death
of a disturber of the peace. And for two or three centuries his church followed in his footsteps, cherishing
his proletarian gospel. The early Christians had "all
things in common, except women;" they lived as social
outcasts, hiding in deserted catacombs, and being
thrown to lions and boiled in oil.

But the devil is a subtle worm; he does not give up
at one defeat, for he knows human nature, and the
strength of the forces which battle for him. He failed
to get Jesus, but he came again, to get Jesus' church.
He came when, through the power of the new revolutionary idea, the Church had won a position of tremendous power in the decaying Roman Empire; and the
subtle worm assumed the guise or no less a person than
the Emperor himself, suggesting that he should become
a convert to the new faith, so that the Church and he
might work together for the greater glory of God. The
bishops and fathers of the Church, ambitious for their
organization, fell for this scheme, and Satan went off

laughing to himself. He had got everything he had asked from Jesus three hundred years before; he had got the world's greatest religion. How complete and swift was his success you may judge from the fact that fifty years later we find the Emperor Valentinian compelled to pass an edict limiting the donations of emotional females to the church in Rome!

From that time on Christianity has been what I have shown in this book, the chief of the enemies of social progress. From the days of Constantine to the days of Bismarck and Mark Hanna, Christ and Caesar have been one, and the Church has been the shield and armor of predatory economic might. With only one qualification to be noted: that the Church has never been able to suppress entirely the memory of her proletarian Founder. She has done her best, of course; we have seen how her scholars twist his words out of their sense, and the Catholic Church even goes so far as to keep to the use of a dead language, so that her victims may not hear the words of Jesus in a form they can understand.

> 'Tis well that such seditious songs are sung
> Only by priests, and in the Latin tongue!

But in spite of this, the history of the Church has been one incessant struggle with upstarts and rebels who have filled themselves with the spirit of the Magnificat and the Sermon on the Mount, and of that bitterly class-conscious proletarian, James, the brother of Jesus.

And here is the thing to be noted, that the factor which has given life to Christianity, which enables it to keep its hold on the hearts of men today, is precisely

this new wine of faith and fervor which has been
poured into it by generation after generation of poor
men who live like Jesus as outcasts, and die like Jesus
as criminals, and are revered like Jesus as founders and
saints. The greatest of the early Church fathers were
bitterly fought by the Church authorities of their own
time. St. Chrysostom, Bishop of Constantinople, was
turned out of office, exiled and practically martyred;
St. Basil was persecuted by the Emperor Valens; St.
Ambrose excommunicated the tyrannical Emperor
Theodosius; St. Cyprian gave all his wealth to the poor,
and was exiled and finally martyred. In the same way,
most of the heretics whom the Holy Inquisition tortured and burned were proletarian rebels; the saints
whom the Church reveres, the founders of the orders
which gave it life for century after century, were men
who sought to return to the example of the carpenter's
son. Let us hear a Christian scholar on this point, Prof.
Rauschenbusch:

> The movement of Francis of Assisi, of the Waldenses, of the
> Humiliati and Bons Hommes, were all inspired by democratic
> and communistic ideals. Wiclif was by far the greatest doctrinal
> reformer before the reformation; but his eyes, too, were first
> opened to the doctrinal errors of the Roman Church by joining
> in a great national and patriotic movement against the alien
> domination and extortion of the Church. The Bohemian revolt,
> made famous by the name of John Huss, was quite as much
> political and social as religious. Savonarola was a great demo-
> crat as well as a religious prophet. In his famous interview with
> the dying Lorenzo de Medici he made three demands as a condi-
> tion for granting absolution. Of the man he demanded a living
> faith in God's mercy. Of the millionaire he demanded restitu-
> tion of his ill-gotten wealth. Of the political usurper he de-
> manded the restoration of the liberties of the people of Florence.
> It is significant that the dying sinner found it easy to assent to

the first, hard to assent to the second, and impossible to concede the last.

Locusts and Wild Honey

This proletarian strain in Christianity goes back to a time long before Jesus; it seems to have been inherent in the religious character of the Jews—that stubborn independence, that stiff-necked insistence on the right of a man to interview God for himself and to find out what God wants him to do; also the inclination to find that God wants him to oppose earthly rulers and their plundering of the poor. What is it that gives to the Bible the vitality it has today? Its literary style? To say that is to display the ignorance of the cultured; for elevation of style is a by-product of passionate conviction; it is what the Jewish writers had to say, and not the way they said it, that has given them their hold upon mankind. Was it their insistence upon conscience, their fear of God as the beginning of wisdom? But that same element appears in the Babylonian psalms, which are as eloquent and as sincere as those of the Hebrews, yet are read only by scholars. Was it their sense of the the awful presence of divinity, of the soul immortal in its keeping? The Egyptians had that far more than the Hebrews, and yet we do not cherish their religious books. Or was it the love of man for all things living, the lesson of charity upon which the Catholics lay such stress? The gentle Buddha had that, and had it long before Christ; also his priests had metaphysical subtlety, greater than that of John the Apostle or Thomas Aquinas.

No, there is one thing and one only which distinguishes the Hebrew sacred writings from all others, and that is their insistent note of proletarian revolt, their furious denunciations of exploiters, and of luxury and wantonness, the vices of the rich. Of that note the Assyrian and Chaldean and Babylonian writing contain not a trace, and the Egyptian hardly enough to mention. The Hindoos had a trace of it; but the true, natural-born rebels of all time were the Hebrews. They were rebels against oppression in ancient Judea, as they are today in Petrograd and New York; the spirit of equality and brotherhood which spoke through Ezekiel and Amos and Isaiah, through John the Baptist and Jesus and James, spoke in the last century through Marx and Lassalle and Jaures, and speaks today through Liebknecht and Rosa Luxemburg and Karl Kautsky and Israel Zangwill and Morris Hillquit and Abraham Cahan and Emma Goldman and the Joseph Fels endowment.

The legal rate of interest throughout the Babylonian Empire was 20%; the laws of Manu permitted 24%, while the laws of the Egyptians only stepped in to prevent more than 100%. But listen to this Hebrew law:

If thy brother be waxen poor, and fallen in decay with thee, then thou shalt relieve him, yea, though he be a stranger or a sojourner, that he may live with thee: Take thou no interest of him, or increase; but fear thy God that thy brother may live with thee. Thou shalt not give him any money upon usury, nor lend him thy victuals for increase.

And so on, forbidding that Hebrews be sold as bond servants, and commanding that at the end of fifty years all debtors shall have their debts forgiven and their lands returned to them. And note that this is not the raving of agitators, the demand of a minority party; it is the law of the Hebrew land.

There has been of late a great deal of new discovery concerning the early Jews. Conrad Noel summarizes the results as follows:

The land-mark law, which sternly forbids encroachment upon peasant rights; consideration for the foreigner; additional sanitary and food laws; tithe regulations on behalf of widows, orphans, foreigners, etc.; that those who have no economic independence should eat and be satisfied; that loans should be given cheerfully, not only without any interest, but even at the risk of losing the principal. To withhold a loan because the year of release is at hand in which the principal is no longer recoverable, is described as a grave sin. When you are compelled to free your slaves, you must give them sufficient capital to embark upon some industry which shall prevent their falling back into slavery. A number of holidays are insisted upon. There must be no more crushing of the poor out of existence, for God cares for these people who have been driven to poverty, and they shall never cease out of the land. Howbeit there shall be no poor with you, for the Lord will bless you, if you will obey these laws.

But then prosperity came, and culture, which meant contact with the capitalist ideas of the heathen empires. The Jews fell from the stern justice of their fathers; and so came the prophets, wild-eyed men of the people, clad in camel's hair and living upon locusts and wild honey, breaking in upon priests and kings and capitalists with their furious denunciations. And always they incited to class war and social disturbance. I quote Conrad Noel again:

Nathan and Gad had been David's political advisers, Abijah had stirred Jeroboam to revolt, Elijah had resisted Ahab, Elisha had fanned the rebellion of Jehu, Amos thunders against the misrule of the king of Israel, Isaiah denounces the landlords and the usurers, Micah charges them with blood-guiltiness; Jeremiah and the latter prophets, though they strike a more intimate note of personal repentance, strike it as the prelude to that national restoration for which they hunger as exiles.

The first chapters of Isaiah are typical of the Old Testament point of view. Just as the prophets of the nineteenth century thundered against the "Christian" employers of Lancashire, and told them their houses were cemented with the blood of little children, so Isaiah cries against his generation: "Your governing classes companion with thieves; behold you build up Sion with blood." Their ceremonial and their Sabbath keeping are an abomination to God. "When ye spread forth your hands, I will hide mine eyes from you. Your hands are full of blood." The poor man is robbed. The rich exact usury. "Woe unto you that lay house to house and field to field, that ye may dwell alone in the midst of the land." "Wash you, make you clean, put away the evil of your doing from before mine eyes; cease to do evil; learn to do well, seek judgment, relieve the oppressed, judge the fatherless, plead for the widow. Come now, let us reason together, saith the Lord. Though your sins be blood-colored, they shall be as white as snow; though they be red like crimson, they shall be as wool. If ye be willing and obedient, ye shall eat the good of the land. But if ye refuse and rebel, ye shall be devoured by the sword.

Mother Earth

And nowadays we have the Socialist and Anarchist agitators, following the same tradition, possessed by the same dream as the ancient Hebrew prophets. I have mentioned Emma Goldman; it may be that the reader is not familiar with her writings, and does not realize how very Biblical she is, both in point of view and style. Let me quote a few sentences from a recent issue of her paper, "Mother Earth", on the subject of our ruling classes and their social responsibility:

Yes, you idle rich, you may howl about what we mean to do to you! Your riches are rotten and your fine clothes are falling from your backs. Your stocks and bonds are so tainted that the ink on them should turn to acid and eat holes in your pockets and your skins. You have piled up your dirty millions, but what wages have you paid to the poor devils of farm hands you have robbed? And do you imagine they won't remember it when the revolution comes? You loll on soft couches and amuse yourselves with your mistresses; you think you are "it" and the world is yours. You send militiamen and shoot down our organizers, and we are helpless. But wait, comrades, our time is coming.

Doubtless the reader is well satisfied that the author of this tirade is now in jail, where she can no longer defy the laws of good taste. They always put the ancient prophets in jail; that is the way to know a prophet when you meet him. Let me quote another prophet who is now behind bars—Alexander Berkman, in his "Prison Memoirs of an Anarchist", discussing the same subject of plutocratic pretension:

Tell me, you four hundred, where did you get it? Who gave it to you? Your grandfather, you say? Your father? Can you go all the way back and show there is no flaw anywhere in your title? I tell you that the beginning and the root of your wealth is necessarily in injustice. And why? Because Nature did not make this man rich and that man poor from the start. Nature does not intend for one man to have capital and another to be a wage-slave. Nature made the earth to be cultivated by all. The idea we Anarchists have of the rich is of highwaymen, standing in the street and robbing every one that passes.

Or take "Big Bill" Haywood, chief of the I. W. W. Hear what he has to say in a pamphlet addressed to the harvest-hands he is seeking to organize:

How much farther do you plutes expect to go with your grabbing? Do you want to be the only people left on earth? Why else do you drive out the workers from all share in Nature, and claim everything for yourselves? The earth was made for all, rich and poor alike; where do you get your title deeds to it? Nature gave everything for all men to use alike; it is only your robbery which makes your so-called "ownership". Capital has no rights. The land belongs to Nature, and we are all Nature's sons.

Or take Eugene V. Debs, three times candidate of the Socialist Party for President. I quote from one of his pamphlets:

The propertied classes are like people who go into a public theatre and refuse to let anyone else come in, treating as private property what is meant for social use. If each man would take only what he needs, and leave the balance to those who have nothing, there would be no rich and no poor. The rich man is a thief.

I might go on citing such quotations for many pages; but I know that Emma Goldman and Alexander Berkman and Bill Haywood and Gene Debs may read this book, and I don't want them to close it in the middle and throw it at me. Therefore let me hasten to explain my poor joke; the sentiments I have been quoting are not those of our modern agitators, but of another group of ancient ones. The first is not from Emma Goldman, nor did I find it in "Mother Earth". I found it in the Epistle of James, believed by orthodox authorities to have been James, the brother of Jesus. It is exactly what he wrote—save that I have put it into modern phrases, and changed the swing of the sentences, in order that those familiar with the Bible might read it without suspicion. The second passage is not in the writings of Alexander Berkman, but in those of St. John Chrysostom, most famous of the early fathers, who lived 374-407. The third is not from the pen of "Big Bill" but from that of St. Ambrose, a father of the Latin Church, 340-397, and the fourth is not by Comrade Debs, but by St. Basil of the Greek Church, 329-379. And if the reader objects to my having fooled him for a minute or two, what will he say to the Christian Church, which has been fooling him for sixteen hundred years?

The Soap Box

This book will be denounced from one end of Christendom to the other as the work of a blasphemous infidel. Yet it stands in the direct line of the Christian tradition: written by a man who was brought up in the Church, and loved it with all his heart and soul, and was driven out by the formalists and hypocrites in high places; a man who thinks of Jesus more frequently and with more devotion than he thinks of any other man that lives or has ever lived on earth; and who has but one purpose in all that he says and does, to bring into reality the dream that Jesus dreamed of peace on earth and good will toward men.

I will go farther yet and say that not merely is this book written for the cause of Jesus, but it is written in the manner of Jesus. We read his bitter railings at the Pharisees, and miss the point entirely, because the word Pharisee has become to us a word of reproach. But this is due solely to Jesus; in his time the word was a holy word, it meant the most orthodox and respectable, the ultra high-church devotees of Jerusalem. The way to get the spirit of the tirades of Jesus is to do with him what we did with the early church fathers—translate him into American. This time, since the reader shares the secret, it will not be necessary to disguise the Bible style, and we may follow the text exactly. Let me try the twenty-third chapter of Matthew, omitting seven verses which refer to subtleties of Hebrew casuistry, for which we should have to go to Lyman Abbott or St. Alphonsus to find a parallel:

Then Jesus mounted upon a soap-box, and began a speech, saying, The doctors of divinity and Episcopalians fill the Fifth Avenue churches; and it would be all right if you were to listen to what they preach, and do that; but don't follow their actions, for they never practice what they preach. They load the backs of the working-classes with crushing burdens, but they themselves never move a finger to carry a burden, and everything they do is for show. They wear frock-coats and silk hats on Sundays, and they sit at the speakers' table at the banquets of the Civic Federation, and they occupy the best pews in the churches, and their doings are reported in all the papers; they are called leading citizens and pillars of the church. But don't you be called leading citizens, for the only useful man is the man who produces. (Applause). And whoever exalts himself shall be abased, and whoever humbles himself shall be exalted.

Woe unto you, doctors of divinity and Catholics, hypocrites! for you shut up the kingdom of Heaven against men; you don't go in yourself and you don't let others go in. Woe unto you, doctors of divinity and Presbyterians, hypocrites! for you foreclose mortgages on widows' houses, and for a pretense you make long prayers. For this you will receive the greater damnation! Woe unto you, doctors of divinity and Methodists, hypocrites! for you send missionaries to Africa to make one convert, and when you have made him, he is twice as much a child of hell as yourselves. (Applause). Woe unto you, blind guides, with your subtleties of doctrine, your transubstantiation and consubstantiation and all the rest of it; you fools and blind! Woe unto you, doctors of divinity and Episcopalians, hypocrites! for you drop your checks into the collection-plate and you pay no heed to the really important things in the Bible, which are justice and mercy and faith in goodness. You blind guides, who strain at a gnat and swallow a camel! (Laughter). Woe unto you, doctors of divinity and Anglicans, hypocrites! for you bathe yourselves and dress in immaculate clothing but within you are full of extortion and excess. You blind high churchmen, clean first your hearts, so that the clothes you wear may represent you. Woe unto you, doctors of divinity and Baptists, hypocrites! for you are like marble tombs which appear beautiful on the outside, but inside are full of dead men's bones and all uncleanness. Even so you appear righteous to men, but inside you are full of hypocrisy and iniquity. (Applause). Woe unto you, doctors of divinity and Unitarians, hypocrites! because you erect statues to dead reformers, and put wreathes upon the tombs of old-time martyrs. You say, if we had been alive in those days, we would not have helped to kill those good men. That ought to show you how to treat us at present. (Laughter). But you are the children of those who killed the good men; so go ahead and kill us too! You serpents, you generation of vipers, how can you escape the damnation of hell?

At this point, according to the report published in the Jerusalem "Times", a police sergeant stepped up to the orator and notified him that he was under arrest; he submitted quietly, but one of his followers attempted to use a knife, and was severely clubbed. Jesus was taken to the station-house followed by a riotous throng, and held upon a charge of disorderly conduct. Next morning the Rev. Dr. Caiaphas of Old Trinity appeared against him, and Magistrate Pilate sentenced him to six months on Blackwell's Island, remarking that from this time on he proposed to make an example of those soapbox orators who persist in using threatening and abusive language. Just as the prisoner was being led away, a detective appeared with a requisition from the Governor, ordering that Jesus be taken to San Francisco, where he is under indictment for murder in the first degree, it being charged that his teachings helped to incite the Preparedness Day explosion.

The Church Machine

The Catholics of His time came to Jesus and said, "Master, we would have a sign of Thee"—meaning that they wanted him to do some magic, to prove to their vulgar minds that his power came from God. He an-

swered by calling them an evil and adulterous generation—which is exactly what I have said about the Papal
machine. The Baptists and Methodists and Presbyterians and other book-worshippers of his time accused
him of violating the sacred commands so definitely set
down in their ancient texts, and to them he answered
that the Sabbath was made for man and not man for
the Sabbath; he called them hypocrites, and quoted
Karl Marx at them—"This people honoreth me with
their lips, but their heart is far from me." Because he
despised the company of the respectables, and went
among the humble and human folk of his own class in
the places where they gathered—the public houses—
the churchly scandal-mongers called him "a man glut-
tonous and a wine-bibber, a friend of publicans and sinners"—precisely as in the old days they used to sneer
at the Socialists for having their meetings in the back-
rooms of saloons, and precisely as they still denounce
us as free-lovers and atheists.

But the longing for justice between man and man,
which is the Kingdom of Heaven on earth, is the deepest instinct of the human heart, and the voice of the
carpenter cannot be confined within the thickest
church-walls, nor drowned by all the pealing organs
in Christendom. Even in these days, when the power
of Mammon is more widespread, more concentrated
and more systematized than ever before in history—
even in these days of Morgan and Rockefeller, there are
Christian clergymen who dare to preach as Jesus
preached. One by one they are cast out of the Church—
Father McGlynn, George D. Herron, Alexander Irvine,
J. Stitt Wilson, Austin Adams, Algernon Crapsey,

Bouck White; but their voices are not silenced, they
are like the leaven, to which Jesus compared the kingdom of God—a woman took it and hid it in three measures of meal till the whole was leavened. The young
theological students read, and some of them understand; I know three brothers in one family who have
just gone into the Church, and are preaching straight
social revolution—and the scribes and the pharisees
have not yet dared to cast them out.

In this book I have portrayed the Christian Church
as the servant and henchman of Big Business, a part of
the system of Mammon. Every church is necessarily a
money machine, holding and administering property.
And it is not alone the Catholic Church which is in politics, seeking favors from the state—the exemption of
church property from taxation, exemption of ministers
from military service, free transportation for them and
their families on the railroads, the control of charity
and education, laws to deprive people of amusements
on Sunday—so on through a long list. As the churches
have to be built with money, you find that in them
the rich possess the control and demand the deference,
while the poor are humble, and in their secret hearts
jealous and bitter; in other words, the class struggle is
in the churches, as everywhere else in the world, and
the social revolution is coming in the churches, just as
it is coming in industry.

It is a fact of deep significance that the majority of
ministers are proletarians, eking out their existence
upon a miserable salary, and beholden in all their comings and goings to the wealthy holders of privilege.
Even in the Roman Catholic Church that is true. The

ordinary priest is a man of the working class, and knows what working people suffer and feel. So in the Catholic Church there are proletarian rebellions; there is many a priest who does not carry out the political orders of his superiors, but goes to the polls and votes for his class instead of for his pope. In Ireland, as I write, the young priests are defying their bishops and joining the Sinn Fein, a non-religious movement for an Irish Republic.

What is it that keeps the average workingman in subjection to the exploiter? Simply terror, the terror of losing his job. And if you could get into the inmost soul of Christian ministers, you would find that precisely the same force is keeping many of them slaves to Tradition. They are educated men, and thousands of them must resent the dilemma which compels them to be either fools or hypocrites. They have caught enough of the spirit of their time not to enjoy having to pose as miracle-mongers, rain-makers and witch-doctors; they would like to say frankly that they do not believe that Jonah ever swallowed the whale, and even that they are dubious about Hercules and Achilles and other demigods. But they are part of a machine, and the old men and the rich men who run the machine have laid down the law. Those who find themselves tempted to think, remember suddenly that they have wives and children; they have only one profession, they have been unfitted for any other by a life-time of study of dead things, as well as by the practice of altruism.

But now the Social Revolution is coming; coming upon swift wings—it may be here before this book sees the light. And who knows but then we may see in

America that wonderful sight which we saw in Russia, when Christian monks assembled and burned their holy books, and petitioned the state to take them in as citizens and human beings? It is my belief that when the power of exploitation is broken, we shall see the Dead Hand crumble into dust, as a mummy crumbles when it is exposed to the air. All those men who stay in the Church and pretend to believe nonsense, because it affords an easy way to earn a living, will suddenly realize that it is possible to earn a living outside; that any man can go into a factory, clean and well-ventilated and humanly run, and by four hours work can earn the purchasing power of ten or fifteen dollars. Do you not think that there may be some who will choose freedom and self-respect on those terms?

And what of those thousands and tens of thousands who join the church because it is a part of the regime of respectability, a way to make the acquaintance of the rich, to curry favor and obtain promotion, to get customers if you are a tradesman, to extend your practice if you are a professional man? And what about the millions who go to church because they are poor, and because life is a desperate struggle, and this is one way to keep the favor of the boss, to get a little better chance for the children, to get charity if you fall into need; in short, to acquire influence with the well-to-do and powerful, who stand together, and like to see the poor humble and reverent, contented in that state of life to which it has pleased God to call them?

The Church Redeemed

Do I mean that I expect to see the Church—all

churches—perish and pass away? I do not, for I believe that the Church answers one of the fundamental needs of man. The Social Revolution will abolish poverty and parasitism, it will make temptations fewer, and the soul's path through life much easier; but it will not remove the necessity of struggle for individual virtue, it will only clear the way for the discovery of newer and higher types of virtue. Men will gather more than ever in beautiful places to voice their love of life and of one another; but the places in which they gather will be places swept clean of superstition and tyranny. As the Reformation compelled the Catholic Church to cleanse itself and abolish the grossest of its abuses, so the Social Revolution will compel it to repudiate its defense of parasitism and exploitation. I will record the prophecy that by the year 1950 all Catholic authorities will be denying that the Church ever opposed Socialism—true Socialism; just as today they deny that the Church ever tortured Galileo, ever burned men for teaching that the earth moves around the sun, ever sold the right to commit crime, ever gave away the New World to Spain and Portugal, ever buried newly-born infants in the cellars of nunneries.

The Social Revolution will compel all churches, Christian, Hebrew, Buddhist, Confuscian, or what you will, to drive out their formalists and traditionalists. If there is any church that refuses so to adapt itself, the swift progress of enlightenment and freedom will leave it without followers. But in the great religions, which have a soul of goodness and sincerity, we may be sure that reformers will arise, prophets and saints who, as of old, will preach the living word of God. In many churches today we can see the beginning of that new Counter-Reformation. Even in the Catholic Church there is a "modernist" rebellion; read the books of the "Sillon", and Fogazzaro's trilogy of novels, "The Saint", and you will see a genuine and vital protest against the economic corruption of the Church. In America, the "Knights of Slavery" have been forced by public pressure to support a "War for Democracy", and even to compete with the Y. M. C. A. in the training camps. They are doing good work, I am told.

This gradual conquest of the old religiosity by the spirit of modern common sense is shown most interestingly in the Salvation Army. William Booth was a man with a great heart, who took his life into his hands and went out with a bass-drum to save the lost souls of the slums. He was stoned and jailed, but he persisted, and brought his captives to Jesus—

> Vermin-eaten saints with mouldy breath,
> Unwashed legions with the ways of death.

Incidentally the "General" learned to know his slum population. He had not wanted to engage in charity and material activities; he feared hypocrisy and corruption. But in his writings he lets us see how utterly impossible it is for a man of real heart to do anything for the souls of the slum-dwellers without at the same time helping their diseased and hunger-racked bodies. So the Salvation army was forced into useful work—old clothes depots, nights lodgings, Christmas dinners, farm colonies—until today the bare list of the various kinds of enterprises it carries on fills three printed pages. It is all done with the money of the rich, and is tainted by subservience to authority, but no one can deny that it is better than "Gibson's Preservative", and the fox-hunting parsons filling themselves with port.

And in Protestant Churches the advance has been even greater. Here and there you will find a real rebel, hanging onto his job and preaching the proletarian Jesus; while even the great Fifth Avenue churches are making attempts at "missions" and "settlements" in the slums. The more vital churches are gradually turning themselves into societies for the practical betterment of their members. Their clergy are running boys clubs and sewing-schools for girls, food conservation lectures for mothers, social study clubs for men. You get prayer-meetings and psalm-singing along with this; but here is the fact that hangs always before the clergyman's face—that with prayer-meetings and psalm-singing alone he has a hard time, while with clubs and educational societies and social reforms he thrives.

And now the War has broken upon the world, and caught the churches, like everything else, in its mighty current; the clergy and the congregations are confronted by pressing national needs, they are forced to take notice of a thousand new problems, to engage in a thousand practical activities. No one can see the end of this —any more than he can see the end of the vast upheaval in politics and industry. But we who are trained in revolutionary thought can see the main outlines of the future. We see that in these new church activities the clergy are inspired by things read, not in ancient Hebrew texts, but in the daily newspapers. They are responding to the actual, instant needs of their boys in

the trenches and the camps; and this is bound to have
an effect upon their psychology. Just as we can say
that an English girl who leaves the narrow circle of
her old life, and goes into a munition factory and joins
a union and takes part in its debates, will never after
be a docile home-slave; so we can say that the clergyman who helps in Y. M. C. A. work in France, or in Red
Cross organization in America, will be less the bigot
and formalist forever after. He will have learned, in
spite of himself, to adjust means to ends; he will have
learned co-operation and social solidarity by the method
which modern educators most favor—by doing. Also
he will have absorbed a mass of ideas in news despatches from over the world. He is forced to read these
despatches carefully, because the fate of his own boys
is involved; and we Socialists will see to it that the despatches are well filled with propaganda!

The Desire of Nations

So the churches, like all the rest of the world, are
caught in the great revolutionary current, and swept on
towards a goal which they do not forsee, and from
which they would shrink in dismay: the Church of the
future, the Church redeemed by the spirit of Brotherhood, the Church which we Socialists will join. They
call us materialists, and say that we think about nothing but the belly—and that is true, in a way; because
we are the representatives of a starving class, which
thinks about its belly precisely as does any individual
who is ravening with hunger. But give us what that
arrant materialist, James, the brother of Jesus, calls
"those things which are needful to the body," and then

we will use our minds, and even discover that we have souls; whereas at present we are led to despise the very word "spiritual", which has become the stock-in-trade of parasites and poseurs.

We have children, whom we love, and whose future is precious to us. We would be glad to have them trained in ways of decency and self-control, of dignity and grace. It would make us happy if there were in the world institutions conducted by men and women of consecrated life who would specialize in teaching a true morality to the young. But it must be a morality of freedom, not of slavery; a morality founded upon reason, not upon superstition. The men who teach it must be men who know what truth is, and the passionate loyalty which the search for truth inspires. They cannot be the pitiful shufflers and compromisers we see in the churches today, the Jowetts who say they used to believe in the Father, the Son and the Holy Ghost. Rather than trust our children to such shameless cynics, we will make shift to train them ourselves—we amateurs, not knowing much about children, and absorbed in the desperate struggle against organized wrong.

It is a statement which many revolutionists would resent, yet it is a fact nevertheless, that we need a new religion, need it just as badly as any of the rest of our pitifully groping race. That we need it is proven by the rivalries and quarrels in our midst—the schisms which waste the greater part of our activities, and which are often the result of personal jealousies and petty vanities. To lift men above such weakness, to make them really brothers in a great cause—that is the work of "personal religion" in the true and vital sense of the words.

We pioneers and propagandists may not live to see the birth of the new Church of Humanity; but our children will see it, and the dream of it is in our hearts; our poets have sung of it with fervor and conviction. Read these lines from "The Desire of Nations," by Edwin Markham, in which he tells of the new Redeemer who is at hand:

> And when he comes into the world gone wrong,
> He will rebuild her beauty with a song.
> To every heart he will its own dream be:
> One moon has many phantoms in the sea.
> Out of the North the norns will cry to men:
> "Baldur the Beautiful has come again!"
> The flutes of Greece will whisper from the dead:
> "Apollo has unveiled his sunbright head!"
> The stones of Thebes and Memphis will find voice:
> "Osiris comes: Oh tribes of Time, rejoice!"
> And social architects who build the State,
> Serving the Dream at citadel and gate,
> Will hail Him coming through the labor-hum.
> And glad quick cries will go from man to man:
> "Lo, He has come, our Christ the artisan,
> The King who loved the lilies, He has come!"

The Knowable

The new religion will base itself upon the facts of life, as demonstrated by experience and reason; for to the modern thinker the basis of all interest is truth, and the wonders of the microscope and the telescope, of the new psychology and the new sociology are more wonderful than all the magic recorded in ancient Mythologies. And even if this were not so, the business of the thinker is to follow the facts. The history of all philos-

ophy might be summed up in this simile: The infant
opens his eyes and sees the moon, and stretches out his
hands and cries for it; but those in charge do not give
it to him, and so after a while the infant tires of crying,
and turns to his mother's breast and takes a drink of
milk.

Man demands to know the origin of life; it is intol-
erable for him to be here, and not know how, or whence,
or why. He demands the knowledge immediately and
finally, and invents innumerable systems and creeds.
He makes himself believe them, with fire and torture
makes other men believe them; until finally, in the confusion of a million theories, it occurs to him to investigate his instruments, and he makes the discovery that
his tools are inadequate, and all their products worth-
less. His mind is finite, while the thing he seeks is infinite; his knowledge is relative, while the First Cause
is absolute.

This realization we owe to Immanuel Kant, the
father of modern philosophy. In his famous "antin-
omies", he proved four propositions: first, that the
universe is limitless in time and space; second, that
matter is composed of simple, indivisible elements;
third, that free will is impossible; and fourth, that
there must be an absolute or first cause. And having
proven these things, he turned round and proved their
opposites, with arguments exactly as unanswerable.
Any one who follows these demonstrations and understands them, takes all his metaphysical learning and
lays it on the shelf with his astrology and magic.

It is a fact, which every one who wishes to think
must get clear, that when you are dealing with abso-

lutes and ultimates, you can prove whatever you want to prove. Metaphysics is like the fourth dimension; you fly into it and come back upside down, hindside foremost, inside out; and when you get tired of this condition, you take another flight, and come back the way you were before. So metaphysical thinking serves the purpose of Catholic cheats like Cardinal Newman and Professor Chatterton-Hill; it serves hysterical women like "Mother" Eddy; it serves the New-thoughters, who wish to fill their bellies with wind; it serves the charlatans and mystagogs who wish to befuddle the wits of the populace. Real thinkers avoid it as they would a bottomless swamp; they avoid, not merely the idealism of Platonists and Hegelians, but the monism of Haeckel, and the materialism of Buechner and Jacques Loeb. The simple fact is that it is as impossible to prove the priority of origin and the ultimate nature of matter as it is of mind; so that the scientist who lays down a materialist dogma is exactly as credulous as a Christian.

How then are we to proceed? Shall we erect the mystery into an Unknowable, like Spencer, and call ourselves Agnostics with a capital letter, like Huxley? Shall we follow Frederic Harrison, making an inadequate divinity out of our impotence? I have read the books of the "Positivists", and attended their imitation church in London, but I did not get any satisfaction from them. In the midst of their dogmatic pronouncements I found myself remembering how the egg falls apart and reveals a chicken, how the worm suddenly discovers itself a butterfly. The spirit of man is a breaker of barriers, and it seems a futile occupation to set limits upon the future. Our business is not to say what men will know ten thousand years from now, but to content ourselves with the simple statement of what men know **now**. What we know is a procession of phenomena called an environment; our life being an act of adjustment to its changes, and our faith being the conviction that this adjustment is possible and worth while.

In the beginning the guide is instinct, and the act of trust is automatic. But with the dawn of reason the thinker has to justify his faith; to convince himself that life is sincere, that there is worth-whileness in being, or in seeking to be; that there is order in creation, laws which can be discovered, processes which can be applied. Just as the babe trusts life when it gropes for its mother's breast, so the most skeptical of scientists trusts it when he declares that water is made of two parts hydrogen and one part oxygen, and sets it down for a certainty that this will always be so—that he is not being played with by some sportive demon, who will today cause $H2O$ to behave like water, and tomorrow like benzine.

Nature's Insurgent Son

Life has laws, which it is possible to ascertain; and with each bit of knowledge acquired, the environment is changed, the life becomes a new thing. Consider, for example, what a different place the world became to the man who discovered that the force which laid the forest in ashes could be tamed and made to warm a cave and make wild grains nutritious! In other words, man can create life, he can make the world and himself into that which his reason decides it ought to be. The means by which he does this is the most magical of all the tools he has invented since his arboreal ancestor made the first club; the tool of experimental science—and when one considers that this weapon has been understood and deliberately employed for but two or three centuries, he realizes that we are indeed only at the beginning of human evolution.

To take command of life, to replace instincts by reasoned and deliberate acts, to make the world a conscious and ordered product—that is the task of man. Sir Ray Lankester has set this forth with beautiful precision in his book, "The Kingdom of Man". We are, at this time, in an uncomfortable and dangerous transition stage, as a child playing with explosives. This child has found out how to alter his environment in many startling ways, but he does not yet know why he wishes to alter it, nor to what purpose. He finds that certain things are uncomfortable, and these he proceeds immediately to change. Discovering that grain fermented dispels boredom, he creates a race of drunkards; discovering that foods can be produced in profusion, and prepared in alluring combinations, he makes himself so many diseases that it takes an encyclopedia to tell about them. Discovering that captives taken in war can be made to work, he makes a procession of empires, which are eaten through with luxury and corruption, and fall into ruins again.

This is Nature's way; she produces without limit, groping blindly, experimenting ceaselessly, eliminating ruthlessly. It takes a million eggs to produce one salmon; it has taken a million million men to produce

one idea—algebra, or the bow and arrow, or democracy.
Nature's present impulse appears as a rebellion against
her own methods; man, her creature, will emancipate
himself from her law, will save himself from her blindness and her ruthlessness. He is "Nature's insurgent
son"; but, being the child of his mother, goes at the
task in her old blundering way. Some men are sched-
uled to elimination because of defective eyesight; they
are furnished with glasses, and the breeding of defective eyes begins. The sickly or imbecile child would perish at once in the course of Nature; it is saved in the
name of charity, and a new line of degenerates is
started.

What shall we do? Return to the method of the
Spartans, exposing our sickly infants? We do not have
to do anything so wasteful, because we can replace the
killing of the unfit by a scientific breeding which
will prevent the unfit from getting a chance at life.
We can replace instinct by self-discipline. We can sub-
stitute for the regime of "Nature red in tooth and claw
with ravin" the regime of man the creator, knowing
what he wishes to be and how to set about to be it.
Whether this can happen, whether the thing which
we call civilization is to be the great triumph of the
ages, or whether the human race is to go back into the
melting pot, is a question being determined by an infin-
itude of contests between enlightenment and ignorance: precisely such a contest as occurs now, when you,
the reader, encounter a man who has thought his way
out to the light, and comes to urge you to perform the
act of self-emancipation, to take up the marvellous new
tools of science, and to make yourself, by means of

exact knowledge, the creator of your own life and in part of the life of the race.

The New Morality

Life is a process of expansion, of the unfoldment of new powers; driven by that inner impulse which the philosophers of Pragmatism call the **élan vital.** Whenever this impulse has its way, there is an emotion of joy; whenever it is balked, there is one of distress. So pleasure and pain are the guides of life, and the final goal is a condition of free and constantly accelerating growth, in which joy is enduring.

That man will ever reach such a state is more than we can say. It is a perfectly conceivable thing that to-morrow a comet may fall upon the earth and wipe out all man's labor's. But on the other hand, it is a conceivable thing that man may some day learn to control the movements of comets, and even of starry systems. It seems certain that if he is given time, he will make himself master of the forces of his immediate environment—

> The untamed giants of nature shall bow down—
> The tides, the tempest and the lightning cease
> From mockery and destruction, and be turned
> Unto the making of the soul of man.

It is a conceivable thing that man may learn to create his food from the elements without the slow processes of agriculture; it is conceivable that he may master the bacteria which at present prey upon his body, and so put an end to death. It is certain that he will ascertain the laws of heredity, and create human qualities as he has created the spurs of the fighting-cock and the legs of the greyhound. He will find out what genius is, and the laws of its being, and the tests whereby it may be recognized. In the new science of psycho-analysis he has already begun the work of bringing an infinity of subconsciousness into the light of day; it may be that in the evidence of telepathy which the psychic researchers are accumulating, he is beginning to grope his way into a universal consciousness, which may come to include the joys and griefs of the inhabitants of Mars, and of the dark stars which the spectroscope and the telescope are disclosing.

All these are fascinating possibilities. What stands in the way of their realization? Ignorance and superstition, fear and submission, the old habits of rapine and hatred which man has brought with him from his animal past. These make him a slave, a victim of himself and of others; to root them out of the garden of the soul is the task of the modern thinker.

The new morality is thus a morality of freedom. It teaches that man is the master, or shall become so; that there is no law, save the law of his own being, no check upon his will save that which he himself imposes.

The new morality is a morality of joy. It teaches that true pleasure is the end of being, and the test of all righteousness.

The new morality is a morality of reason. It teaches that there is no authority above reason; no possibility of such authority, because if such were to appear, reason would have to judge it, and accept or reject it.

The new morality is a morality of development. It teaches that there can no more be an immutable law of conduct, than there can be an immutable position for the steering-wheel of an aeroplane. The business of the pilot of an aeroplane is to keep his machine aloft amid shifting currents of wind. The business of a moralist is to adjust life to a constantly changing environment. An action which was suicide yesterday becomes heroism today, and futility or hypocrisy tomorrow.

This new morality, like all things in a world of strife, is fighting for existence, using its own weapons, which are reason and love. Obviously it can use no others, without self-destruction; yet it has to meet enemies who fight with the old weapons of force and fraud. Whether it will prevail is more than any prophet can say. Perhaps it is too much to ask that it should succeed—this insolent effort of the pigmy man to leap upon the back of his master and fit a bridle into his mouth. Perhaps it is nothing but a dream in the minds of a few, the scientists and poets and inventors, the dreamers of the race. Perhaps the nerve of the pigmy will fail him at the critical moment, and he will fall from the back of his master, and under his master's hoofs.

The hour of the decision is now; for this we can see plainly, and as scientists we can proclaim it—the human race is in a swift current of degeneration, which a new morality alone can check. The struggle is at its height in our time; if it fails, if the fibre of the race continues to deteriorate, the soul of the race to be eaten out by poverty and luxury, by insanity and disease, by prostitution, crime and war—then mankind will slip back into the abyss, the untamed giants of Nature will resume their ancient sway, and the tides, the tempest and the lightning will sweep the earth clean again. I do not believe that this calamity will befall us. I know that in the diseased social body the forces of resistance are gathering—the Socialist movement, in the broad sense—the activities of all who believe in the possibility of reconstructing society upon a basis of reason, justice and love. To such people this book goes out: to the truly religious people, those who hunger and thirst after righteousness here and now, who believe in brotherhood as a reality, and are willing to bear pain and ridicule and privation for the sake of its ultimate achievement.

> From the edge of harsh derision,
>   From discord and defeat,
> From doubt and lame division,
>   We pluck the fruit and eat;
> And the mouth finds it bitter, and the spirit sweet....
>   O sorrowing hearts of slaves,
>   We heard you beat from far!
>   We bring the light that saves,
>   We bring the morning star;
> Freedom's good things we bring you, whence all good things
>   are....

Envoi

I have come to the end of my task; but one question troubles me. I think of the "young men and maidens meek" who will read this book, and I wonder what they will make of it. We have had a lark together; we have gone romping down the vista of the ages, swatting every venerable head that showed itself, beating the dust out of ancient delusions. You would like all your life to be that kind of lark; but you may not find it so, and perhaps you will suffer disillusionment and vexation.

I have known hundreds of young radicals in my life; they have nearly all been gallant and honest, but they have not all been wise, and therefore not so happy as they might have been. In the course of time I have formulated to myself the peril to which young radicals are exposed. We see so much that is wrong in ancient things, it gets to be a habit with us to reject them. We have only to know that a thing is old to feel an impulse of impatient scorn; on the other hand, we are tempted to welcome anything which can prove itself to be unprecedented. There is a common type of radical whose aim in life is to be several jumps ahead of mankind; whose criterion of conduct is that it shocks the bourgeois. If you do not know that type, you may find him—and her—in the newest of the Bohemian cafes, drinking the newest red chemicals, smoking the newest brand of cigarettes, and discussing the newest form of **psycopathia sexualis.** After you have watched them a while, you realize that these ultra-new people have fallen victim to the oldest form of logical fallacy, the non sequitur, and likewise to the oldest form of slavery, which is self-indulgence.

If it is true that much in the old moral codes is based upon ignorance, and cultivated by greed, it is also true that much in the old moral codes is based upon facts which will not change so long as man is what he is—a creature of impulses, good and bad, wise and foolish, selfish and generous, and compelled to make choice between these impulses; so long as he is a material body and a personal consciousness, obliged to live in society and adjust himself to the rights of others. What I would like to say to young radicals—if there is any way to say it without seeming a prig—is that in choosing their own path through life, they will need not merely enthusiasm and radical fervor, but wisdom and judgment and hard study.

It is our fundamental demand that society shall cease to repeat over and over the blunders of the past, the blunders of tyranny and slavery, of luxury and poverty, which wrecked the ancient societies; and surely it is a poor way to begin by repeating in our own persons the most ancient blunders of the moral life. To light the fires of lust in our hearts, and let them smoulder there, and imagine we are trying new experiments in psychology! Who does not know the radical woman who demonstrates her emancipation from convention by destroying her nerves with nicotine? Who does not know the genius of revolt who demonstrates his repudiation of private property by permitting his lady loves to support him? Who does not know the man who finds in the phrases of revolution the most effective devices for the seducing of young girls?

You will have read this book to ill purpose if you draw the conclusion that there is anything in it to spare you the duty of getting yourself moral standards and holding yourself to them. On the contrary, because your task is the highest and hardest that man has yet undertaken—for this reason you will need standards the most exacting ever formulated. Let me quote some words from a teacher you will not accuse of holding to the slave-moralities:

Free dost thou call thyself? Thy ruling thoughts will I hear, and not that thou hast escaped a yoke.
Art thou such a one that can escape a yoke?

Free from what? What is that to Zarathustra! Clear shall your eye tell me: free to what?

Canst thou give to thyself thy good and thine evil, and hang thy will above thee as thy law? Canst thou be thine own judge, and avenger of thy law?

Fearful it is to be alone with the judge and the avenger of thy law. So is a stone flung out into empty space and into the icy breath of isolation.

Out of the pit of ignorance and despair we emerge into the sunlight of knowledge, to take control of a world, and to make it over, not according to the will of any gods, but according to the law in our own hearts. For that task we have need of all the resources of our being; of courage and high devotion, of faith in ourselves and our comrades, of clean, straight thinking, of discipline both of body and mind. We go to this task with a knowledge as old as the first moral impulse of mankind—the knowledge that our actions determine the future of life, not merely for ourselves but for all the race. For this is one of the laws of the ancient Hebrews which modern science has not repealed, but on the contrary has reinforced with a thousand confirmations—that the sins of the fathers are visited upon the children unto the third and fourth generations.

I get letters from the readers of my books; nearly always they are young people, so I feel like the father of a large family. I gather them now about my knee, and pronounce upon them a benediction in the ancient patriarchal style. Children and grandchildren of my hopes, for ages men suffered and fought, so that the world might be turned over to you. Now the day is coming, the glad, new day which blinds us with the shining of its wings; it is coming so swiftly that I am afraid of it. I thought we should have more time to get ready for the taking over of the world! But the old managers of it went insane, they took to tearing each other's eyes out, and now they lie dead about us. So, whether we will or not, we have to take charge of the world; we have to decide what to do with it, even while we are doing it. Let us not fail, young comrades; let us not write on the scroll of history that mankind had to go through yet new generations of wars and tumults and enslavements, because the youth of the international revolution could not lift themselves above those ancient personal vices which wrecked the fair hopes of their fathers—bigotry and intolerance, vindictiveness and vanity, envy, hatred and malice and all uncharitableness!

GREAT BOOKS IN PHILOSOPHY PAPERBACK SERIES

ESTHETICS

- ❏ Aristotle—*The Poetics*
- ❏ Aristotle—*Treatise on Rhetoric*

ETHICS

- ❏ Aristotle—*The Nicomachean Ethics*
- ❏ Marcus Aurelius—*Meditations*
- ❏ Jeremy Bentham—*The Principles of Morals and Legislation*
- ❏ John Dewey—*The Moral Writings of John Dewey, Revised Edition* (edited by James Gouinlock)
- ❏ Epictetus—*Enchiridion*
- ❏ Immanuel Kant—*Fundamental Principles of the Metaphysic of Morals*
- ❏ John Stuart Mill—*Utilitarianism*
- ❏ George Edward Moore—*Principia Ethica*
- ❏ Friedrich Nietzsche—*Beyond Good and Evil*
- ❏ Plato—*Protagoras, Philebus,* and *Gorgias*
- ❏ Bertrand Russell—*Bertrand Russell On Ethics, Sex, and Marriage* (edited by Al Seckel)
- ❏ Arthur Schopenhauer—*The Wisdom of Life* and *Counsels and Maxims*
- ❏ Benedict de Spinoza—*Ethics* and *The Improvement of the Understanding*

METAPHYSICS/EPISTEMOLOGY

- ❏ Aristotle—*De Anima*
- ❏ Aristotle—*The Metaphysics*
- ❏ Francis Bacon—*Essays*
- ❏ George Berkeley—*Three Dialogues Between Hylas and Philonous*
- ❏ W. K. Clifford—*The Ethics of Belief and Other Essays* (introduction by Timothy J. Madigan)
- ❏ René Descartes—*Discourse on Method* and *The Meditations*
- ❏ John Dewey—*How We Think*
- ❏ John Dewey—*The Influence of Darwin on Philosophy and Other Essays*
- ❏ Epicurus—*The Essential Epicurus: Letters, Principal Doctrines, Vatican Sayings, and Fragments* (translated, and with an introduction, by Eugene O'Connor)
- ❏ Sidney Hook—*The Quest for Being*
- ❏ David Hume—*An Enquiry Concerning Human Understanding*
- ❏ David Hume—*Treatise of Human Nature*
- ❏ William James—*The Meaning of Truth*
- ❏ William James—*Pragmatism*
- ❏ Immanuel Kant—*The Critique of Judgment*
- ❏ Immanuel Kant—*Critique of Practical Reason*
- ❏ Immanuel Kant—*Critique of Pure Reason*
- ❏ Gottfried Wilhelm Leibniz—*Discourse on Metaphysics* and the *Monadology*
- ❏ John Locke—*An Essay Concerning Human Understanding*
- ❏ Charles S. Peirce—*The Essential Writings* (edited by Edward C. Moore, preface by Richard Robin)
- ❏ Plato—*The Euthyphro, Apology, Crito,* and *Phaedo*
- ❏ Plato—*Lysis, Phaedrus,* and *Symposium*
- ❏ Bertrand Russell—*The Problems of Philosophy*
- ❏ George Santayana—*The Life of Reason*
- ❏ Sextus Empiricus—*Outlines of Pyrrhonism*

PHILOSOPHY OF RELIGION

❏ Marcus Tullius Cicero—*The Nature of the Gods* and *On Divination*
❏ Ludwig Feuerbach—*The Essence of Christianity*
❏ David Hume—*Dialogues Concerning Natural Religion*
❏ John Locke—*A Letter Concerning Toleration*
❏ Lucretius—*On the Nature of Things*
❏ John Stuart Mill—*Three Essays on Religion*
❏ Friedrich Nietzsche—*The Antichrist*
❏ Thomas Paine—*The Age of Reason*
❏ Bertrand Russell—*Bertrand Russell On God and Religion* (edited by Al Seckel)

SOCIAL AND POLITICAL PHILOSOPHY

❏ Aristotle—*The Politics*
❏ Mikhail Bakunin—*The Basic Bakunin: Writings, 1869–1871*
  (translated and edited by Robert M. Cutler)
❏ Edmund Burke—*Reflections on the Revolution in France*
❏ John Dewey—*Freedom and Culture*
❏ John Dewey—*Individualism Old and New*
❏ John Dewey—*Liberalism and Social Action*
❏ G. W. F. Hegel—*The Philosophy of History*
❏ G. W. F. Hegel—*Philosophy of Right*
❏ Thomas Hobbes—*The Leviathan*
❏ Sidney Hook—*Paradoxes of Freedom*
❏ Sidney Hook—*Reason, Social Myths, and Democracy*
❏ John Locke—*Second Treatise on Civil Government*
❏ Niccolo Machiavelli—*The Prince*
❏ Karl Marx (with Friedrich Engels)—*The German Ideology*, including
  Theses on Feuerbach and *Introduction to the Critique of Political Economy*
❏ Karl Marx—*The Poverty of Philosophy*
❏ Karl Marx/Friedrich Engels—*The Economic and Philosophic Manuscripts of 1844*
  and *The Communist Manifesto*
❏ John Stuart Mill—*Considerations on Representative Government*
❏ John Stuart Mill—*On Liberty*
❏ John Stuart Mill—*On Socialism*
❏ John Stuart Mill—*The Subjection of Women*
❏ Friedrich Nietzsche—*Thus Spake Zarathustra*
❏ Thomas Paine—*Common Sense*
❏ Thomas Paine—*Rights of Man*
❏ Plato—*The Republic*
❏ Jean-Jacques Rousseau—*The Social Contract*
❏ Mary Wollstonecraft—*A Vindication of the Rights of Men*
❏ Mary Wollstonecraft—*A Vindication of the Rights of Women*

GREAT MINDS PAPERBACK SERIES

CRITICAL ESSAYS

❏ Desiderius Erasmus—*The Praise of Folly*
❏ Jonathan Swift—*A Modest Proposal and Other Satires*
  (with an introduction by George R. Levine)
❏ H. G. Wells—*The Conquest of Time* (with an introduction by Martin Gardner)

ECONOMICS

❏ Charlotte Perkins Gilman—*Women and Economics: A Study of the Economic Relation
  between Women and Men*
❏ John Maynard Keynes—*The General Theory of Employment, Interest, and Money*

- ❏ John Maynard Keynes—A Tract on Monetary Reform
- ❏ Thomas R. Malthus—An Essay on the Principle of Population
- ❏ Alfred Marshall—Principles of Economics
- ❏ Karl Marx—Theories of Surplus Value
- ❏ David Ricardo—Principles of Political Economy and Taxation
- ❏ Adam Smith—Wealth of Nations
- ❏ Thorstein Veblen—Theory of the Leisure Class

HISTORY

- ❏ Edward Gibbon—On Christianity
- ❏ Alexander Hamilton, John Jay, and James Madison—The Federalist
- ❏ Herodotus—The History
- ❏ Thucydides—History of the Peloponnesian War
- ❏ Andrew D. White—A History of the Warfare of Science with Theology in Christendom

LAW

- ❏ John Austin—The Province of Jurisprudence Determined

PSYCHOLOGY

- ❏ Sigmund Freud—Totem and Taboo

RELIGION

- ❏ Thomas Henry Huxley—Agnosticism and Christianity and Other Essays
- ❏ Ernest Renan—The Life of Jesus
- ❏ Upton Sinclair—The Profits of Religion
- ❏ Elizabeth Cady Stanton—The Woman's Bible
- ❏ Voltaire—A Treatise on Toleration and Other Essays

SCIENCE

- ❏ Nicolaus Copernicus—On the Revolutions of Heavenly Spheres
- ❏ Charles Darwin—The Autobiography of Charles Darwin
- ❏ Charles Darwin—The Descent of Man
- ❏ Charles Darwin—The Origin of Species
- ❏ Charles Darwin—The Voyage of the Beagle
- ❏ Albert Einstein—Relativity
- ❏ Michael Faraday—The Forces of Matter
- ❏ Galileo Galilei—Dialogues Concerning Two New Sciences
- ❏ Ernst Haeckel—The Riddle of the Universe
- ❏ William Harvey—On the Motion of the Heart and Blood in Animals
- ❏ Werner Heisenberg—Physics and Philosophy: The Revolution in Modern Science (introduction by F. S. C. Northrop)
- ❏ Julian Huxley—Evolutionary Humanism
- ❏ Edward Jenner—Vaccination against Smallpox
- ❏ Johannes Kepler—Epitome of Copernican Astronomy and Harmonies of the World
- ❏ Isaac Newton—The Principia
- ❏ Louis Pasteur and Joseph Lister—Germ Theory and Its Application to Medicine and On the Antiseptic Principle of the Practice of Surgery
- ❏ Alfred Russel Wallace—Island Life

SOCIOLOGY

- ❏ Emile Durkheim—Ethics and the Sociology of Morals (translated with an introduction by Robert T. Hall)